IMAGES
of America

RALLS COUNTY

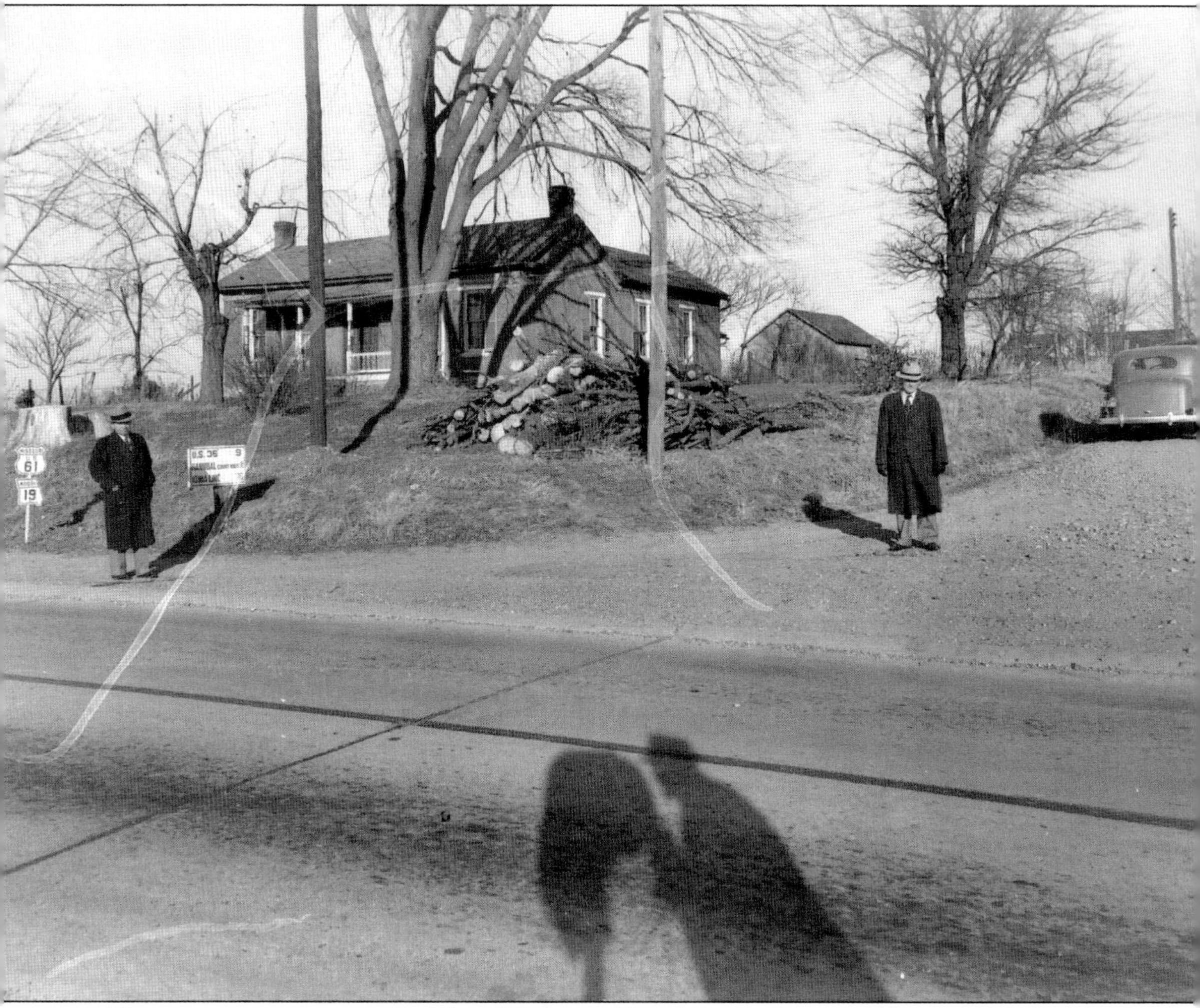

This moment was captured at Main (Highway 61) and Rector Streets in New London, Missouri, following a fatal pedestrian-auto accident. Veterinarian Gay Bird Megowen lived in the 1858 J.G. Rector house owned by the Clara Elzea family around this time. This brick home still stands today. The November 17, 1937, photograph includes the shadow of photographer John Hermann Herring of Hannibal, Missouri. (Author.)

On the Cover: Looking east from Main and Palmyra Streets is the 1912 Corn Carnival in Perry, Missouri. Corn Carnivals and Chautauquas were popular events across the Midwest. In 1908, attendance over the three-day event was estimated at 6,000, 10,000, and 6,000. James O. Allison, a New London lawyer, was behind the origins of Ralls County Corn Carnivals, gaining experience as one of 10 commissioners for the successful 1904 World's Fair in St. Louis, Missouri. (Author.)

IMAGES
of America

RALLS COUNTY

K. Allen Ballard

ARCADIA
PUBLISHING

ISBN 978-0-7385-9402-6

Published by Arcadia Publishing
Charleston, South Carolina

Printed in the United States of America

Library of Congress Control Number: 2012933253

For all general information, please contact Arcadia Publishing:
Telephone 843-853-2070
Fax 843-853-0044
E-mail sales@arcadiapublishing.com
For customer service and orders:
Toll-Free 1-888-313-2665

Visit us on the Internet at www.arcadiapublishing.com

This book is dedicated in fond memory of Ruth (Oaks) Lehenbauer (1941–2011), Jerry Welch (1954–2011), and Jess the Wonder Lab (2003–2011); each one fought courageous battles with cancer.

CONTENTS

ACKNOWLEDGMENTS

This book would not have been possible without the contributions, knowledge, wisdom, and expertise of my friends in time and history. While I have always been a student of history, I am a relative newcomer to documenting Ralls County history. I grew up in Quincy, Adams County, Illinois; and La Grange, Lewis County, Missouri. My wife and I recently arrived in New London, Missouri, in February 1993, pursuing a quality assurance engineering job. But I'm a quick learner, and fortunately, several people fluent in Ralls history accepted me and shared their knowledge and resources freely. For that, I am deeply grateful.

Those people include the following: Ron Leake of Ralls County Historical Society; Rev. Conrad Cheatham, Andy Sisk, Bob McNeill, Wayne Clark, and Becker Spaun of St. Louis & Hannibal Railroad; railroader Archie Hayden, who owns the J.P. Fisher scrapbook; Arcadia author and Mark Twain Postcard Club member Steve Chou; David and Sally Polc, Dave and Demi Black, Nancy Bowman, Robert Spaun, the late Kathy Threlkeld, and James Morton of the Postcard Club; Ben Akers of Lick Creek Antiques; the *Hannibal Courier-Post* (Jack Whitaker, Mary Lou Montgomery, Danny Henley, Bev Darr, Debbie Quinlin, Janet Willet, and Shirley Jackson); Kurt Van Winkle, Capt. Steve Terry, and crew at Broadway Digital Photos; Picture This! (for professional reprints from antique negatives); Sharon Wingate and Walgreens Photo Lab, Hannibal; Martha Adrian of the Mark Twain Book & Gift Shop; Roberta Hagood for personal stories and knowledge; Gene and Judy Stadtler and Carolyn Trower of the *Ralls County Herald Enterprise*; Liz Gingry and Mary Jane White; Jim and Dorothy Quinlin; Judge David Mobley; our families at The Crossing-Hannibal, New London First & Second Christian Churches, Oakwood and Clover Road; and the entire staff of the Hannibal, Missouri Free Public Library.

Images courtesy of Ralls County Historical Society are noted as (RCHS); others are noted directly.

A big THANX goes to my family, my bride, Connie, for her encouragement and patience; Ken for research assistance; and Jess the Wonder Lab for being man's best friend. Unexpectedly, we lost Miss Jess Peabody Ballard to an aggressive canine cancer as this book began. She left us some great history.

INTRODUCTION

Though Ralls County is now smaller in area and population, it has a disproportionately large history. The county and the impact of its citizens are inscribed upon the history of Missouri, America, and even the world. This impact touched diverse areas like politics, the freedom and independence of Texas, religion, entertainment, natural resources, the building of the Panama Canal, vital minerals, farm produce, transportation routes, timber, sand, gravel and more. Today, Ralls County is a major north-south US highway corridor, agricultural resource, and tourist draw. Some of the recreation opportunities include hunting and fishing areas that surround a man-made watershed retained by the Clarence Cannon Dam, which also provides vital flood prevention extending to the Mississippi River. The Ralls County Historical Society is very influential, with a wide, active membership and visionary leadership. RCHS has three storefronts with thousands of artifacts, photographs, and one of the largest genealogical libraries in Northeast Missouri.

Ralls County is Northeast Missouri's cradle of civilization; its original boundaries stretched from the Pike County line in the south to the Iowa state line in the north, and from the Mighty Mississippi in the east to the sources of the major Salt Rivers and East Chariton River branches in the west.

In 1820, Ralls County was born a "Benton Baby," the product of a brokered political deal via the powerful Thomas Hart Benton, who was Missouri's US senator for 30 years. As a result, Ralls is one of the few counties in Missouri named for something other than a famous American of the day. In fact, no other US county is named Ralls.

Its namesake was an ordinary farmer, Daniel Ralls, who lived west of New London. Ralls County, originally part of Pike County, was in turn taken from St. Charles territory. On October 2, 1820, Daniel Ralls, a Pike County representative, voted from his deathbed after having been carried to the St. Louis legislative chamber by four slaves. Thus, he provided the singular margin needed to elect Benton as Missouri's first US senator. Legislative records on October 31 report Ralls had died in Benton's home, and his funeral was at 4:00 p.m. On November 9, the Missouri Senate named the newest county after the deceased Ralls, and the House concurred.

Yet Daniel Ralls remains a mystery today. His gravesite is unknown, and no account exists of his funeral; therefore, Ralls County is his only monument. Ralls's son John tried but never could ascertain the location of his father's remains. Beginning in 1826, the county was carved into eight full counties and five partial counties from a northeastern super county. Today, Ralls County comprises 307,740 acres or 481 square miles, with a population of 10,167 residents in 2010.

More importantly, the Salt River, "Ohaha" or "Laughing Waters," runs through it, physically dividing Ralls into halves. This division of dry ground is both blessing and curse. Providing an unending source of life-giving water and an early transportation route hastening growth and development to the northern interior of Missouri before roads and rails arrived, it certainly gave rise to diverse, well-placed communities, which lay where they fell. Also, the sand and gravel deposits were plentiful for building, and the numerous saline springs meant salt for food preservation.

The river also carries a curse. Obviously, flooding poses the biggest threat of loss to things like farmland, crops, homes, infrastructure, roads, and people who necessarily cross its flowing waters when it "got up out of its banks." Scores of travelers and citizens lost their lives and property crossing in the dark or during high, swift water, and others drowned while gathering food or enjoying the Salt for relaxation. These aforementioned conditions are accepted facts of life when committed to establishing life near a moving body of water.

Not so obvious are the social implications of natural barriers on people living along the Salt's riverbanks. While asking one image contributor about a small community gone only 30 years distant, I received an unexpected answer. The paraphrased response went as follows: "Oh, well, that's on the other side of the Salt River, which was almost a different part of the world. In this town, we conducted our lives this side of the Salt; we did our schooling, shopping, worshipping, doctoring, celebrating, and mourning around this place. Folks on the other side did likewise around another town on their side. Even with a bridge there, you didn't cross over unless you had to. You just conducted life that way."

Using an imaginary time travel machine, consider how much more this physical water barrier affected our ancestors who had no hard roads, bridges, automobiles, or electronic devices. And yet, they made do; most thrived, prospered, and grew Ralls County to what it is today.

Today, we still conduct life "that way" on our respective sides, despite having infrastructure to cross over safely and quickly. In truth, we, their descendants, can no longer use the Salt River as a valid impediment to our crossing over. A richer quality of life waits to be discovered, enabling us to cross more difficult barriers of the will and mind, such as hatred, racism, and man's natural tendency toward despotism. Tyranny always means the loss of personal liberty and a divine right to live free of oppression. No doubt early Ralls citizens struggled with these too, but first they conquered physical barriers leaving behind a better future through rugged individualism. Hopefully, we, their descendants, will rededicate ourselves to that purpose.

I am honored to have this opportunity to select, research, interpret, and present images within this book. I tried not to tread areas covered by Goldena Howard's *Ralls County Missouri History* (1980), although some people, places, structures, and events deserved repetition to a wider audience. Necessarily, information was researched from her lifetime work; other facts came from archival newspapers, Internet sources, and self-published local histories. The 10 chapters are meant to finely dissect Ralls County's enigmatic qualities. Each chapter is chronological; each image intended to be illustrative of the chapter title. The final chapter, Here and Now, is meant to help us recognize that history is still around us if we look for it.

While few photographs exist of Ralls County prior to 1880, there are plenty after. They are drawn from the collections of the Ralls County Historical Society, my personal collection, and local history collectors. Many were taken by professional photographers like Herb Tomlinson, Hal and Jean Fraser, John Hermann Herring, Minnie and Nelson Stehle, Otis Howell of the *Hannibal Courier-Post*, John Porter Fisher of the *Ralls County Times*, itinerant postcard photographers, and ordinary citizens like Liz Gingry, Anna Schnitzlein, and Phil Conn. We are historically richer because these photographers captured images as points on history's timeline. Furthermore, we are fortunate these images survived because of those who preserved them, fully understanding their intrinsic value.

As with any historical endeavor, some wonderful images failed the selection process or factual errors may have occurred. Memories, newspapers, and reliable sources are sometimes wrong. One of my favorite adages says, "Logic is a systematic method of coming to the wrong conclusion with confidence." My only defense is that the images and information were the best that could be acquired and ascertained through careful research and photograph examination at press time. Any errors are regretted.

—K. Allen Ballard, April 2012

"History is not WAS, it IS." —William Faulkner

One
Small Footprint and Big Impact

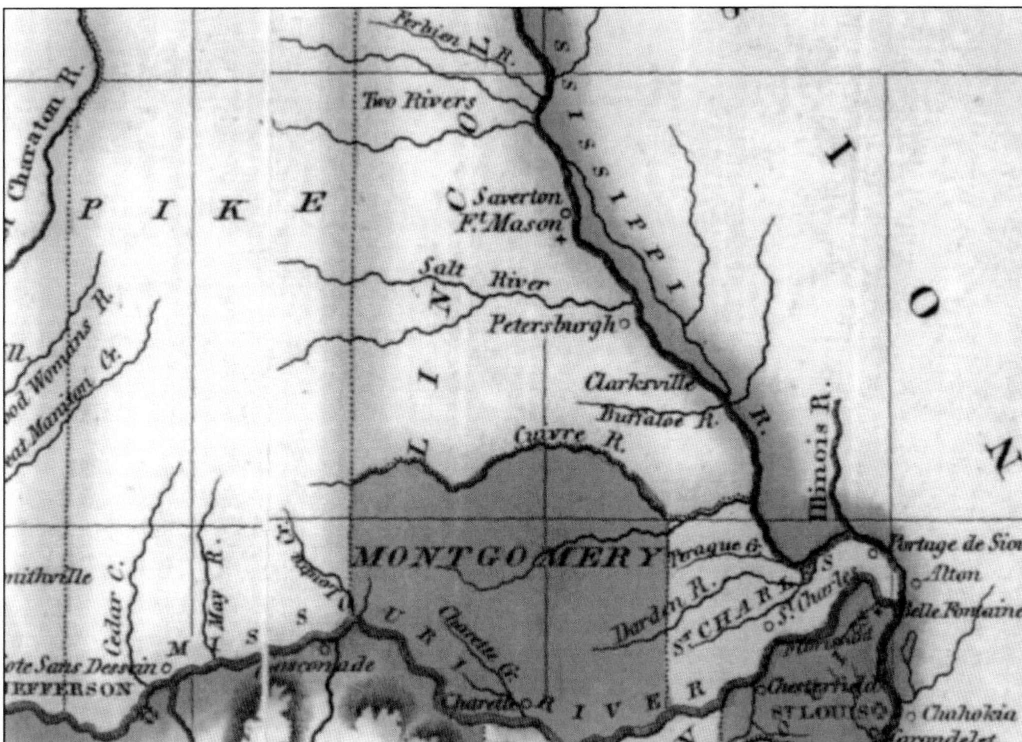

This 1812 map is of Northeast Missouri before the earliest settlements, including New London and Palmyra. Fort Mason was built two miles south of the Saverton Saltworks during the War of 1812 to protect against raiding Indian parties but burned shortly after. Hannibal is not yet established, but Clarksville is. Likewise, Waconda (near present-day LaGrange) and Louisiana are not shown but were early trading posts in the newly designated Missouri Territory. (RCHS.)

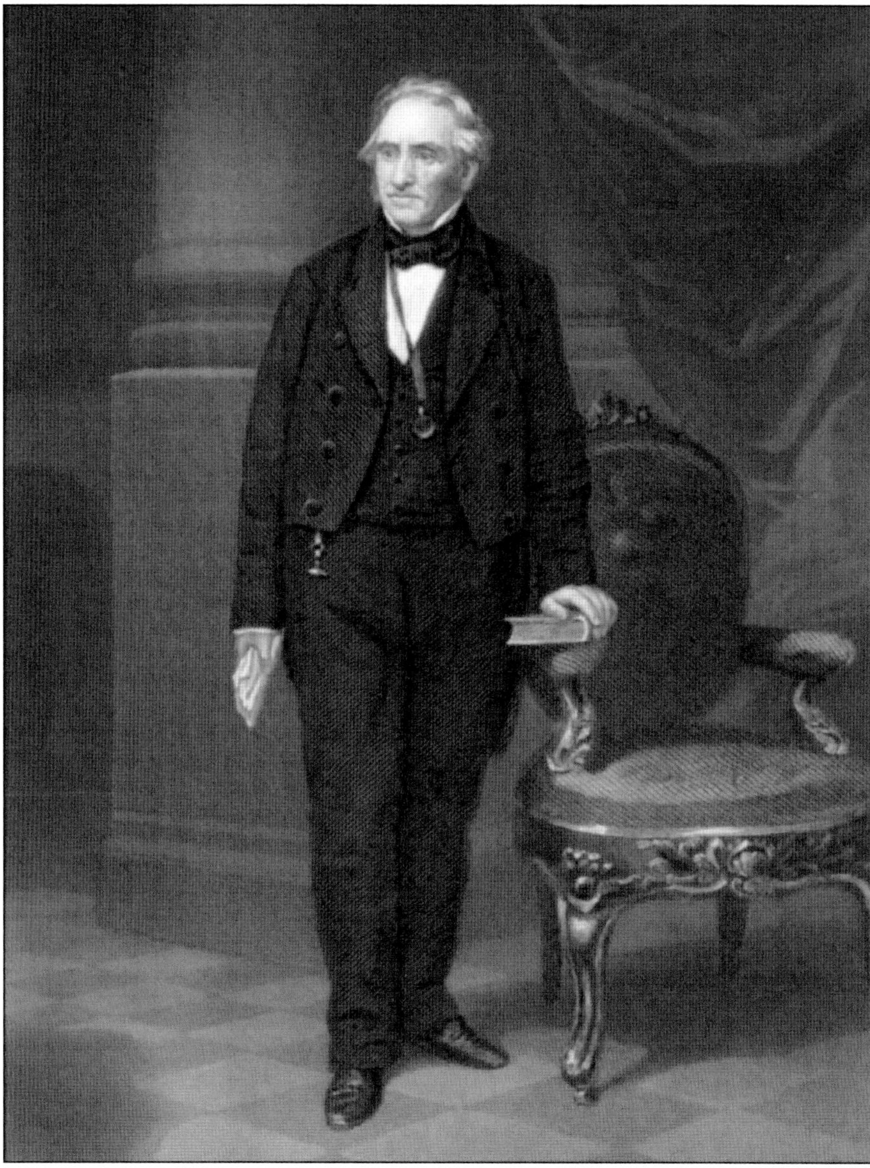

Born in North Carolina, Thomas Hart Benton (1782–1858) was kicked out of law school for stealing and then moved to Tennessee. He became Andrew Jackson's aide-de-camp, serving as lieutenant colonel in the War of 1812. He was assigned to represent Jackson's interests in Washington, DC, which kept Benton from combat experience. Benton felt slighted and so he feuded with Jackson, who was wounded by Benton's brother Jesse. Thereafter, Benton moved to St. Louis, Missouri. In 1817, Benton faced fellow lawyer Charles Lucas in court, where each accused the other of lying. Benton was offended and challenged Lucas to a duel twice on Bloody Island, mortally wounding Lucas in the second challenge. On October 2, 1820, State Representative Daniel Ralls voted for Benton from his deathbed, which was physically carried into the legislative chamber. Ralls's vote clinched Benton's election as Missouri's first US senator; he served five terms from 1821 to 1851. Senator Benton reciprocated, making Ralls immortal by naming the new county for him. Benton was a leading supporter of Manifest Destiny policies and opposed the Democrat Party, denouncing slavery in 1850. (Author.)

This early-1820s map of Northeast Missouri shows most of the original boundaries and early settlements of Ralls County, which stretched from Pike County to the Iowa border and from the Mississippi River to the eastern branch of the Chariton River near present-day Macon. By 1826, eight full and five partial counties had been carved from Ralls County. (RCHS.)

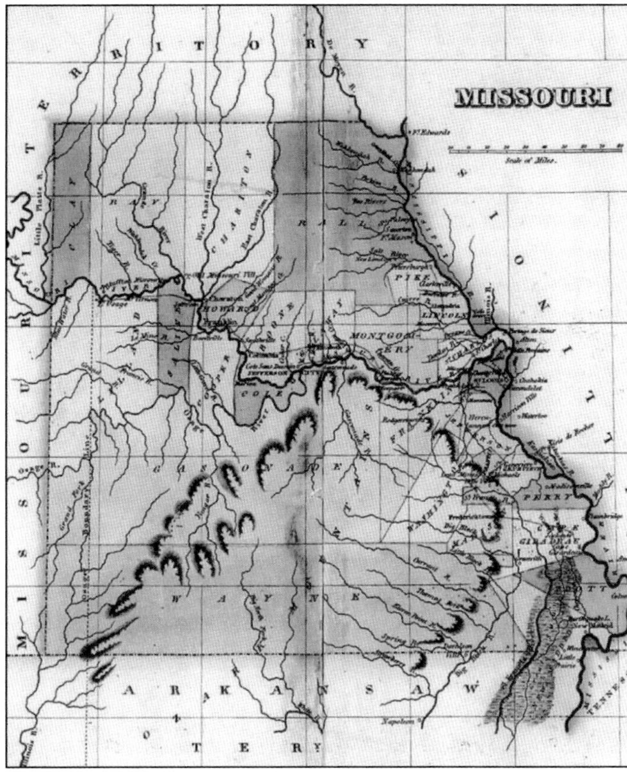

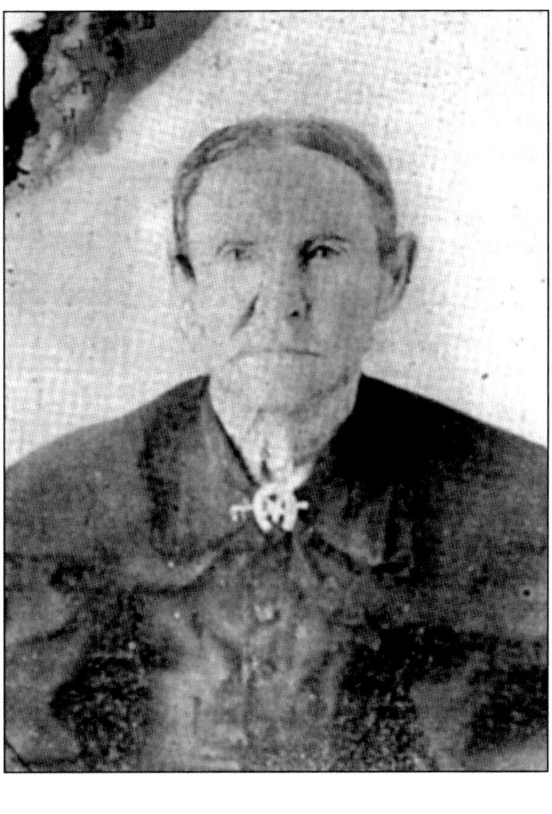

On August 6, 1818, Nancy Jeffries was the first white child born in New London to Robert and Elizabeth (Jamison) Jeffries. She remembered Native Americans still living in the county. Nancy possessed a very industrious, hard-working nature, a quality that meant not just survival but also prosperity for early settlers. She married Washington Epperson in 1838, who built a log cabin near Madisonville. (RCHS.)

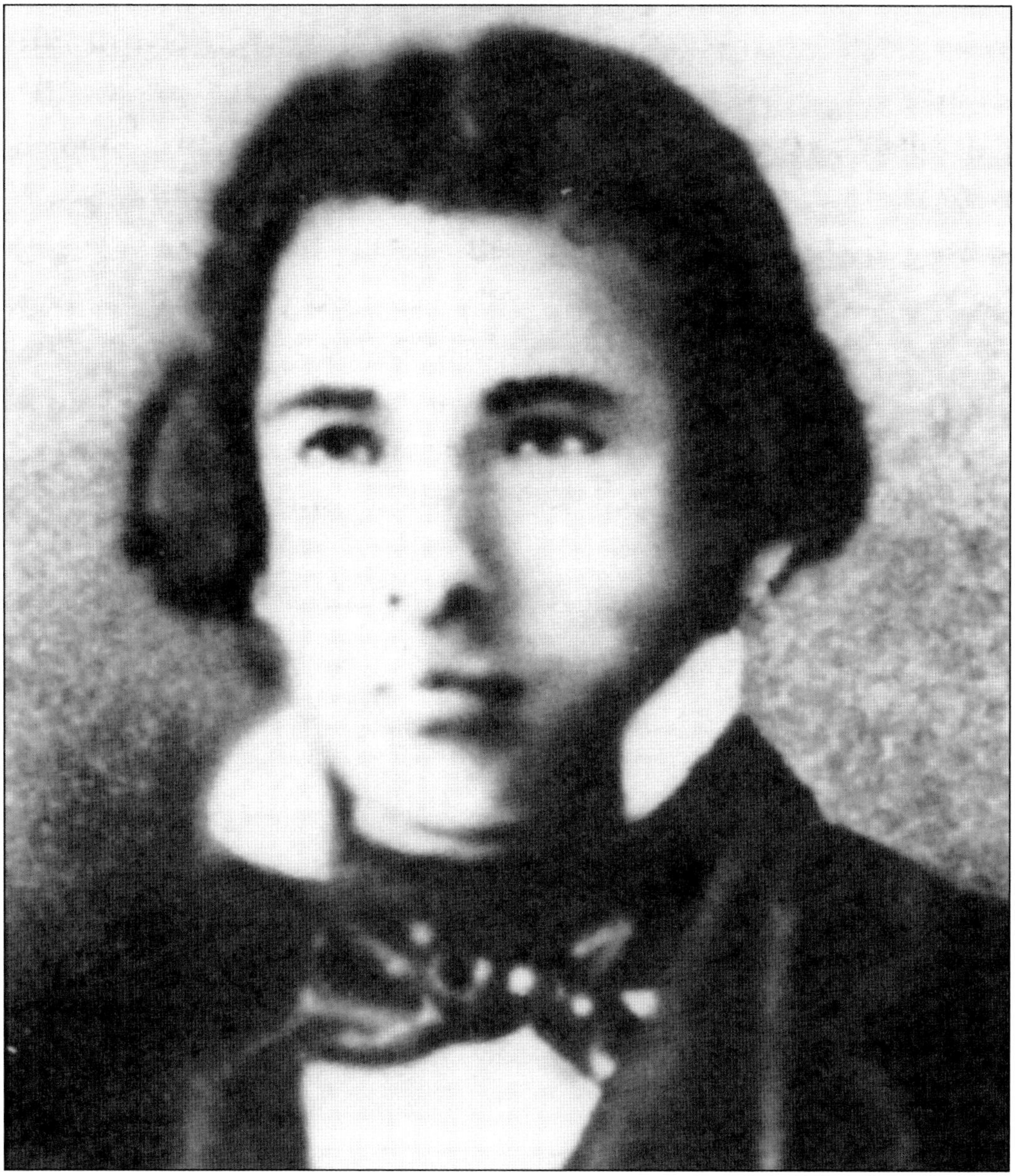

The second Ralls County sheriff, William W. Smith, also known as John W. Smith, abandoned his family for the promise of Texas lands. In Texas, Smith became a military storekeeper, surveyor, land clerk, and engineer for Bexar County. More importantly, he became guide and courier for Col. William Barrett Travis, commander of the fortified Alamo. On March 1, 1836, Smith led Captain Dickinson and 31 Gonzales, Texas, men past Mexican pickets under Gen. Antonio Santa Ana into the besieged Alamo. On March 3, Smith was one of the last men out of the Alamo carrying a plea for reinforcements from Barrett to Gen. Sam Houston. He also carried letters naming him as estate administrator for Will Lysander and Col. David Crockett. On March 6, he reached General Houston at the Texas Convention, who could provide nothing to the Alamo defenders. Smith immediately recruited 50 volunteers and rode back to Cibolo Creek, but the Alamo had already fallen on March 6. Smith later fought at San Jacinto and became mayor of San Antonio three times. He died in 1845, a Texas Republic senator and Texas's second largest landowner. (Bert Howard.)

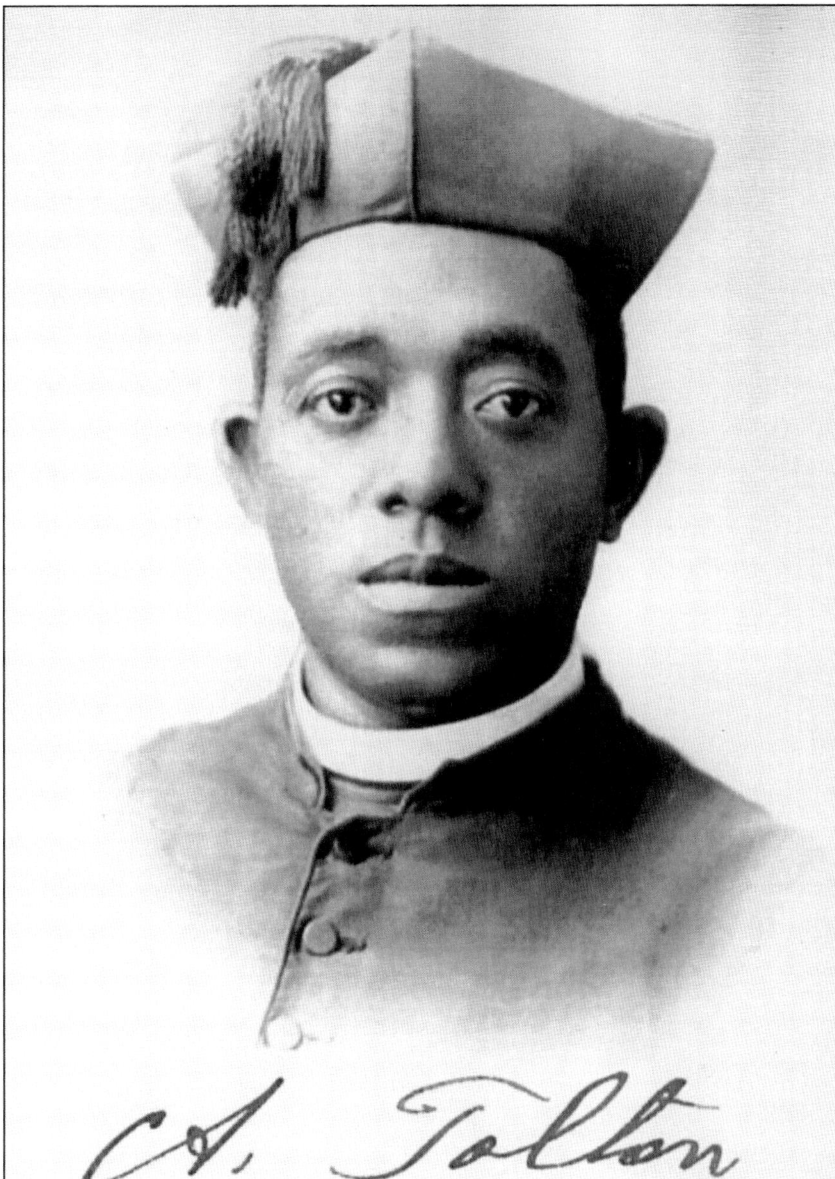

In 1854, Augustus Tolton was born into slavery to Peter and Martha Chisley Tolton, slaves of the Stephen Eliot family in Ralls County near Brush Creek. Peter escaped in 1861 but died serving in the Union army; Martha escaped with her four children to Quincy, Illinois. In Quincy, sisters at St. Boniface tutored Gus until he enrolled in St. Peter's. Racism kept him from attending an American seminary, so Father McGirr and Franciscan father Richardt secured his entry to Rome's Collegia Urbanum de Propaganda Fide. America's first black Catholic priest was ordained on April 24, 1886, and returned to pastor St. Joseph's in Quincy. In 1888, he was sent to the Chicago Diocese and a small chapel at Thirty-sixth and Dearborn Streets. "Good Father Gus" was a passionate, popular preacher, speaking at conferences in Boston, Galveston, and Washington, DC. Tragically, jealousy and racism followed him closely his entire ministry. He died of heatstroke in Chicago July 9, 1897, and was buried in a shared grave in Quincy. In February 2011, the Catholic Church began the canonization process toward sainthood for Father Tolton. (RCHS.)

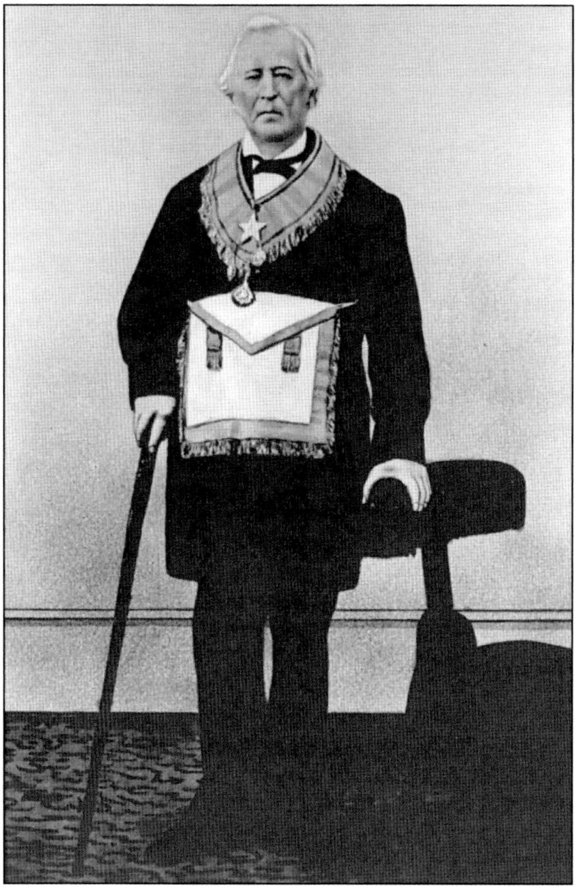

Col. John Ralls (left), eldest son of Daniel Ralls, was raised by Kentucky grandparents. In 1828, he took advantage of his father's political favors beginning as doormaster for the Missouri Senate. As Missouri's grand master, he established Masonic lodges statewide and nationally. He served during the Blackhawk War and participated in the 1847 capture of Santa Cruz, Mexico, receiving the sabers of the vanquished for Gen. Sterling Price. (Ralls Lodge No. 33.)

Below is an 1890s portrait of Judge Rueben F. Roy (1854–1922) and Margaret "Maggie" Hays (1863–1925) of New London. Roy was a lawyer, judge, and commissioner to the Missouri Supreme Court from 1911 to 1919. Judge Roy, originally Democrat, switched to Republican and ran unsuccessfully against Bowling Green's Champ Clark for US Congress, yet both were lifelong friends. (RCHS.)

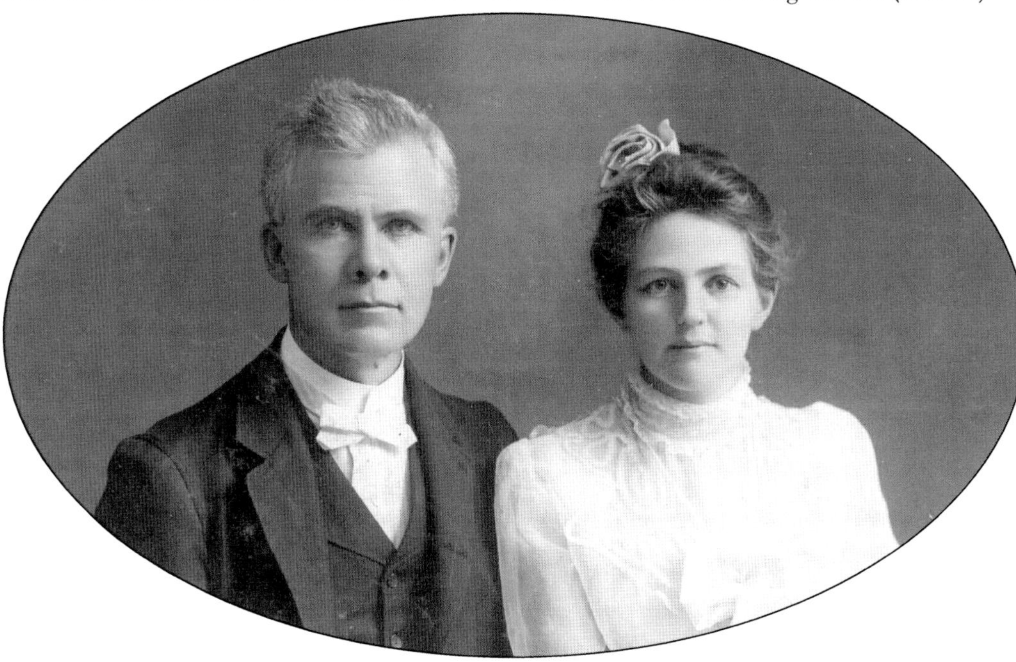

This 1893 Tomlinson photograph is of New London's Harry Carstarphen (1891–1989). He became a brilliant attorney who argued and won a landmark case, Baldwin versus the State of Missouri, before the US Supreme Court. On May 26, 1930, the court declared that only one state could impose estate taxes on a deceased person's estate. Harry was the final attorney for the St. Louis & Hannibal Railroad and partners with Frank Harvey in Hannibal. (Author.)

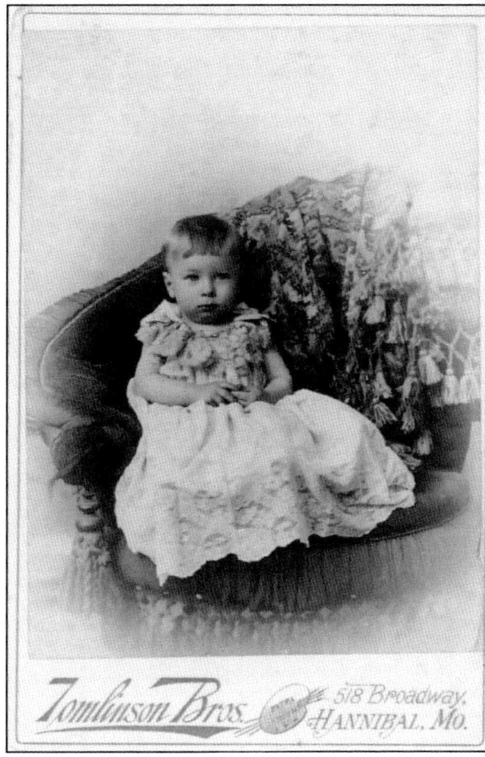

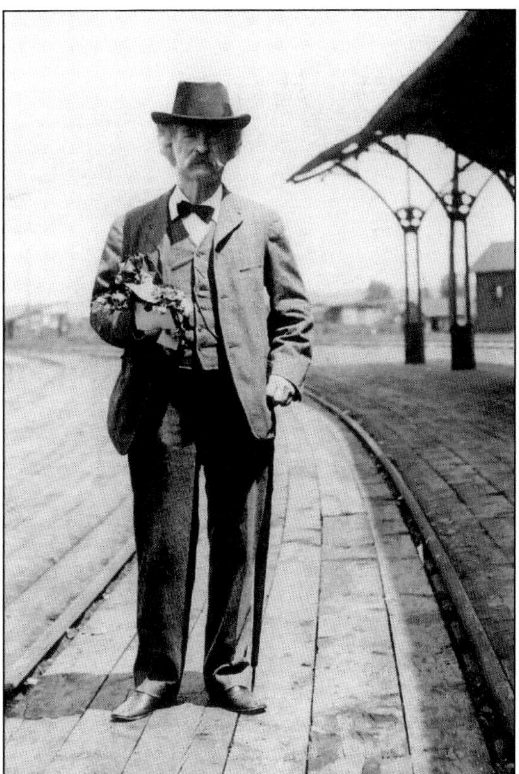

Samuel Clemens and Absalom Grimes were Confederate soldiers briefly in Ralls County with the Salt River Rangers near Florida, Missouri. The Rangers dissolved two weeks later, so Clemens went to his brother Orion's in Keokuk. Thereafter, both left for Nevada Territory, where Orion was appointed secretary and Clemens became Mark Twain, later recalling this adventure in "The Private History of a Campaign That Failed." Twain is shown here at Hannibal's Union Depot in 1902. (Steve Chou.)

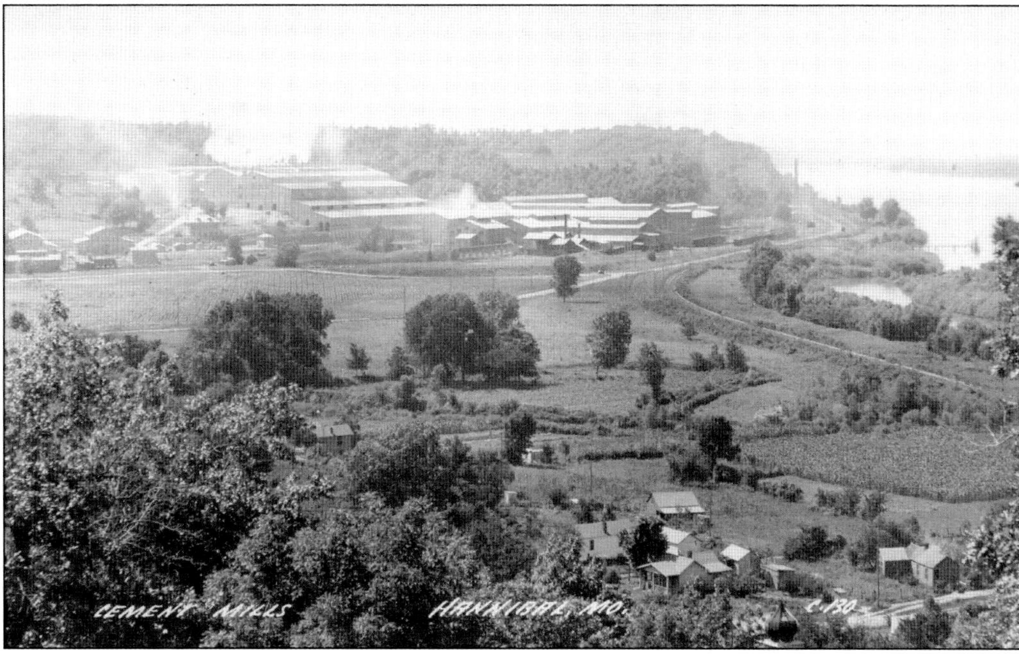

This L.L. Cook real-photo postcard from the 1910s is of the Atlas Cement plant and the village of Monkey Run in the foreground. About 6.5 million barrels of cement from Atlas went into the concrete construction of the Panama Canal (1909–1914). In addition, Atlas cement was used for New York City's Empire State Building (1930–1931). (David Polc.)

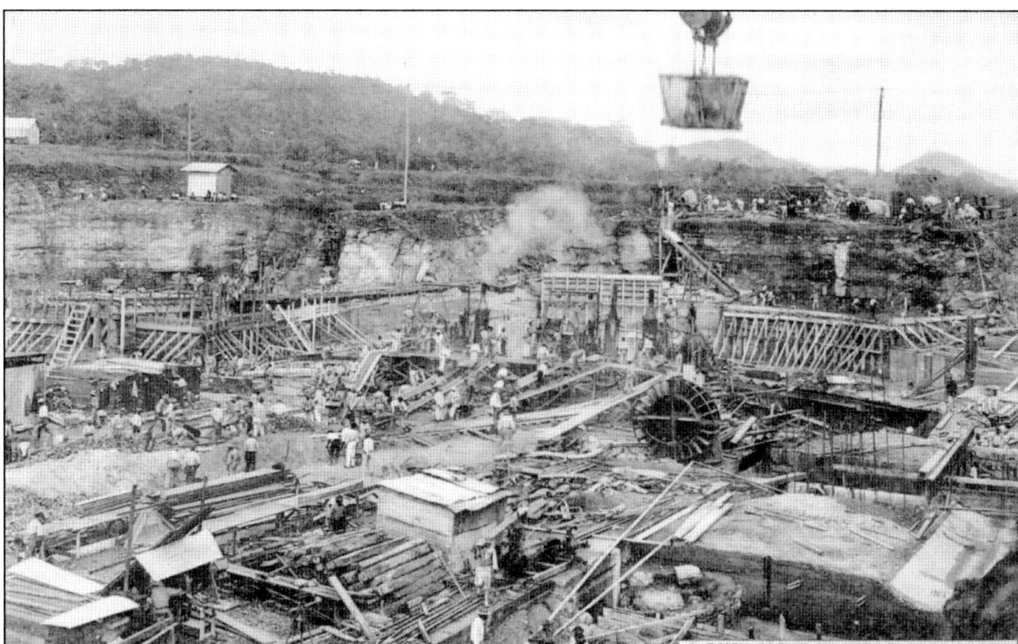

This real-photo postcard shows construction of the Miraflores Canal Locks in the Panama Canal Zone around 1912. The cement used to build the canal was mined and manufactured by the immigrant men who worked in Ilasco, Missouri. (Author.)

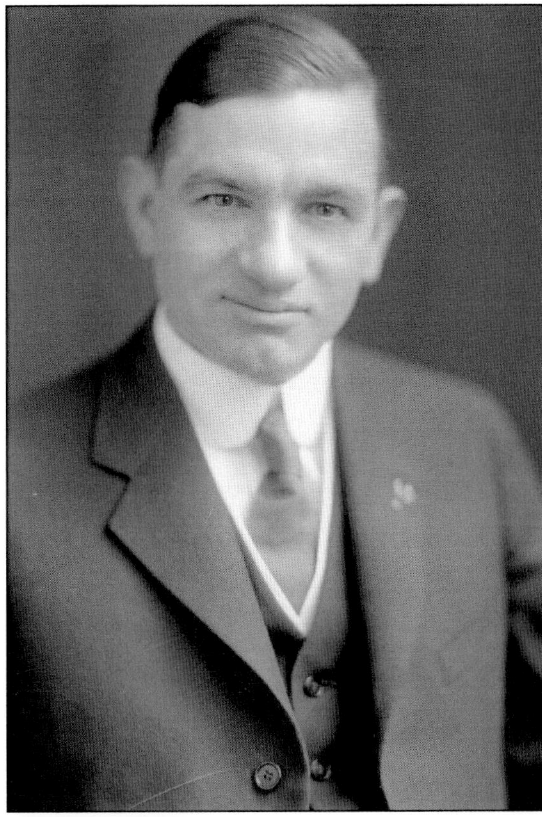

Clarence Cannon (1871–1964) of Elsberry, Missouri, attended LaGrange (Missouri) College, William Jewell in Liberty, Missouri, and and earned a law degree from the University of Missouri. He went from being a teacher, principal, and then clerk to Champ Clark, finally winning election to Congress in 1922. As appropriations committee chairman, he supported soil conservation, rural electrification, and flood control projects, like the dam built and named for him in Ralls County. This photograph was taken in the 1910s. (Author.)

Joe Douglass (1821–1923), "Old Indian Joe," emphatically denied resemblance to Mark Twain's "Injun Joe" character. Both Native American and African American, he was found abandoned in a Callaway County Indian campsite by a man named Douglass. Joe farmed near Center, invested in real estate, was widowed twice, and moved to Hannibal. In 1902, Joe met Twain at his hotel with a gift of flowers. (Author.)

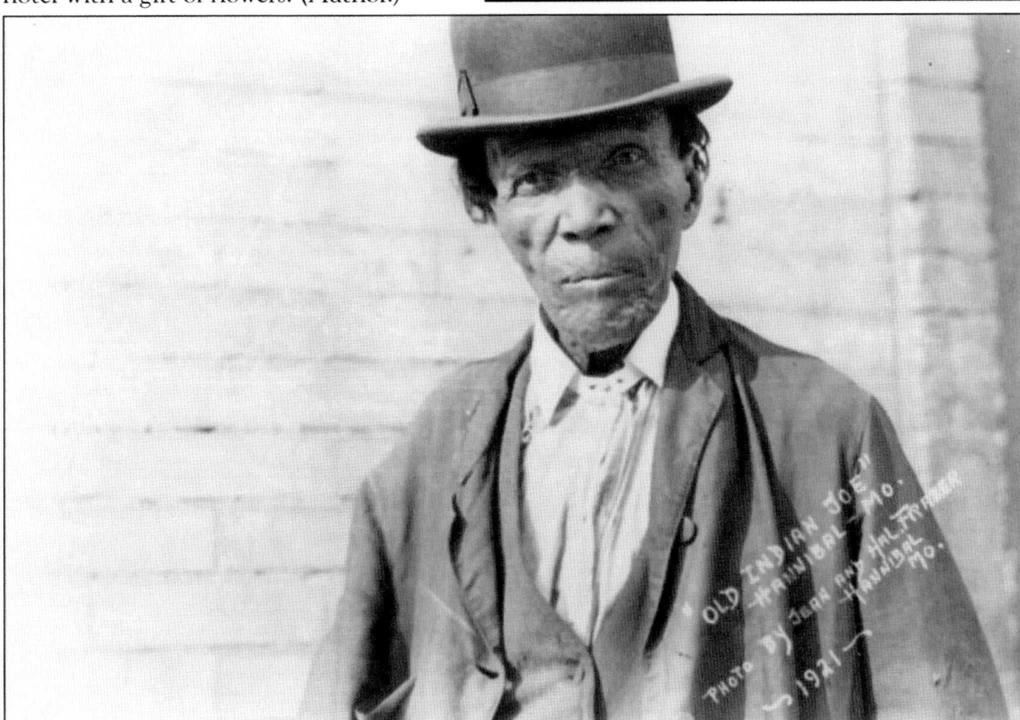

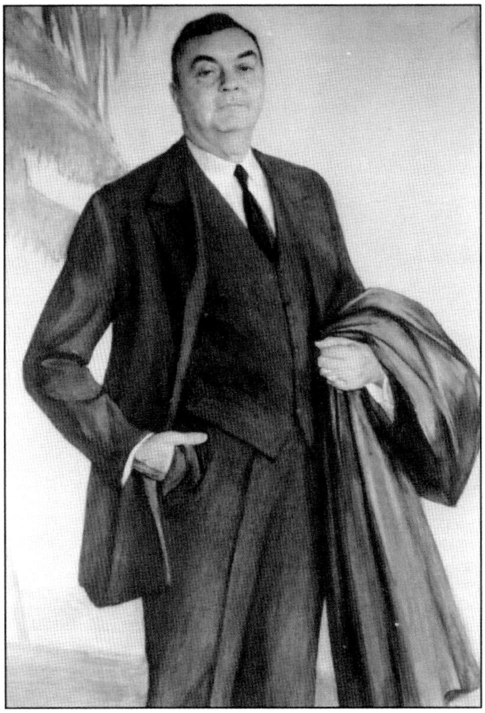

John Ringling (1886–1936) was the surviving brother of Ringling Bros. Circus. As one of the wealthiest men in America, he bought Barnum & Bailey's Circus for $400,000 in 1907, collected Baroque art and bourbon, and invested millions in American communities. In 1919, he bought and updated the St. Louis & Hannibal Railroad, partnered in Perry-Hannibal Coal Co., and began Northeast Missouri Sand and Gravel near Organ Ferry Ford. (Author.)

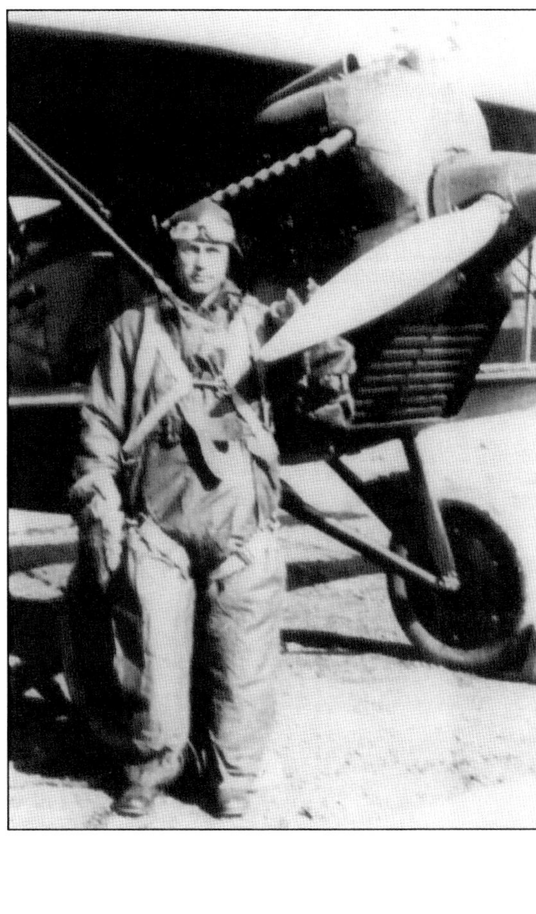

Here is Joanna resident 2nd Lt. Okle Rouse of the Army Air Reserve. As a mechanic, he helped prepare Charles Lindbergh's Ryan N-X 211, the *Spirit of St. Louis*, for his not-as-famous December 13–14, 1927, nonstop flight from Washington, DC, to Mexico City. Okle is shown with a Curtiss Falcon, the same type of aircraft that Lindbergh flew to Mexico in 1928. Okle later helped Dee Paul West, author of *The End of a Way of Life*. (RCHS.)

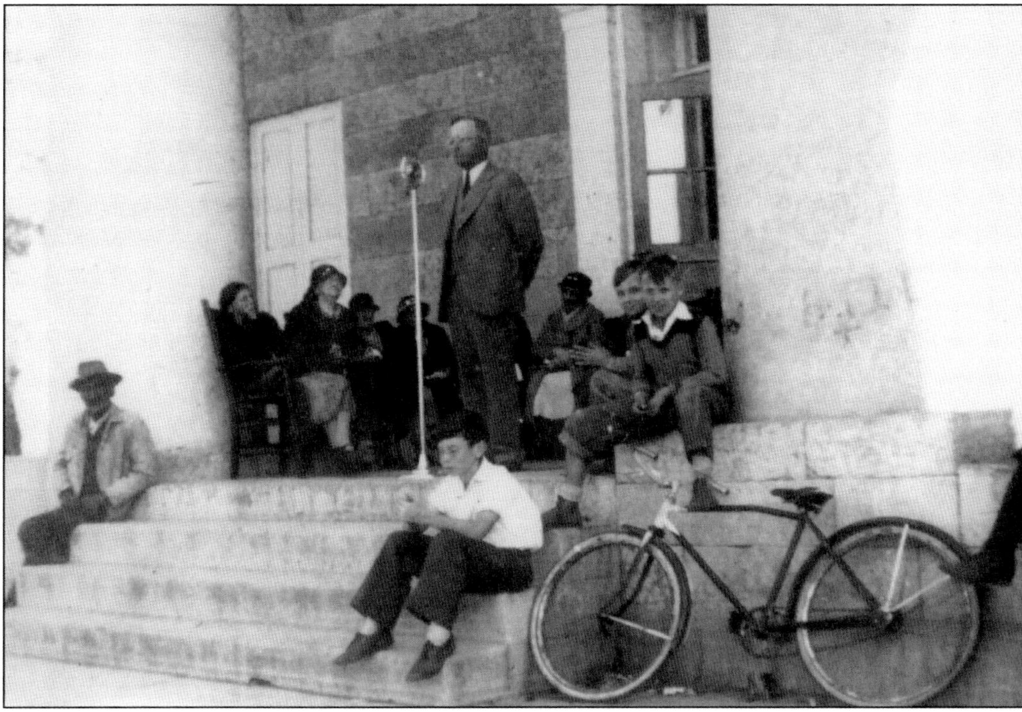

Harry Truman is seen campaigning for US Senate from the courthouse steps on October 13, 1934. Truman was then presiding judge of Jackson County, Missouri. In 1940, while campaigning for reelection, he bought a round of beers at Al's Tavern in Ilasco. Identified are Caroll Willey (boy on steps); Onie Newlon (man right of column); and Mabel Stout (middle woman seated looking at Truman). (Harry S. Truman Library.)

Egbert Van Alstyne (1878–1951), born in Chicago, moved with his family to near Fools Creek in 1885, which was where he attended Centenary School. An early musical prodigy, "Bert" became the most diverse composer of his era, writing comic tunes, ragtimes, and operettas. Recalling his boyhood days and an apple tree on a hill south of Centenary School, he wrote "In the Shade of the Old Apple Tree" in 1905. (Author.)

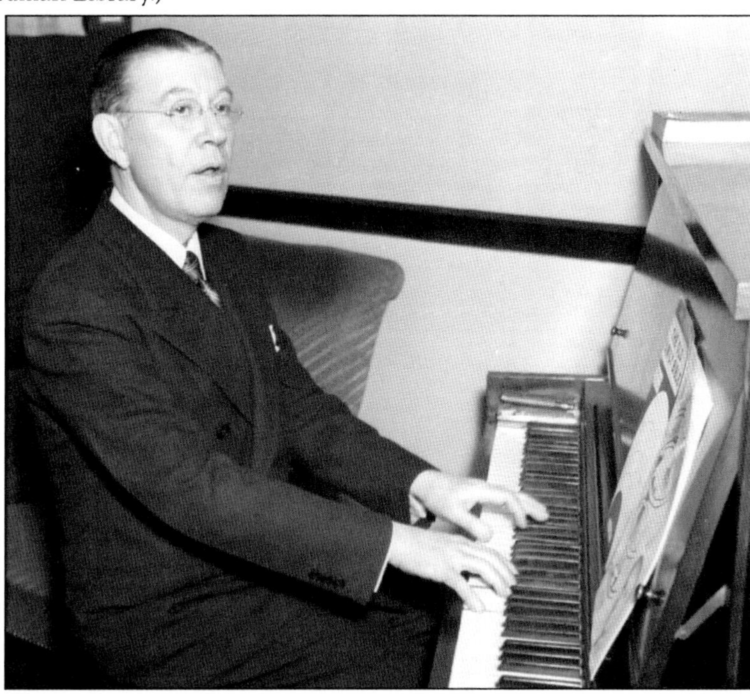

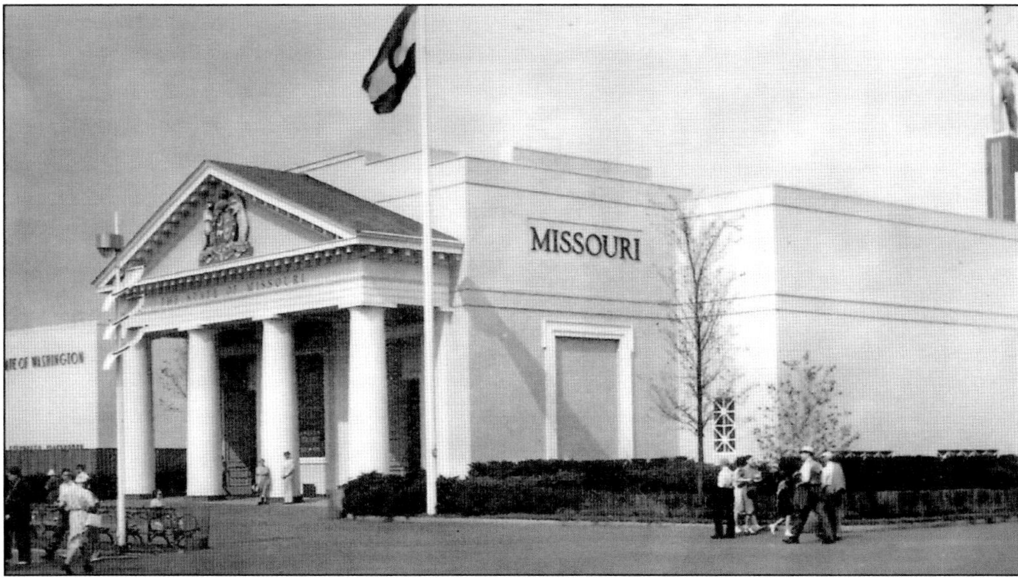

At the 1939 World's Fair in New York City, the Missouri State Building featured the facade of the Ralls County Courthouse. This building housed exhibits of minerals, resources, and agricultural and manufacturing products from the Show Me State, as well as a Mark Twain exhibit. Only 23 of 48 American states participated in the 1939 fair. (RCHS.)

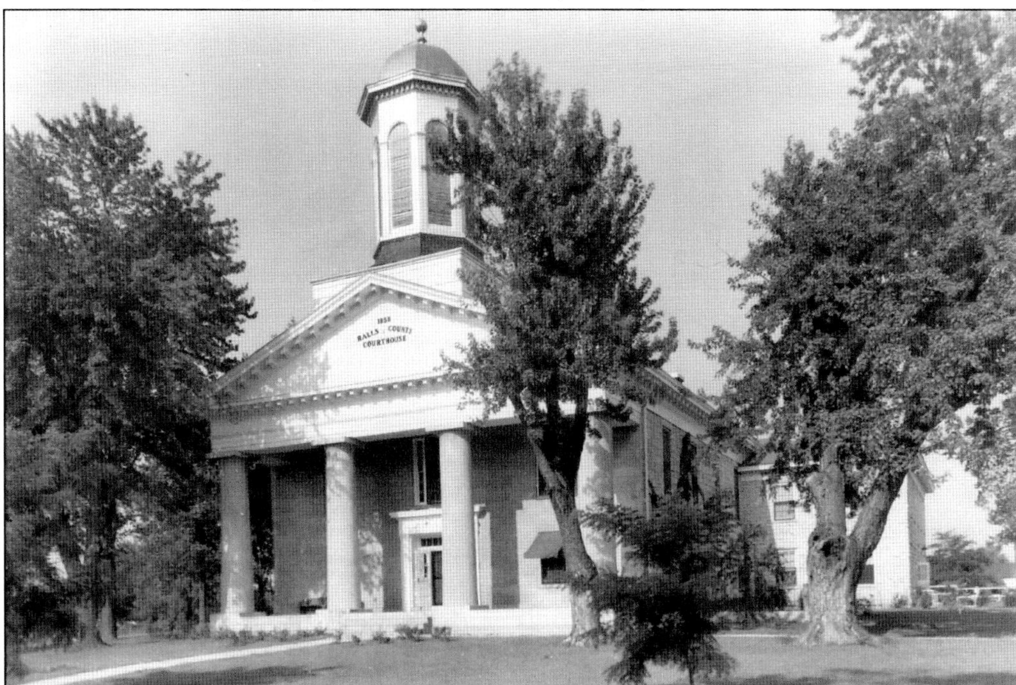

The 1858 Ralls County Courthouse is classic Greek Revival architecture from locally quarried limestone. The third seat of Ralls County government was built in 1856–1858 at a cost of $18,000. Chapel Carstarphen, William Fagan, and Kemper Shumate oversaw construction. Today, it is one of the oldest courthouses still in continuous use west of the Mississippi River. It is pictured on July 21, 1939. (Author.)

Two
Hither and Yon

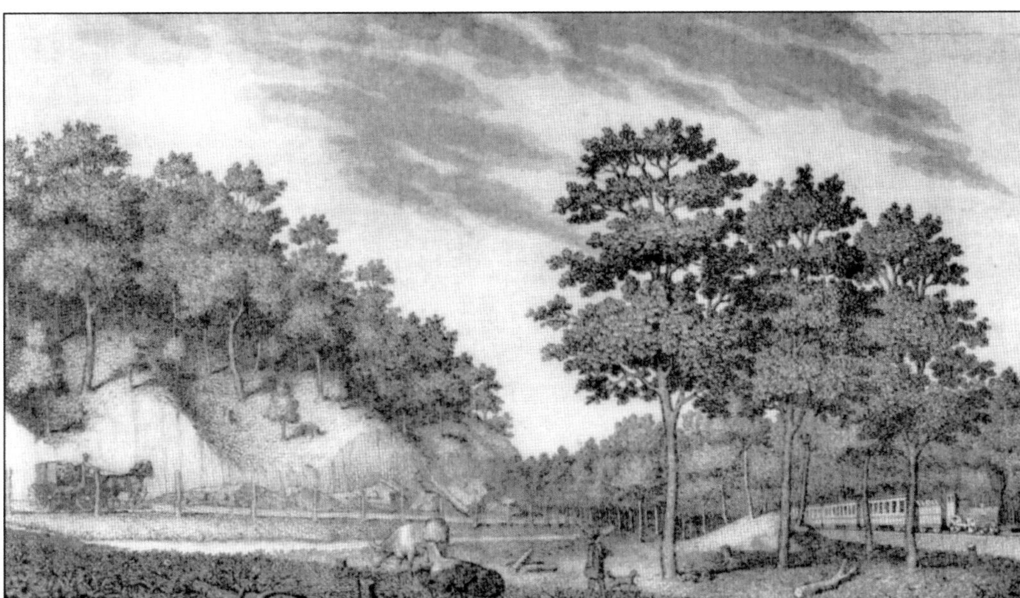

This 1855 newspaper engraving shows the Hannibal, Ralls County, Paris Plank Road west of Oakwood. This 55-mile-long pike passed through Hydesburg, Pidgeon Creek, Saline, Sidney, Monroe City, Indian Creek, and Florida before reaching Paris, Missouri. Sufficient investment capital and toll money never materialized to completely plank or maintain the road, so around 1870, gravel became the practical road surface. (Author.)

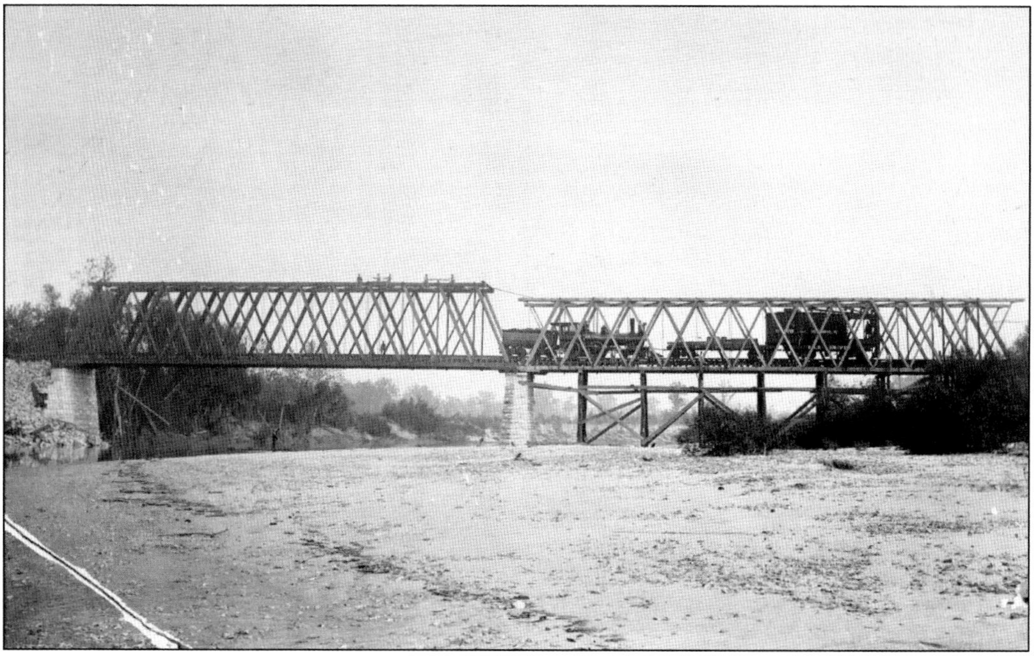

Salt River Railroad Bridge, three miles north of New London, is pictured here in the 1890s. This 294-foot Double Howe Truss span was built in 1871, costing $8,900, and was rebuilt in 1917 with two 147-foot through-riveted spans. In 1925, a section crew informed Sheriff John Palmer that they found a frozen moonshine still in the woods nearby. Though the bridge was scrapped in the late 1940s, the abutments remain today near the Steve Lake Farm. (Archie Hayden.)

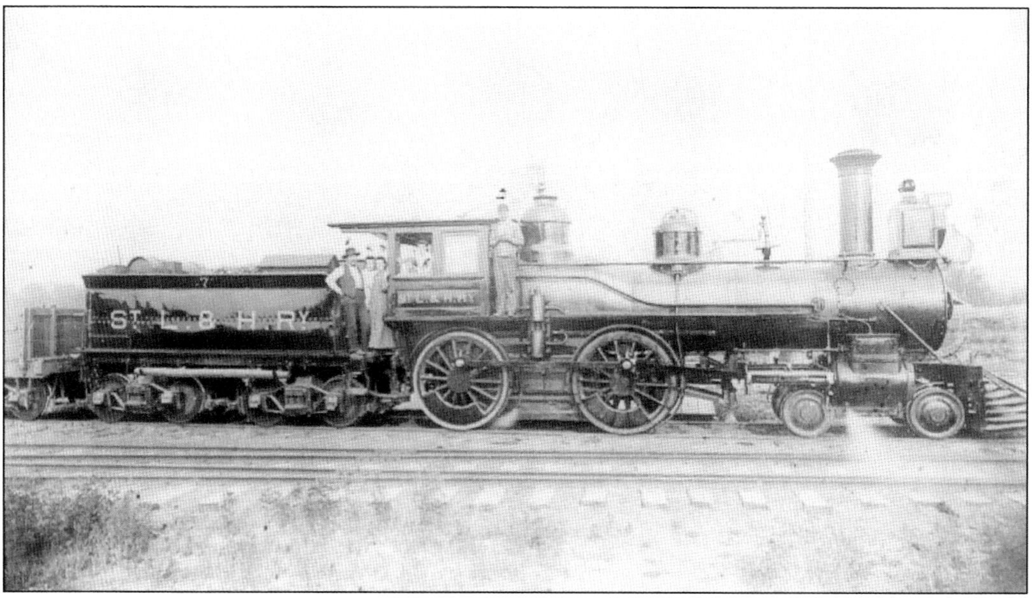

On July 25, 1892, engine No. 7 arrived in Perry following completion of St. Louis & Hannibal's 19-mile branch line from New London. From left to right, engineer Mirt Tierney, Mable, Anna, and Myrle Crim, and Charles Poole pose on the 4-4-0 locomotive, built by Schenectady Locomotive in 1884. L.J. "Snow" Stark was conductor. Trains arrived in Perry facing forward but backed into Hannibal until a 60-foot turntable was installed at Perry. (RCHS.)

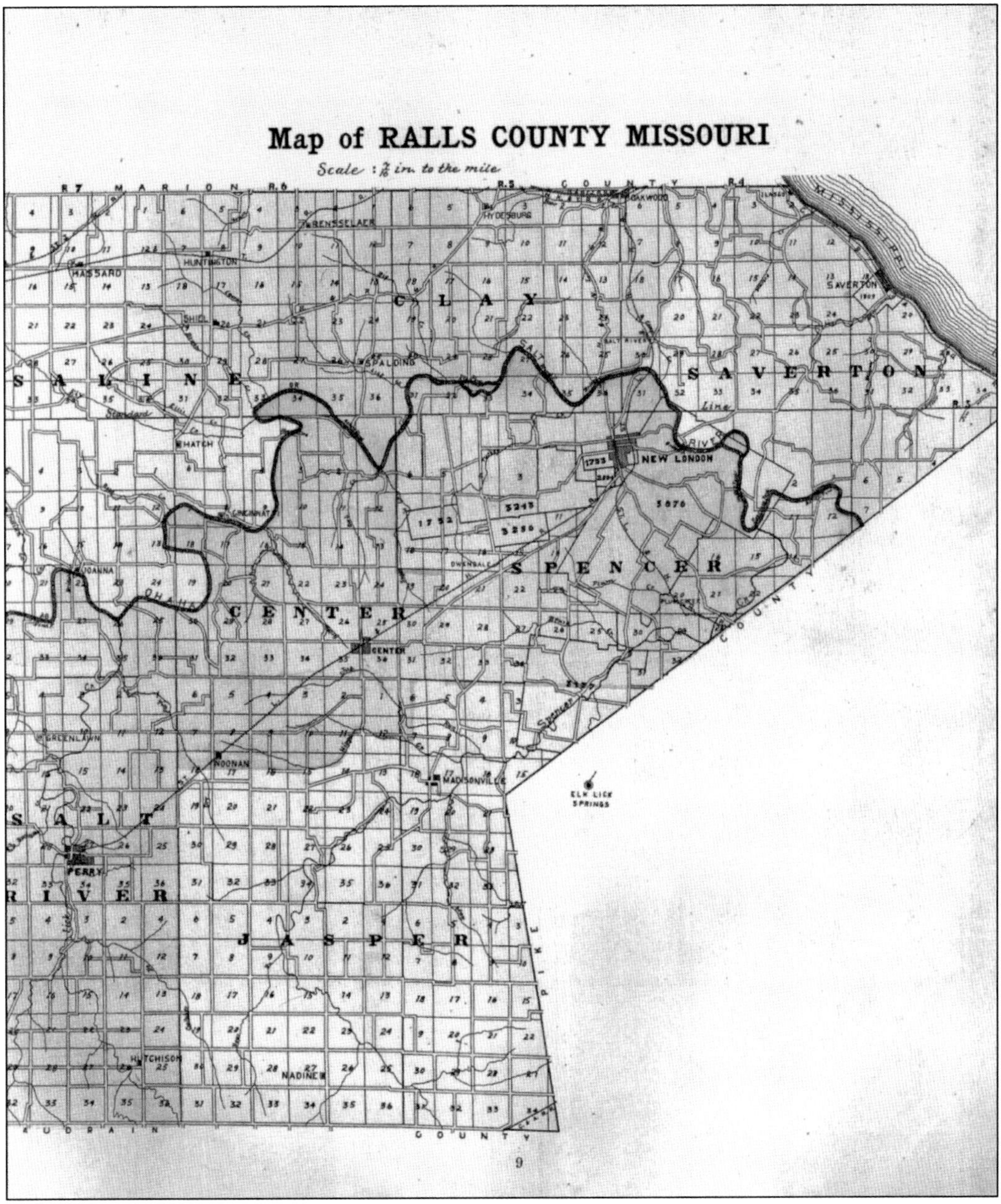

The 1904 Ralls County Plat Book has this full sectional map of Ralls County within. Present-day roads are taking shape, and others are starting to fade into the past. Note that Missouri Route 19 has yet to be constructed. Today, Highway 19 closely connects all three major Ralls towns of New London, Center, and Perry. By 1904, there were three bridges over the Salt—the 1853 covered toll bridge, a new steel bridge at Joanna, and a second bridge completed at Organ Ferry east of New London. Asher Bridge had not been erected by the time of this map. Of special interest are the named river fords: Lower Hogg, Asher, Ely, Woods, Haden, Epperson, and Bailey. Upper Hogg is not shown but was located at the present-day dam site near the Joanna community. (RCHS.)

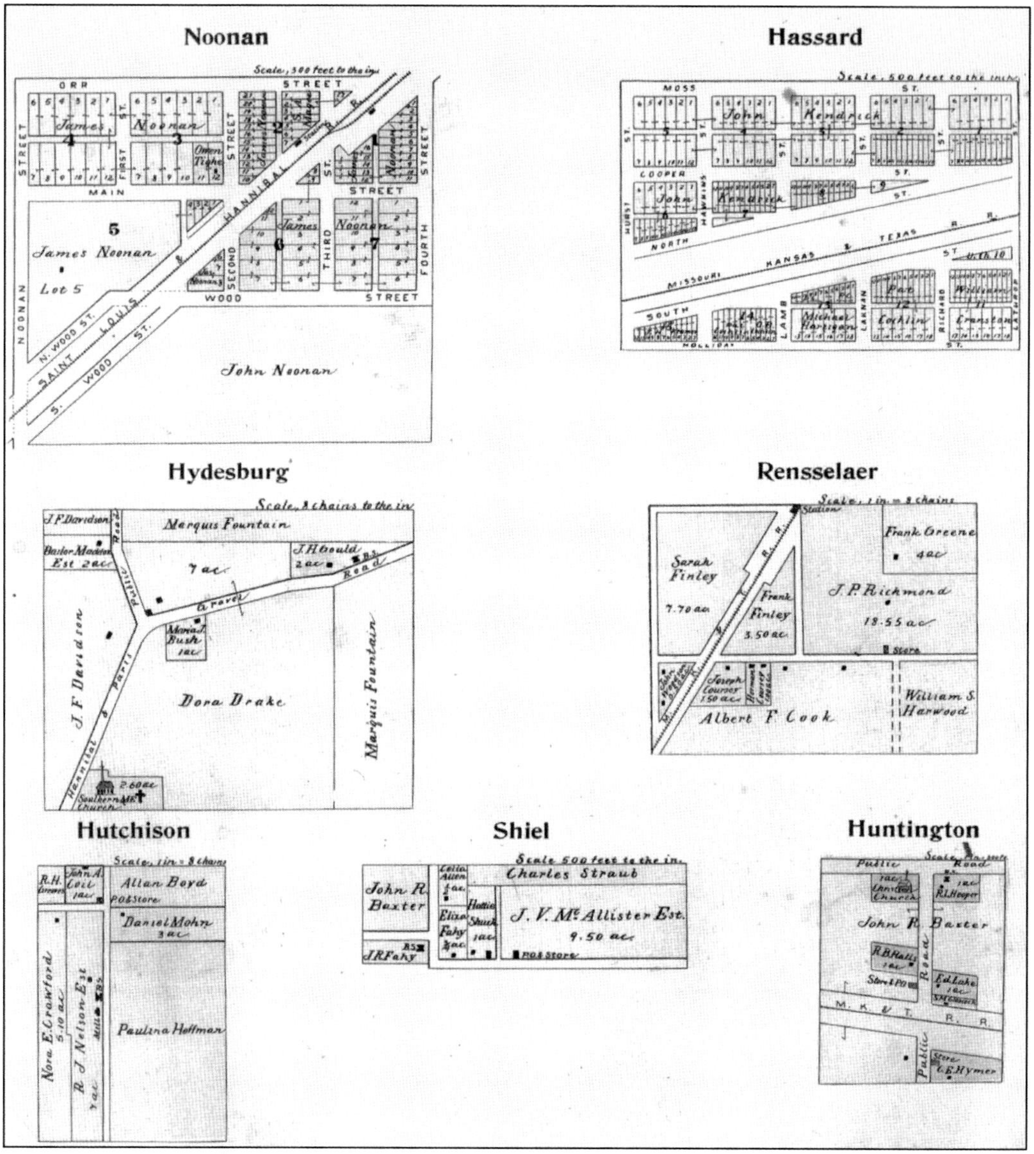

Here are seven smaller communities from the 1904 Ralls Plat Book. Essentially, these are true pictures of actual layouts with the exception of Noonan and Hassard. Neither ever achieved the lot occupancy shown. There are some errors too: Big Creek Church and both schools are not shown in Rensselaer; the same is true of Hassard and the Kendrick Store. (RCHS.)

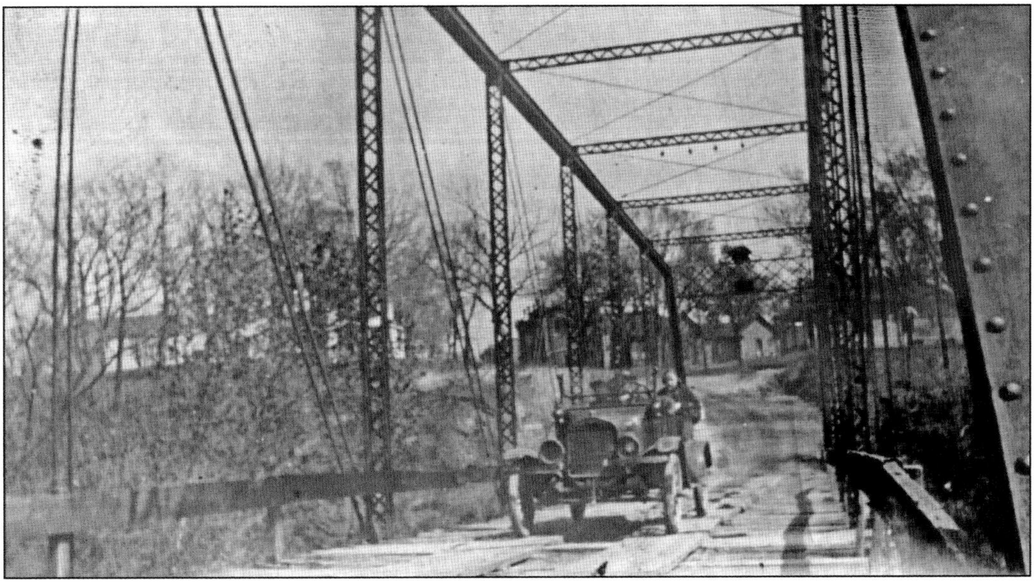

The main western door to Perry was crossing Lick Creek over this first bridge. Two more have succeeded it on present-day Missouri Route 154 on this picturesque entrance along Lick Creek's bluffs. If one were to go uphill from here, the view would be similar to what is found in the next image. (RCHS.)

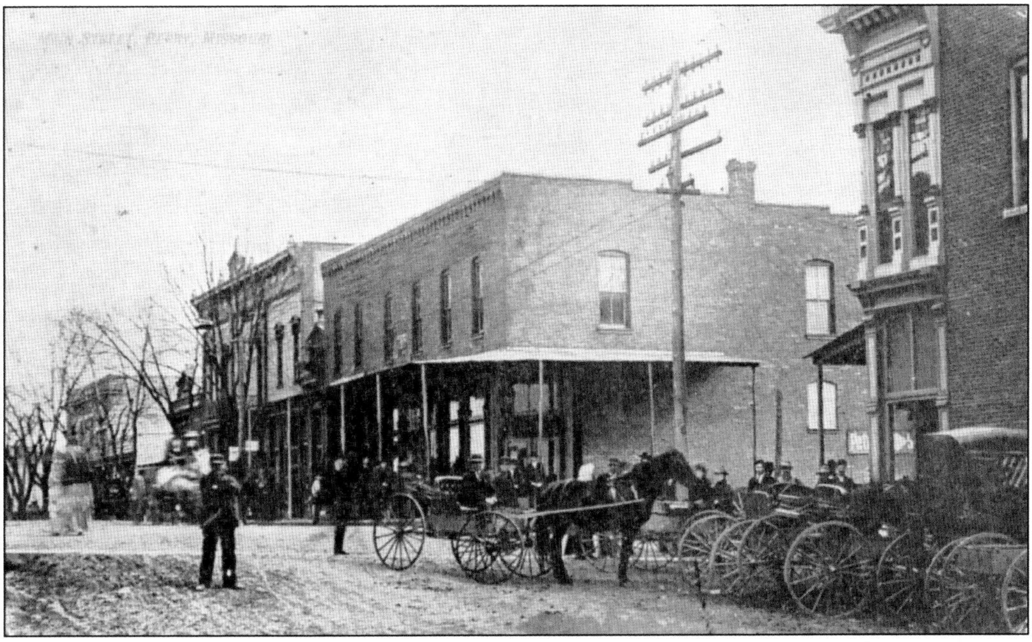

Here is a 1905 postcard view looking southeast at the intersection of Main and Palmyra Streets in Perry, Missouri. Buildings in view are, from left to right, Richards Store, Perry State Bank, Elliott Goss, Hanna Store, and the Young and Menefee store across the street. (David Polc.)

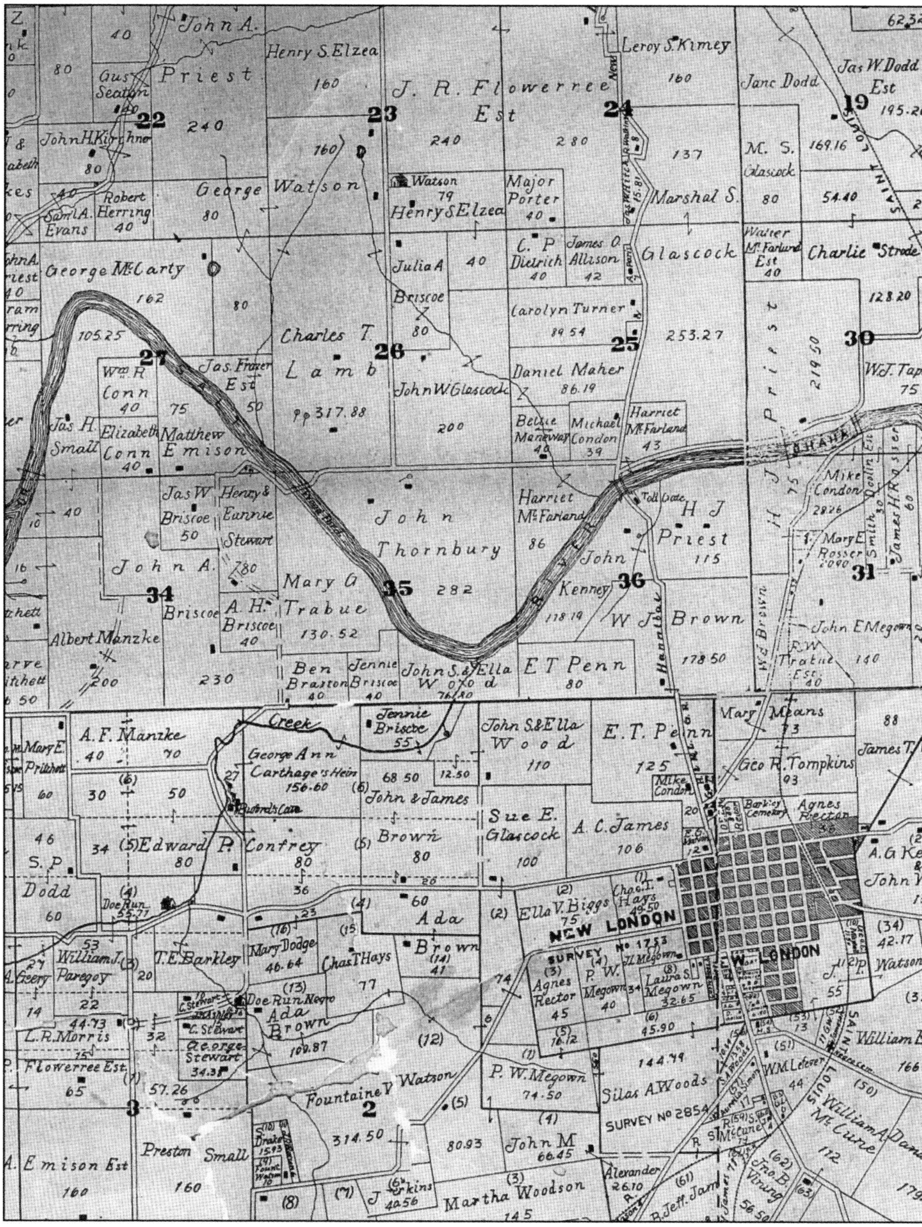

Here is partial view of a 1905 Bank of New London 35-inch-square plat map that once hung in Dr. Tom Waters's office. It shows a portion of the Hannibal–New London Gravel Road heading north out of New London. Some notable landmarks are the 1853 covered bridge and tollgate; several low-water crossings of Salt River, with one marked as "Woods Ford," later Lemon Ford; the St. Louis & Hannibal Railroad route including Ralls Junction; homes, schools, churches, and cemeteries; and the location of Buford Cave. The map includes homes, landowners, and roads around New London. Of special interest is land near Buford Cave on Turkey Creek denoted as "George Ann Carthage's Heirs." George Ann Cartridge was a slave of the James Buford family. She started Doe Run Colored School and was the only female school board member. Upon Buford's death in 1870, he left this property to George Ann Cartridge and her descendants. Lastly, note that the Salt River is labeled as "Ohaha." (Author.)

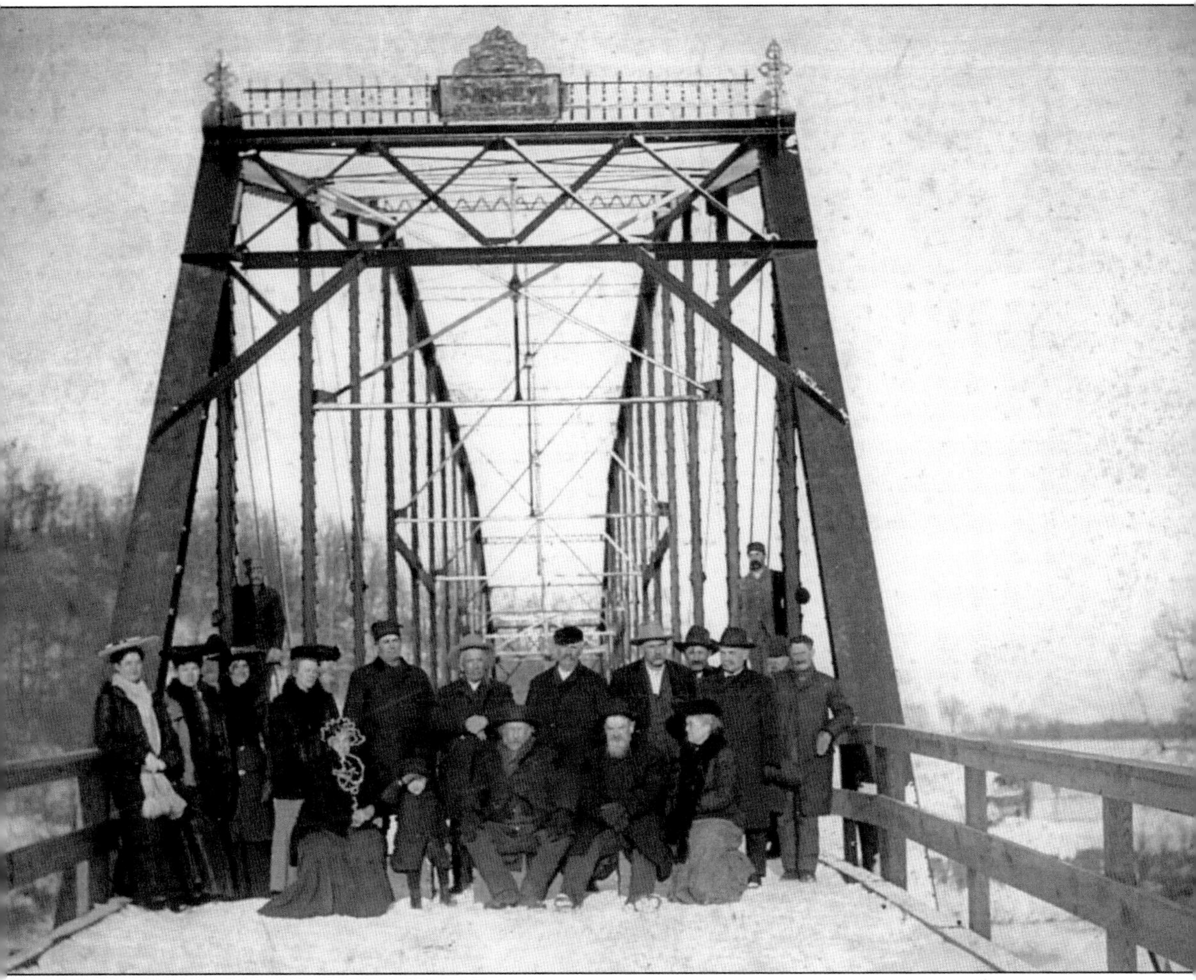

Locals gather on the newly completed 280-foot-long Asher Bridge in 1905. Before Asher Bridge was built, travelers used a nearby low-water crossing that could only be forded three months of the year. Asher was the fourth bridge spanning the lower Salt, the third Ralls steel span, and the longest bridge constructed by a county commission in Missouri. Construction was greatly welcomed by residents, who brought workers hot meals. A man named Meissert working for the St. Louis bridge builder married a local Coontz girl. This part of the river was deep and treacherous, as was the crossing upstream near the later Norton Bridge. Norton was knocked off its abutments twice, once by flash flood and the second by ice jam; it was replaced in 1925 due to the extreme punishment. More than 1,000 people attended opening day at Asher; 300 pounds of fried fish, boiled hams, slaw, bread, pie, cake, ice cream, tea, and coffee were served. The vehicle procession backed up a mile on both sides. From the deck to the water, it was 40 feet, but Marcus Crousore and others dove from it often. (RCHS.)

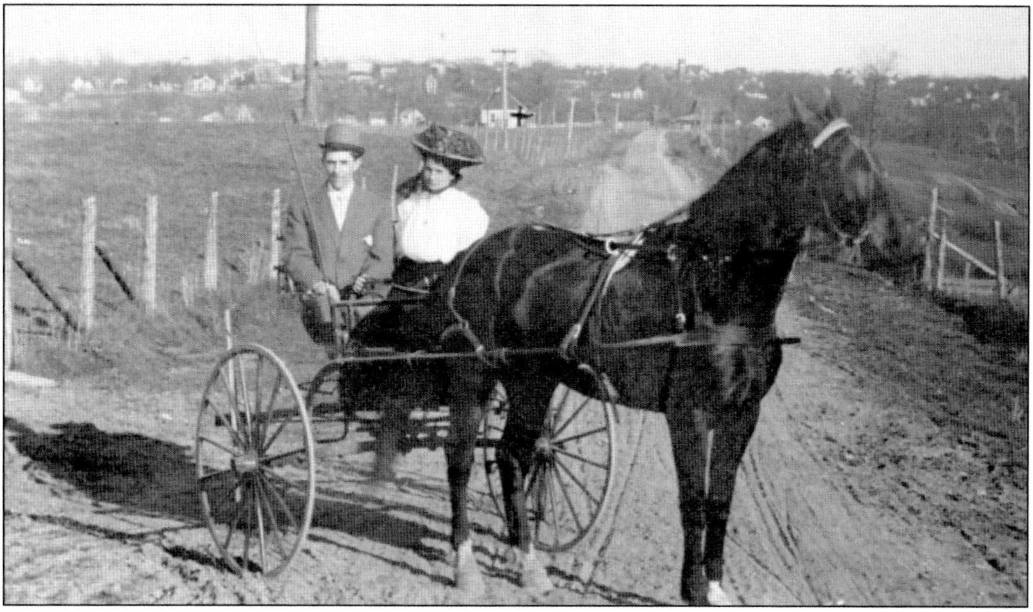

Roxie (1884–1958) and Bertha Rogers (1887–1981) are seen in this postcard riding in a two-wheeled gig west of Perry on present-day Missouri 154. Roxie was the son of Thomas and Anna Rogers. This dirt road was typical of those in Ralls until the mid-1920s. William H. Robey mailed this card on April 21, 1903. He remarks that the "+" indicates a house recently completed. (David Polc.)

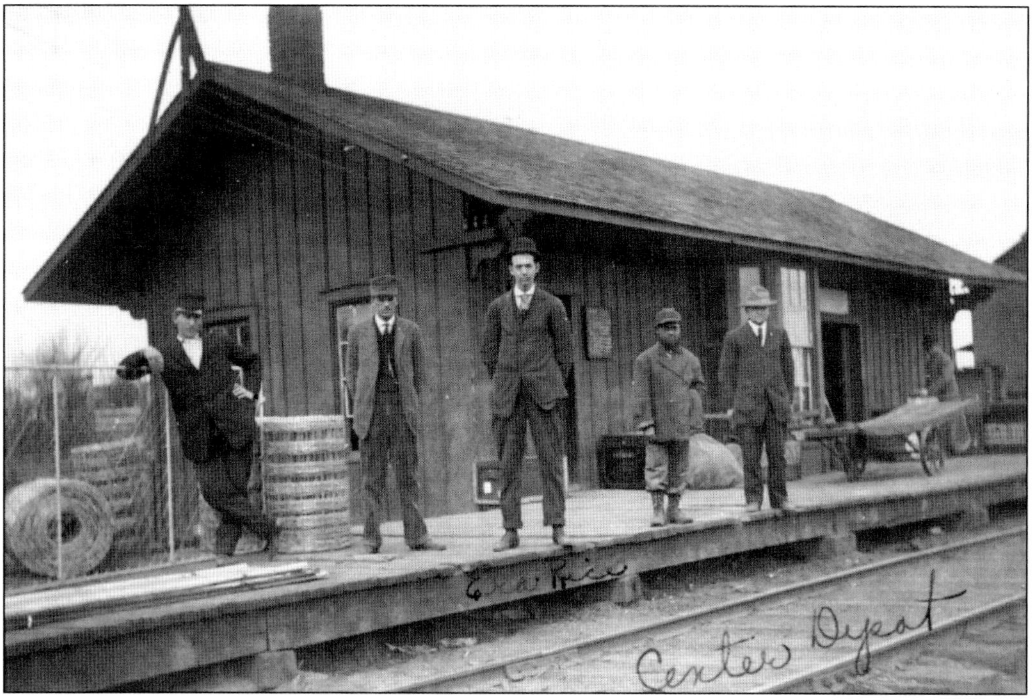

This is the first St. Louis & Hannibal depot at Center in 1908. Standing at center is agent Arah J. Rice, with brother Roy K. Rice to his right. On June 19, 1910, lightning struck and burned the depot. Rice placed a note in a sealed bottle within a corner block as "Doc" Acoff's crew built a new depot in June 1911. Rice noted his salary as $35 monthly. (David Polc.)

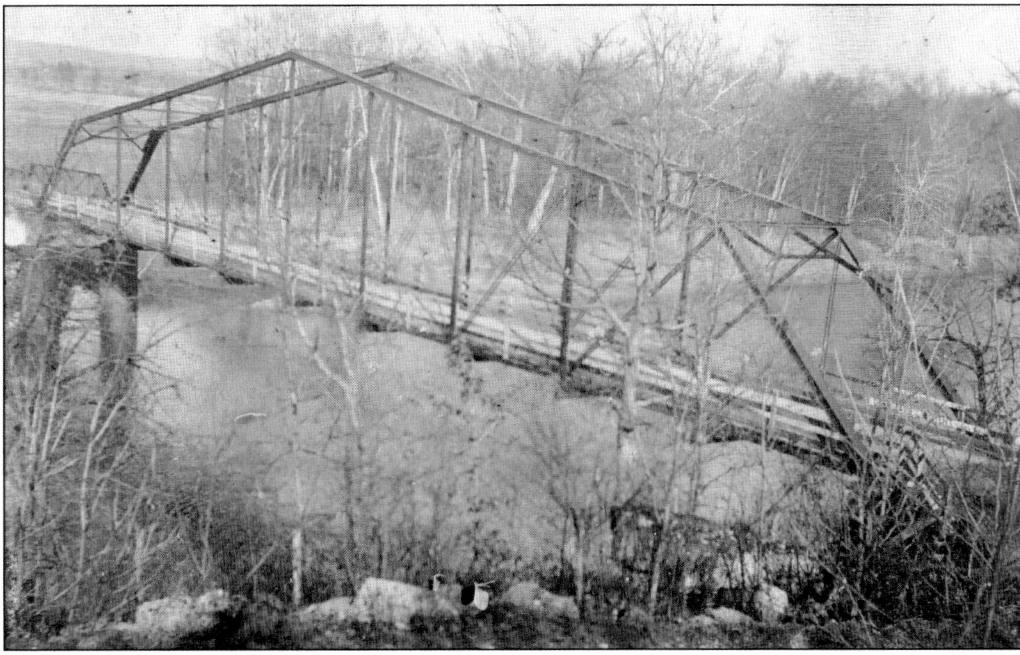

Ralls County's infamous Organ Ferry Bridge is viewed from the bluffs above Salt River in 1909. It hosted some rather bizarre incidents during its service life. The first was the 1905 murder trial of Dr. Taylor Jones Watson of Denver. He was found not guilty of killing his wife, Amanda, after St. Louis forensics expert Dr. Rutherford B. Hayes Gradwohl determined the Watsons were accident victims on the bridge. (Archie Hayden.)

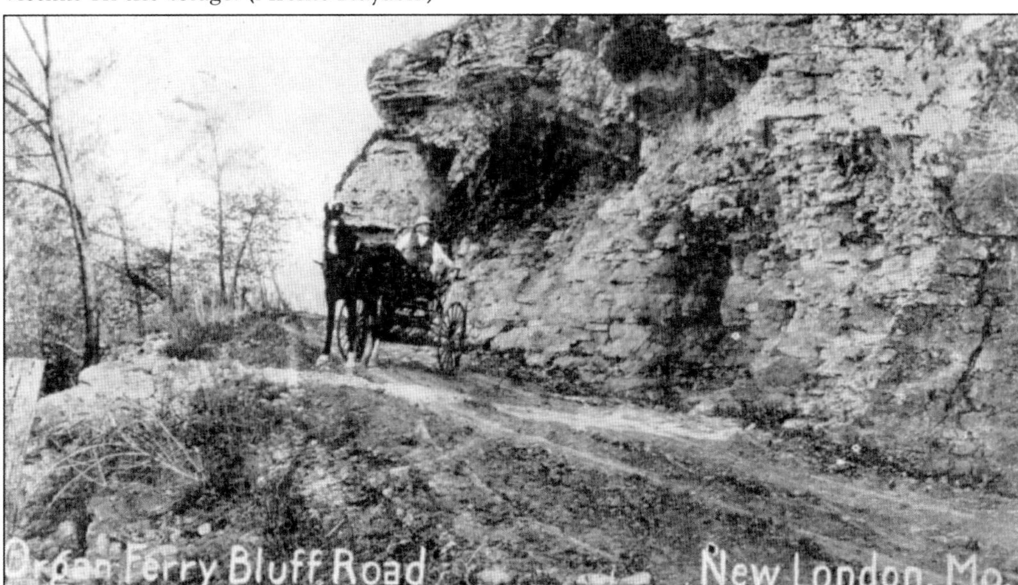

This is a postcard view of the western approach to Organ Ferry Bridge in 1910. The road east from New London was different from traveling Route V today. Leaving town, travelers crossed the Short Line tracks, down present-day Carver Drive, passing Douglass School, the city dump, a limestone quarry, and scattered homes until reaching the Salt River. Then one turned right up Organ Ferry Bluff Road and left onto the bridge. (Author.)

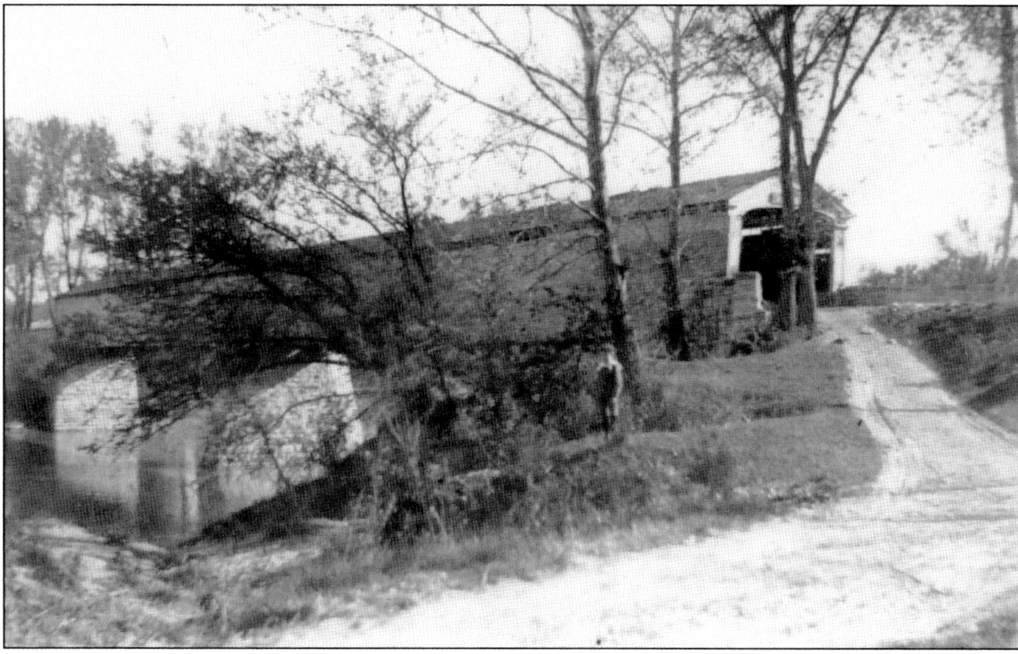

Here is the Hannibal–New London Toll Bridge over Salt River about 1909. This 300-foot Howe truss covered bridge, built by John Morris, was the first to span the Salt on April 9, 1853, surviving until June 1931, when a Works Progress Administration steel span was completed during concrete surfacing of the Red Ball Route. George D. Clayton Jr., later Hannibal lawyer and state senator, stands below the northern abutments, which survive today. (Steve Chou.)

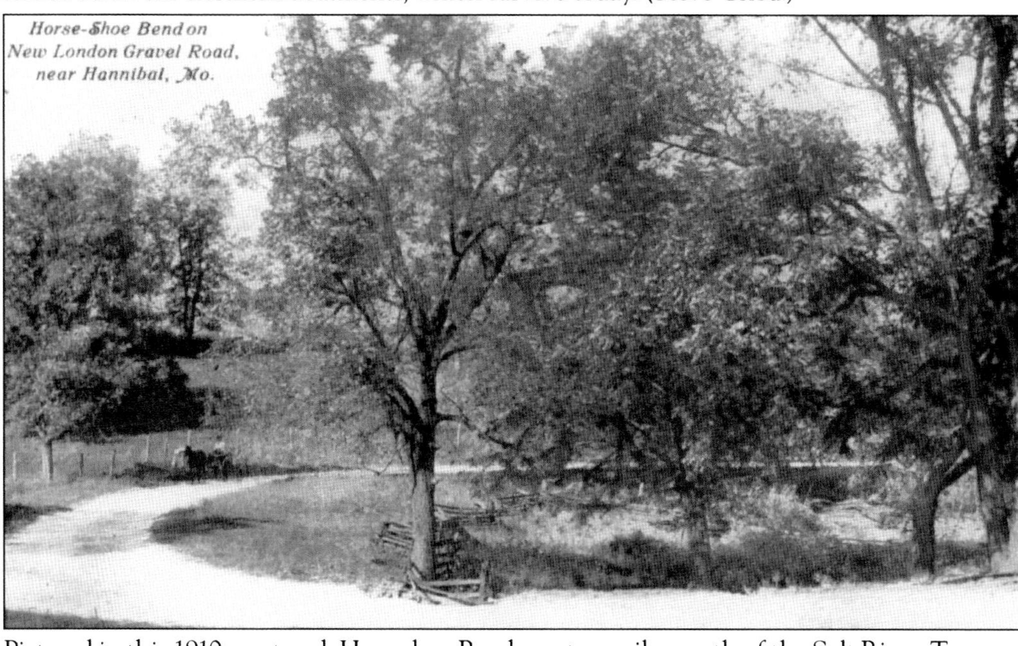

Pictured in this 1910s postcard, Horseshoe Bend was two miles north of the Salt River. Traces of the bend remain south of present-day Camp Creek Road on New London Gravel, just uphill from Rivere Au Sel (River of Salt) Road. The *Hannibal Messenger* of July 15, 1852, noted 100 men were "at work on the New London Plank Road." Today, this is New London Gravel Road. (Steve Chou.)

This is a view from Jefferson and Palmyra Streets looking north at Main Street during the 1908 Perry Corn Carnival. Temporary electric light towers were erected at the corners of Main, Gill, Jefferson, and Palmyra Streets to better facilitate night activities. All enjoyed the Corn Carnivals. (David Polc.)

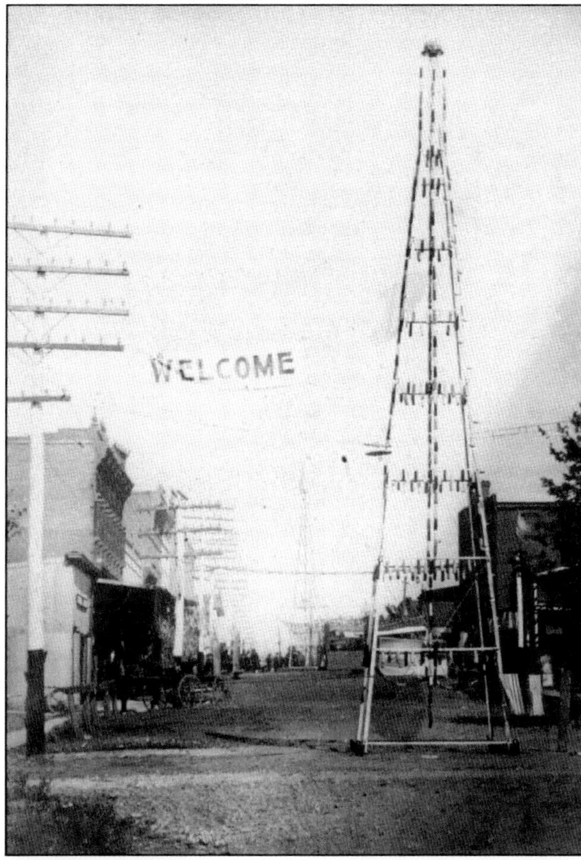

An ingenious early Perry mechanic has made his own roadster from a cast off automobile, evidence that being green is nothing new. This is one of several glass-plate negatives found in the Perry VFW Building and developed by Ralph and Fred Omer. It dates to the 1920s. (RCHS.)

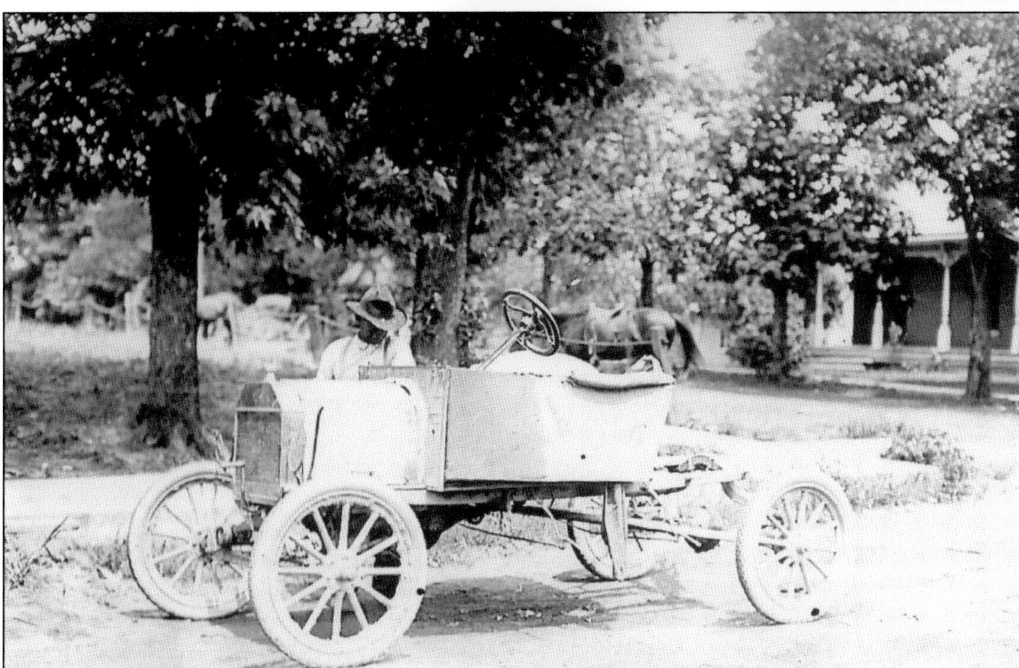

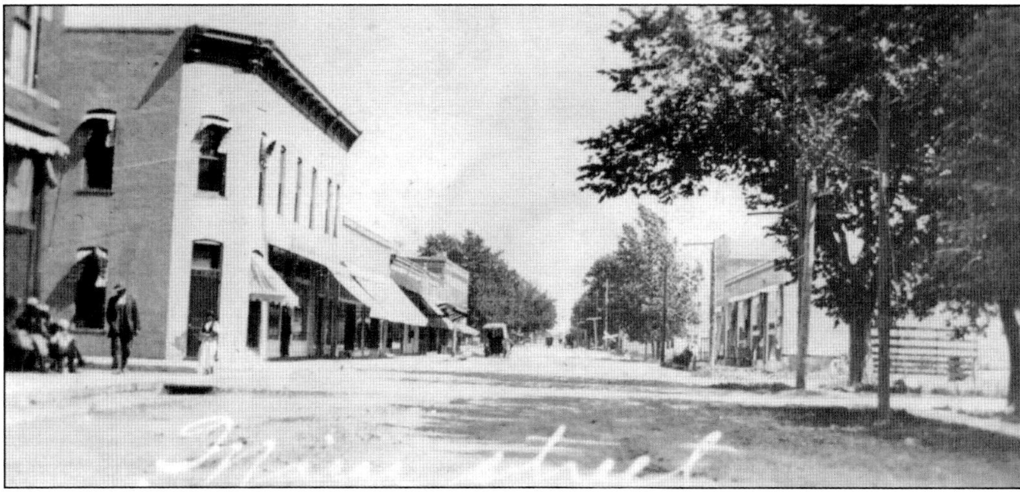

At left is the new Center Bank on the southwest corner of South Public and Lamb Streets about 1909. Visible is the barber pole of John Teall Sr.'s barbershop. Neither Farmers & Merchants Bank, on the southeast corner of Public and Lamb Streets, or the People's Bank of Center (which later became the Ralls County Library), located just across the Short Line tracks, has been built yet. (RCHS.)

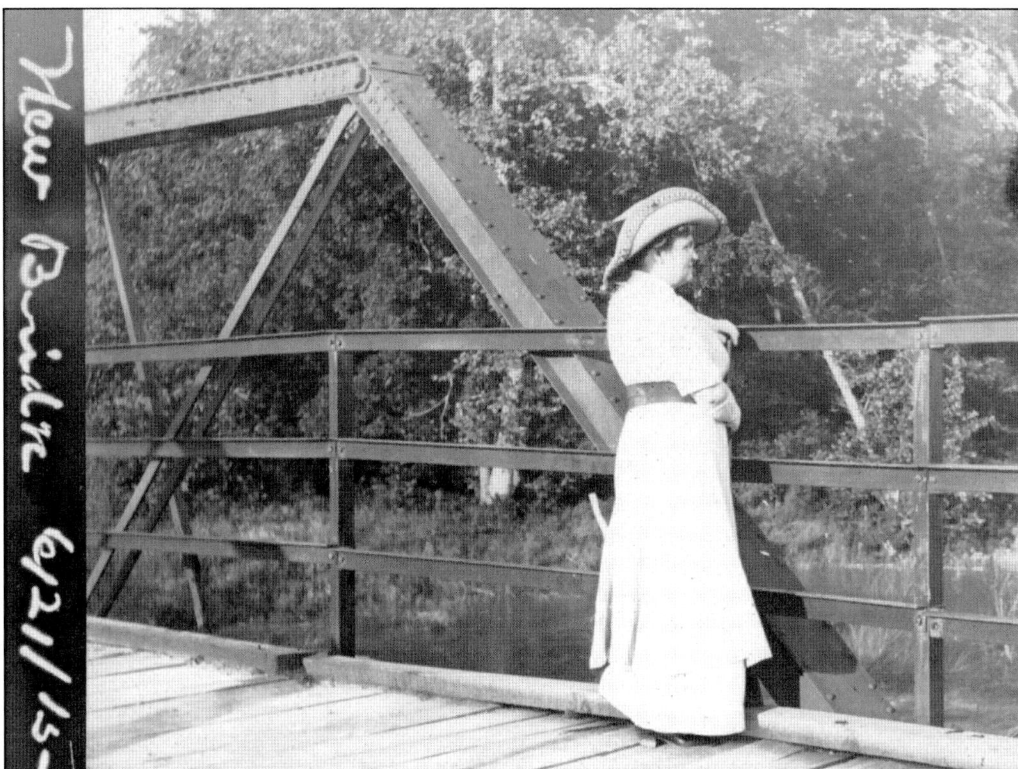

Zora (Jameson) Fisher gazes over Turkey Creek from the newly completed Briscoe Bridge pony span on Buford Cave Lane west of New London. The date is June 21, 1915. Buford Cave Road continued north, crossing the Salt River north of the covered bridge at Woods Ford (later Lemon Ford). (Archie Hayden.)

Pictured in 1922, Liz Crawford (left) and Lucy Glascock pose on a motorcycle with sidecar. The location is New London's Seventh Street; the St. Joseph Catholic Church is visible in the background, with its tall steeple no longer there. (Liz Gingry.)

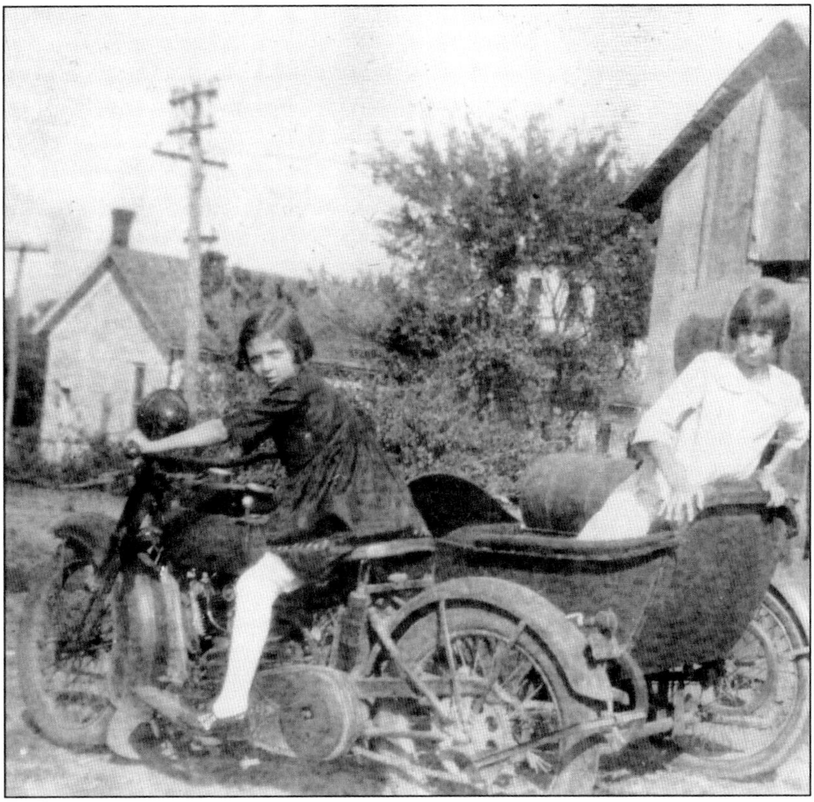

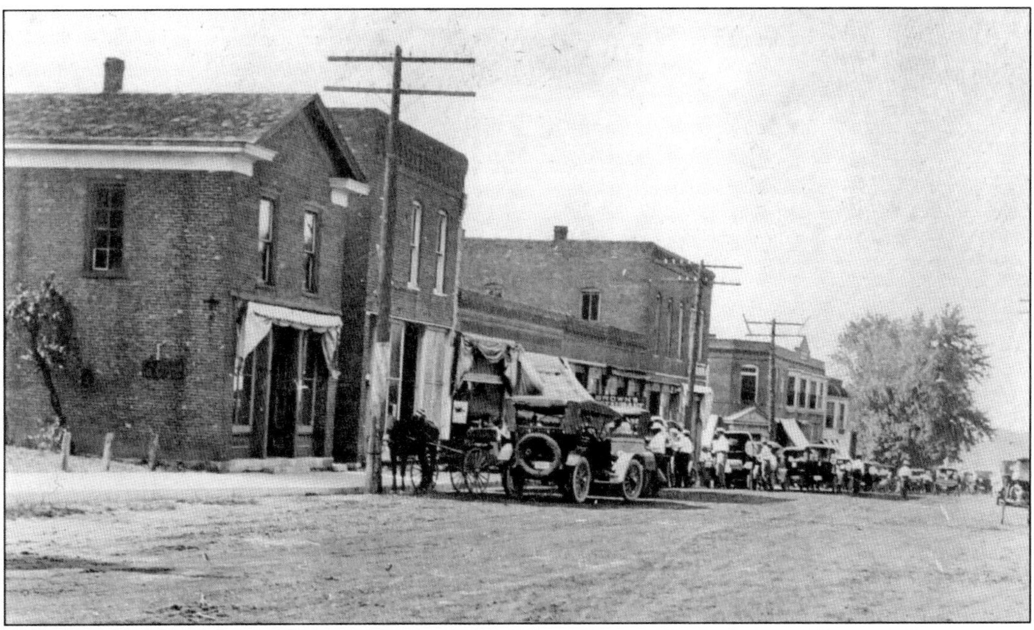

Here is New London at Fifth and Main Streets looking north in front of Brown's Restaurant. Judging by the mix of horse-drawn and horseless carriages, a large auto-touring club appears to be passing through on the Red Ball Route. The date of this image is certainly after 1923, as more two-story buildings existed on the west side of Main until being lost to fire. (David Polc.)

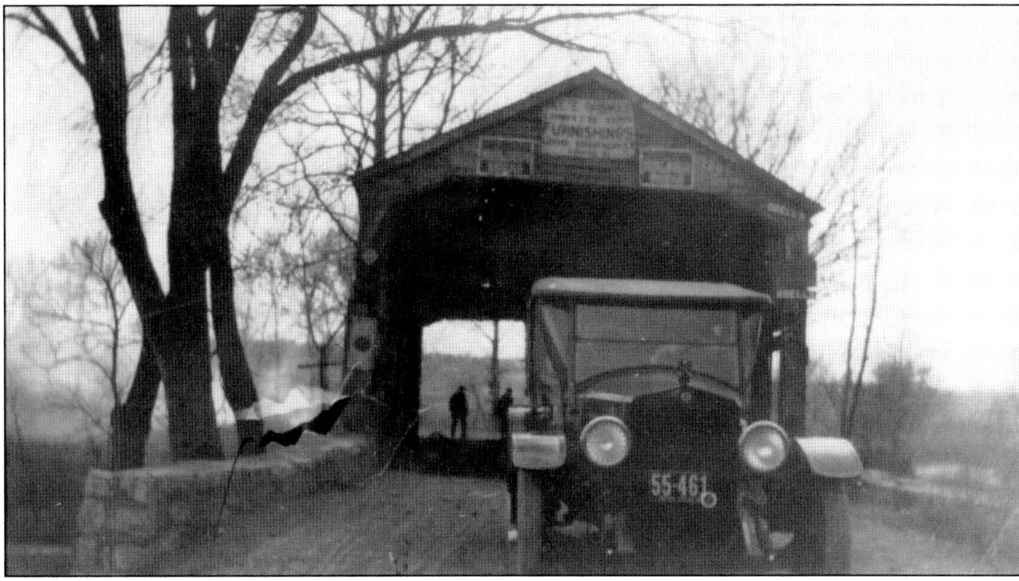

A.J. Key built Ralls's other covered bridge (pictured) in 1859 over Bear Creek. In 1928, much of the siding was blown off during a storm. However, being situated on busy Red Ball Route 1, it continued to serve travelers until the summer of 1931, when a concrete box culvert replaced it upon completion of US 61. The car's license plate is dated 1923. (RCHS.)

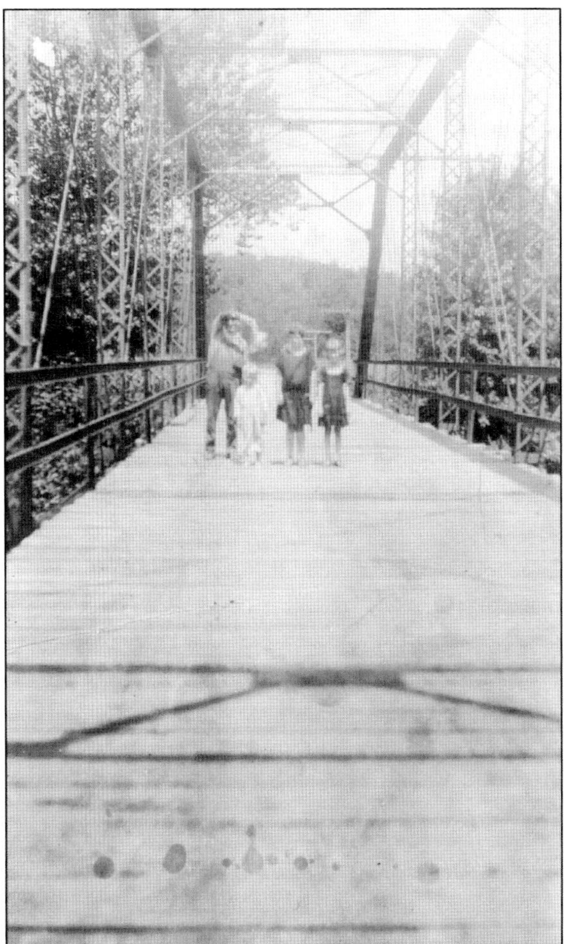

At a cost of $10,000, the 325-foot-long Bailey Bridge was built in 1910 over the Salt River, 10 miles southeast of New London. On the left is Arthur Epperson who lived nearby; the children are unidentified. The photograph dates to the 1930s. Bailey Bridge Road starts at Route T and crosses the Salt River heading south into Frankford as Missouri Route ZZ. (Jim and Dorothy Quinlin.)

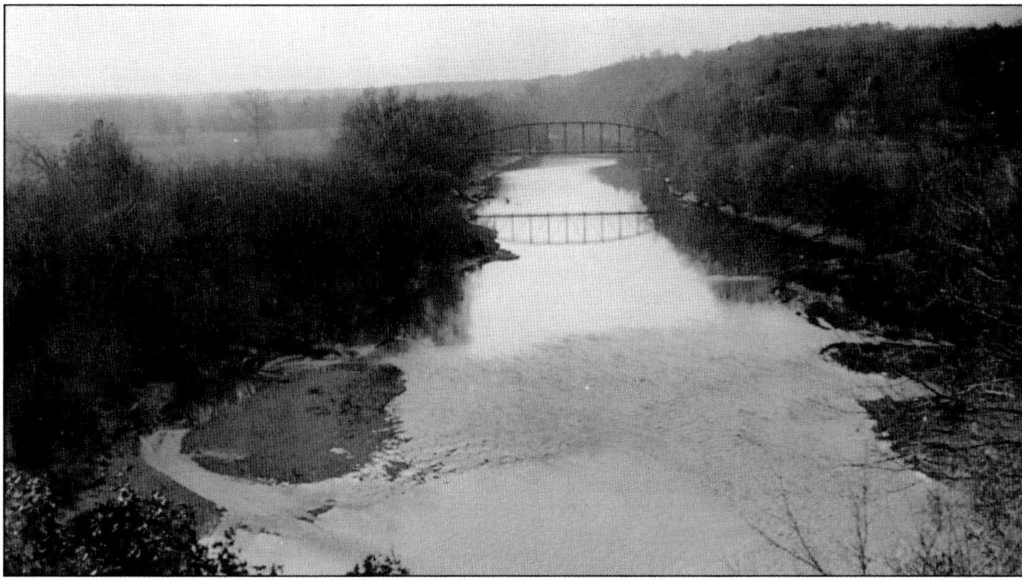

Along Salt River and Cow Creek, Joanna is in the distance on the right. John Lyle received a presidential land grant, building a home here in 1834. By 1844, he established a trading post and became postmaster of New Portland, Missouri, shortened to Newport. Closed in 1853, it reopened in 1886 as Utter, closing in 1891. It became Joanna in 1895. In 1984, Joanna slipped beneath Mark Twain Lake. (RCHS.)

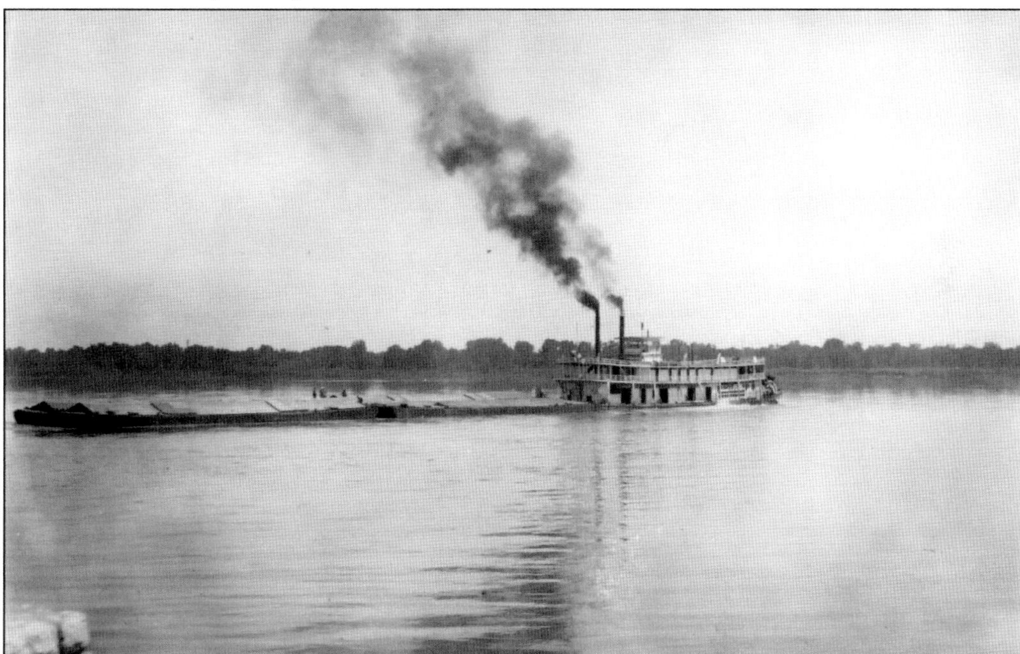

Ralls originally had Mississippi River frontage stretching 63 miles to Iowa, but then the county was broken up, borders were changed, and suddenly it had none. Finally, in the late 1820s, the borders were finalized with Marion and Pike, but only the Ilasco-Saverton port area was returned. River traffic still has the same purpose today; it is just performed with different means than seen here on June 6, 1933. (Author.)

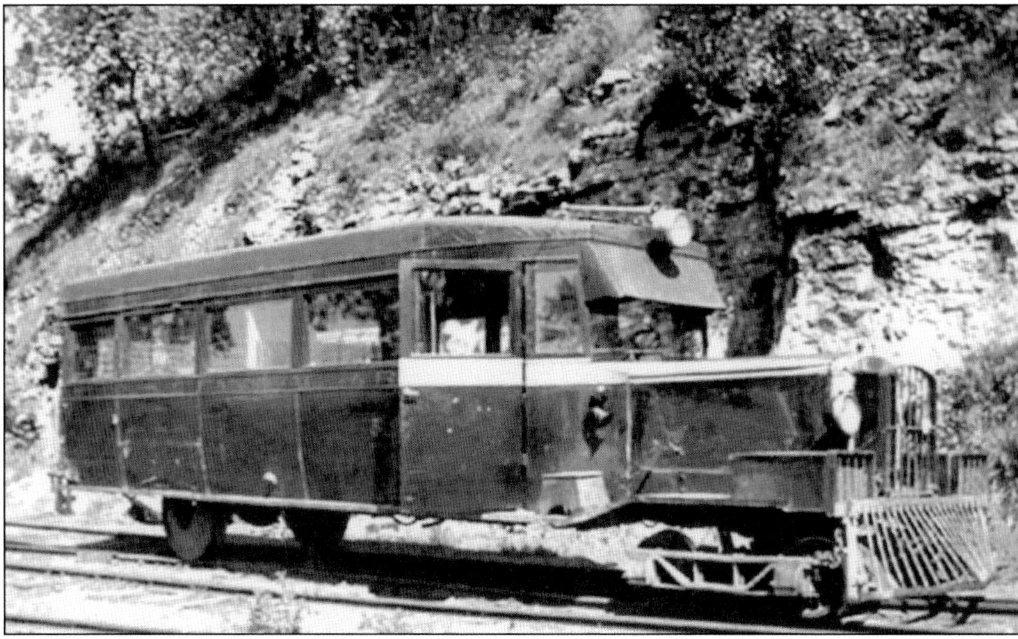

In 1935, Mack motor coach No. 54 allowed travelers to commute over the St. Louis & Hannibal Railroad system. In 1900, busses were adapted to rail usage around America, allowing more flexible schedules. Nos. 53 and 54 were the last in use on the Short Line. People are still living who recall riding them, their colorful nicknames, such as Hurdy-Gurdys, Puddle Jumpers, Hoopies, and Dinkys, and the men who drove them. (Author.)

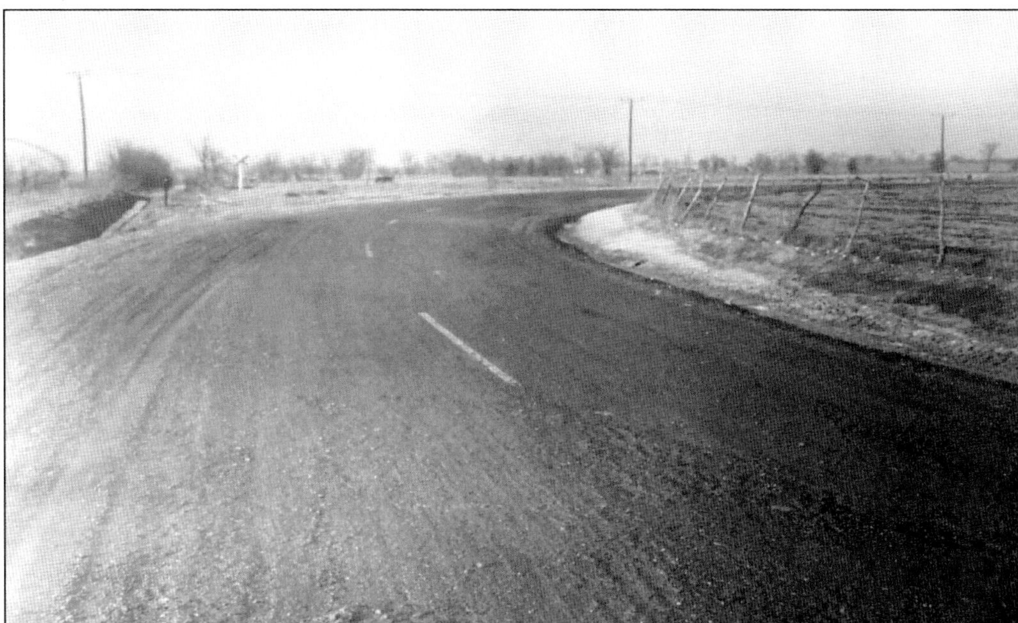

Highway 19 has double curves at Olivet Road and the St. Louis & Hannibal Railroad's Briggs flag stop crossing near present-day Palmer Farms. On February 6, 1937, the road surface is still gravel, witnessed by tire ruts and the cameraman's footprints; however, the centerline stripe is painted. (Author.)

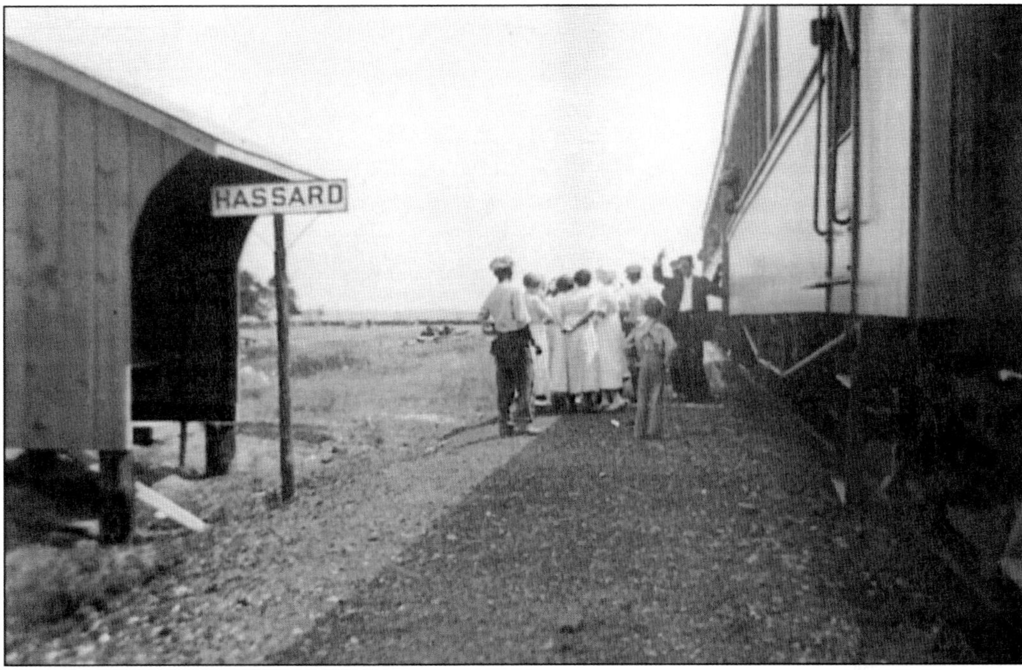

The Missouri, Kansas & Texas Railroad (MK&T, or "Katy") crossed the upper half of Ralls County beginning in 1869. It had a flag station at Hassard and depots at Huntington and Rensselaer. This is the shelter at Hassard around 1940. The Katy was eventually sold to the Wabash, the Norfolk & Western, and finally the Norfolk & Southern. (David Polc.)

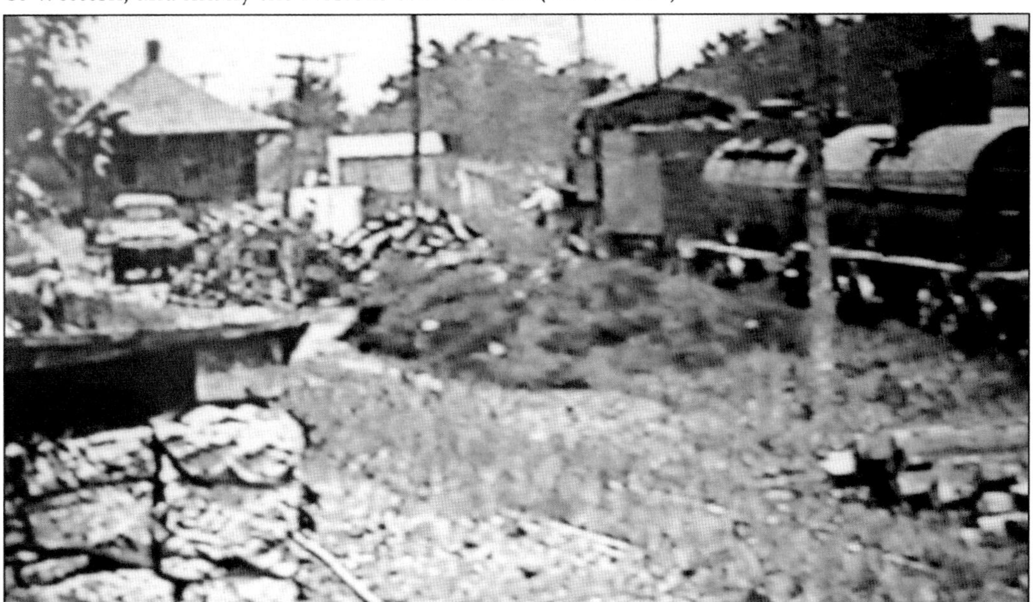
New London Depot at First and Depot Streets is seen looking north in the summer of 1942. A crewman jumps from engine No. 625 arriving from the south. This is the only known image of the depot, which was the second one built here. In 1914, "Doc" Acoff, an African American contractor from Frankford, built this granitoid block structure. This still is from an eight-millimeter film by Phil Conn, the Gem Theatre projectionist. (Author.)

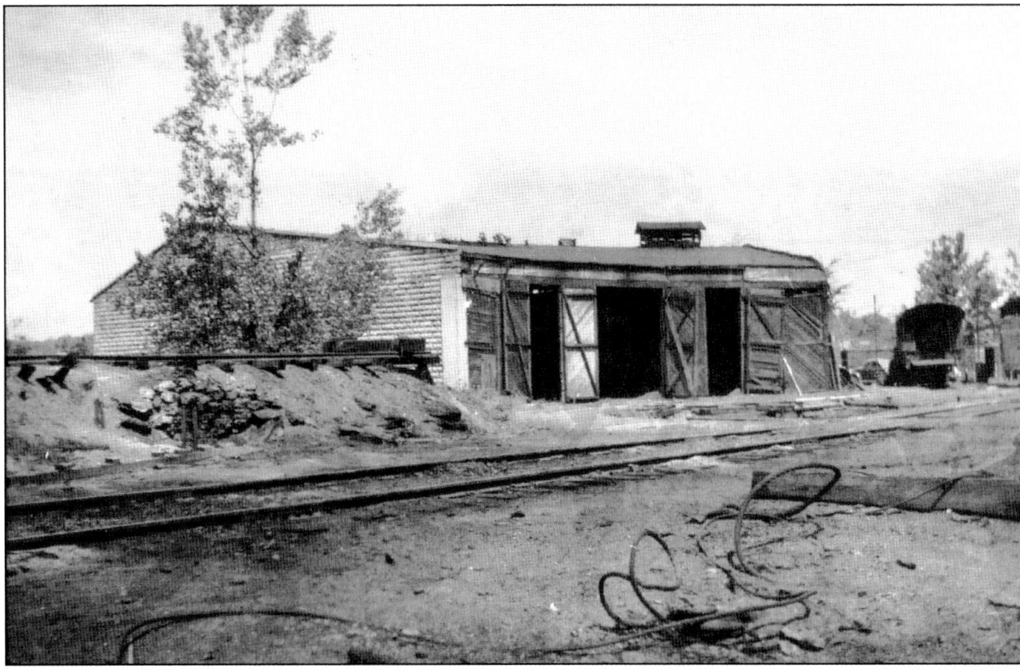

Here is the St. Louis & Hannibal Railroad's roundhouse as it appeared in 1944 when the railroad was abandoned in May. The original Oakwood roundhouse burned in 1890 but was rebuilt with a 10-stall building. By 1944, this is all that was left. Today, Althorfer's Caterpillar service occupies this site, and part of the roundhouse wall remains as a separator between the front service desk area and the repair shop. (Steve Chou.)

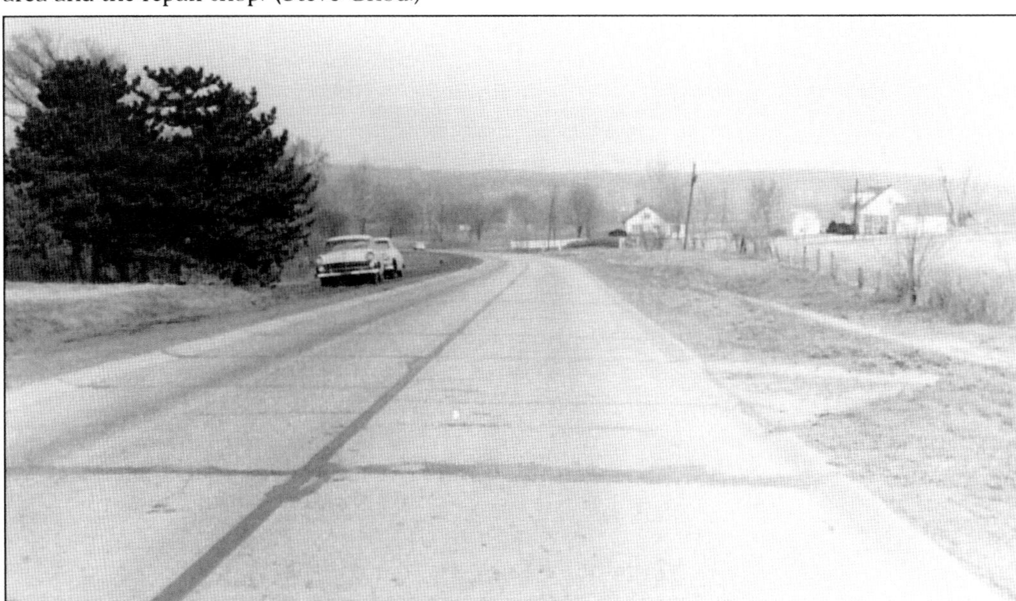

US Highway 61 is seen heading north out of New London toward the Salt River. Today, the house remains; however, the road is present-day Northside Drive. The driveway on the left led to the Brown farm buildings, which were removed to make way for the US 61 bypass of New London in 1970. It was also the location of a March 30, 1955, accident. (Author.)

Three
Citizens, Characters, and Founders

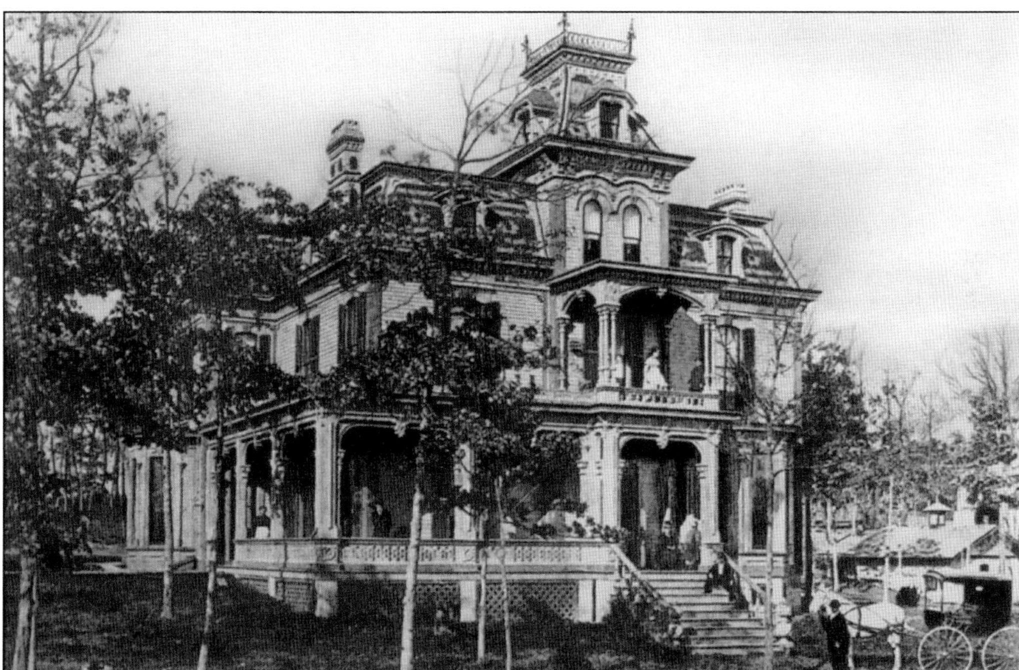

Seen here is a postcard view of the John Garth Woodside Mansion on the Hannibal–New London Plank Road in 1871. The Garths were wealthy Hannibalians involved in the lumber business. John Garth, an early promoter of roads, was on the Plank Road Co. board and owned the Hannibal Trolley Co. John and Julie Rolsen currently own this fine home listed in the National Register of Historic Places and operate a bed & breakfast and restaurant here. (Author.)

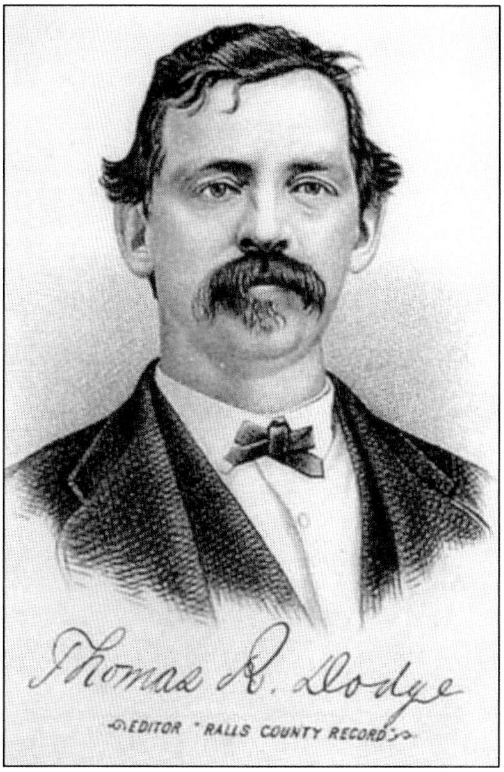

Thomas Dodge founded the *Beacon* in 1860, but it ceased when he enlisted in the Union army. Upon returning from the Civil War, it was resumed as the *Ralls County Record* in 1865. He later partnered with brother-in-law Clay "Men" Mayhall but sold out to Joe Burnett of Paris in 1895. In 1916, John Porter Fisher and Guilford Harris bought the paper from Burnett. (RCHS.)

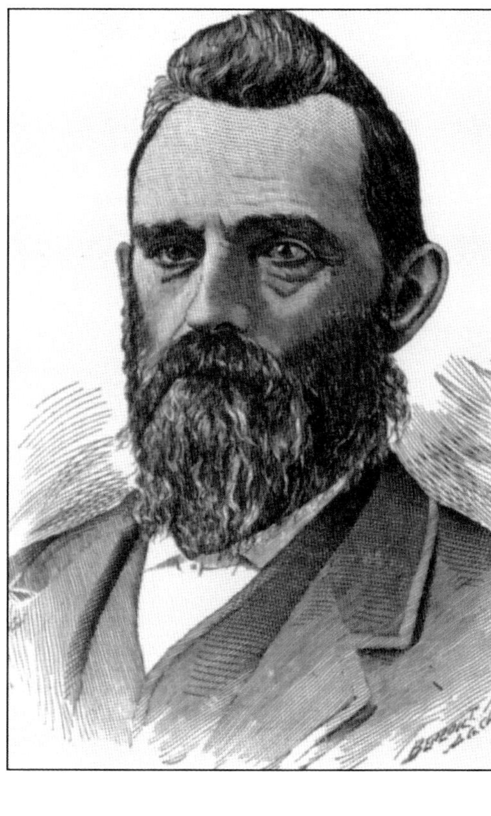

This is an engraving of Thomas F. Gill (1831–1893) of Perry, Missouri. Gill came to Perry around 1864 and built the first store on the southeast corner of Main and Palmyra Streets. He also started the first bank, the People's Bank of Perry, in 1885. It is noted that Thomas Gill had built, financed, and/or sold more than half the homes and business buildings in Perry. (RCHS.)

This is a c. 1873 tintype of young Tom Waters, son of Nimrod and Mary Alford Waters of New London. He attended Kentucky Medical School and served New London as a physician his entire career. Dr. Tom was involved in community affairs, such as coroner, St. Louis & Hannibal Railroad surgeon, the Red Cross, and the World War II Rationing Board, and ran for mayor in 1940. (Author.)

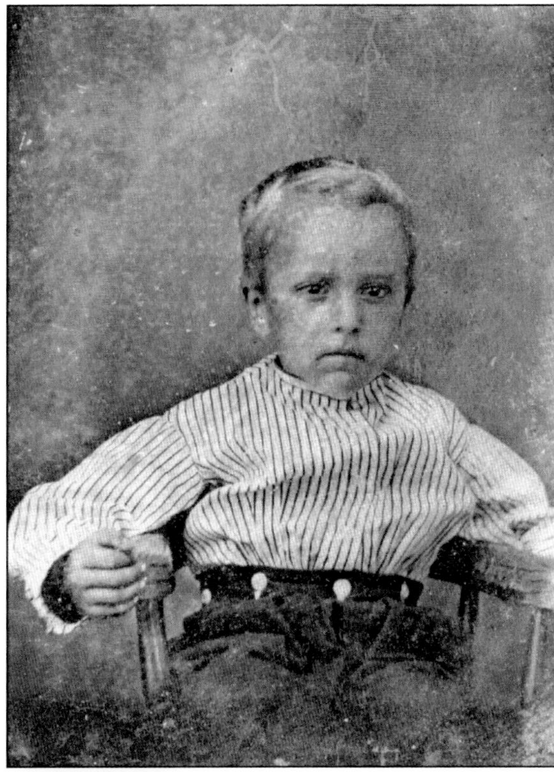

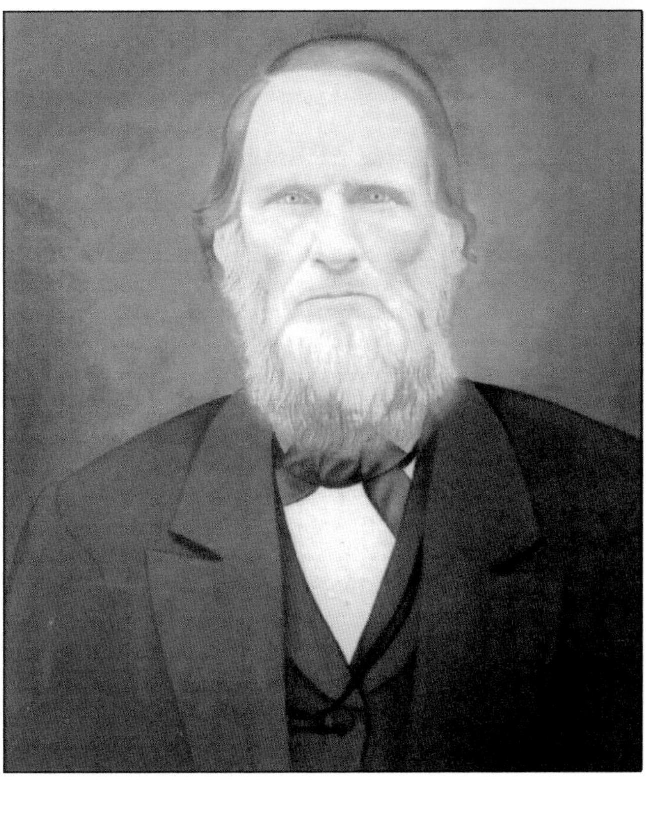

Nimrod Waters (1826–1901) was born in Tennessee to George and Polly Waters. George was a War of 1812 veteran and Christian minister who settled north of Center in 1831. In 1844, Nimrod taught at Cold Spring School and then accompanied Ralls men to the 1850 California goldfields. Returning in 1852, he married Mary Alford. In 1866, he was elected county judge, serving with Nathan Dimmitt and William E. Harris. (Author.)

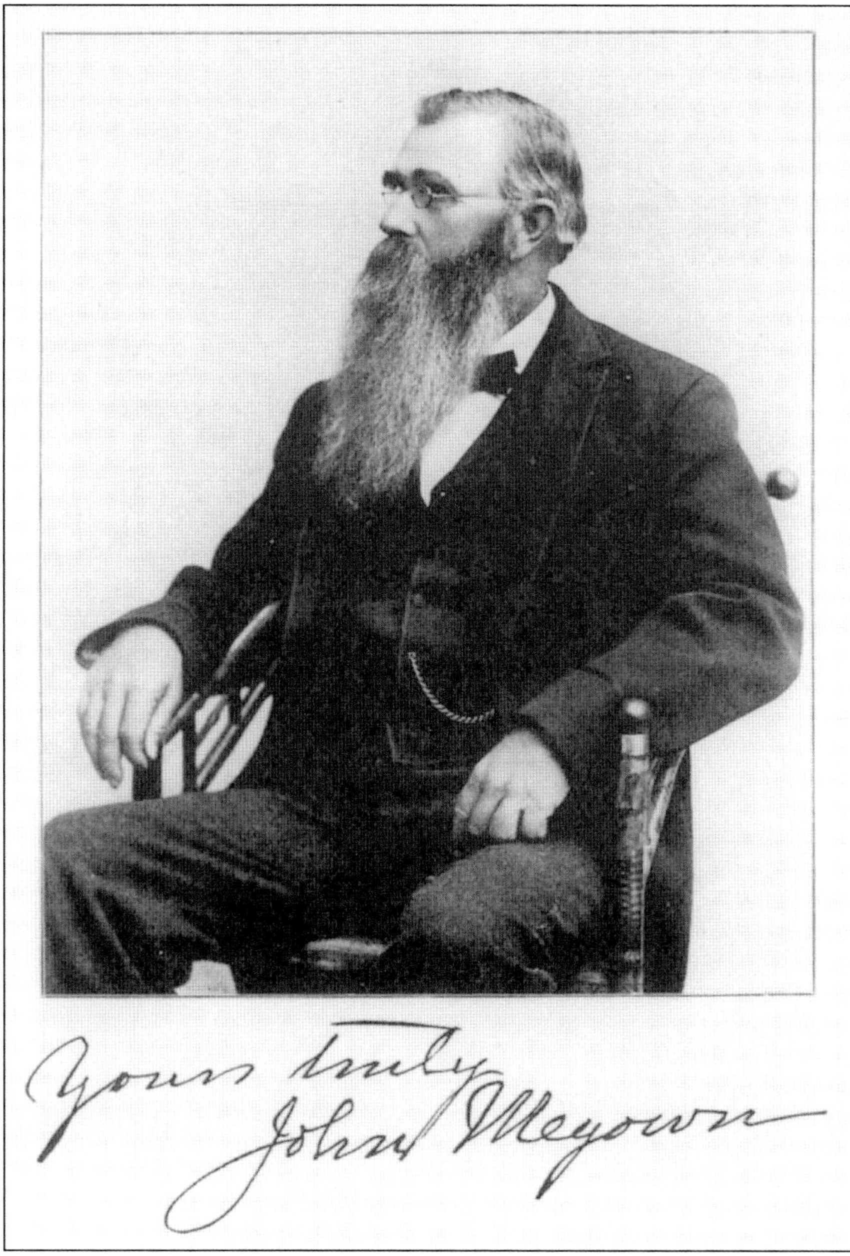

Judge John Megown, born in 1834, was the son of Samuel and Julia Anne (McReady) Megown, who settled in Clay Township in 1836. He learned the family trades of brickmaking and farming. His great-great-grandfather Samuel erected the first brick building in Pittsburgh, Pennsylvania. John had an interest in education, teaching school in Center Township while pursuing law studies. He was admitted to the bar in 1857. In 1860, he was appointed US deputy marshal in New London and was elected county assessor in 1862–1863 and 1866. In 1870, he was elected probate judge serving until 1883, when he returned to farming and practicing law. Megown married Mary E. Conn on April 4, 1856. They had 11 children; many became involved in early mercantile, banking, and newspaper interests in New London and Hannibal. Judge Megown also recorded early New London and Ralls history for our benefit. (Author.)

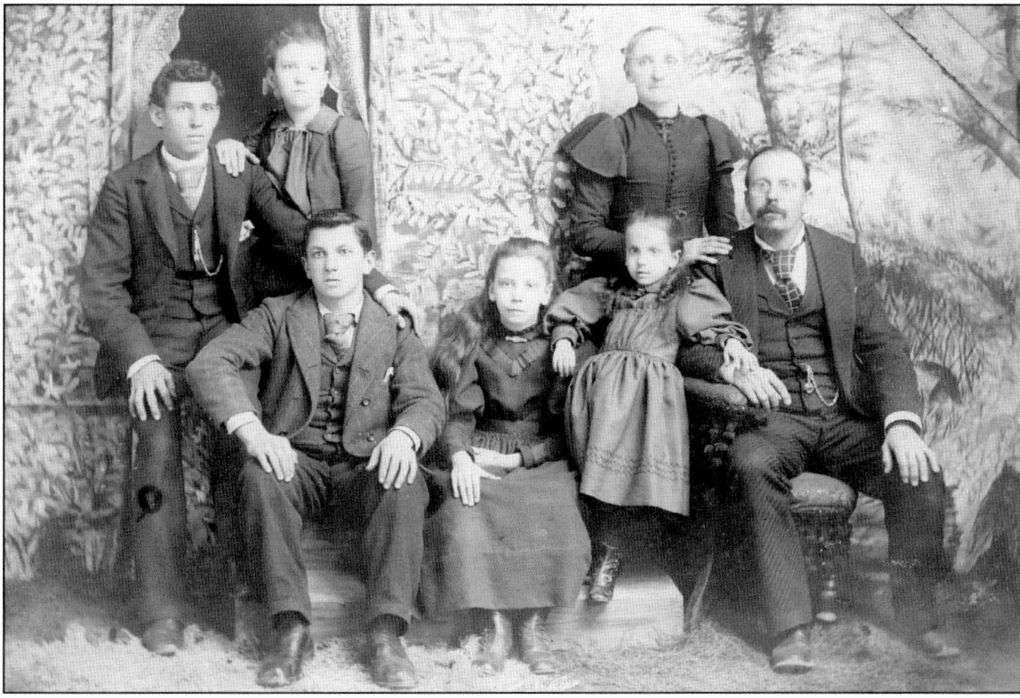

The Martin Stehle Jr. family is pictured in 1893. His parents were tinsmiths from Alsace Lorrain, France, who settled in Kirkwood. Martin, born in St. Louis, married Adeline Hocar, moved to Perry, and operated Stehle and Sons Stove Co. From left to right are (first row) George Joseph, Anna Catherine, Margaret Lee, and Martin; (second row) William "Will" Nelson, Mary Adeline, and Adeline. Son Frank James died in 1872 as an infant. (Ben Akers.)

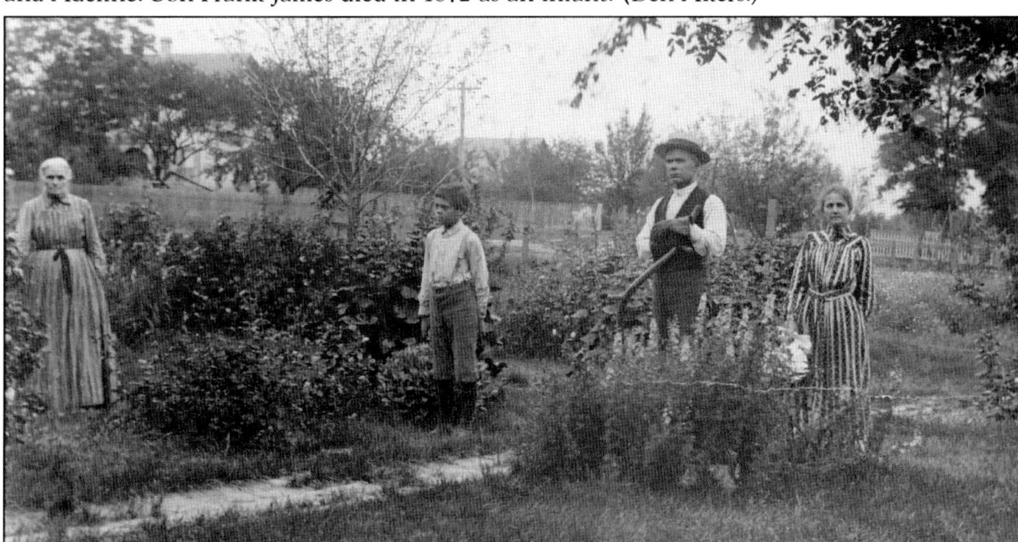

Shown around 1900, from left to right, Mary Hays, George Roy, Rueben Roy, and Maggie (Hays) Roy are in their garden on Fourth and Clay Streets, which is now New London's Ruth Roy Wright Park. George died in a hunting accident at age 12 on November 28, 1902. Margaret "Ruth" was later born to the Roys; she married Bailey Wright. Hundreds of the Roys' personal letters to each other survive in private and university collections. (RCHS.)

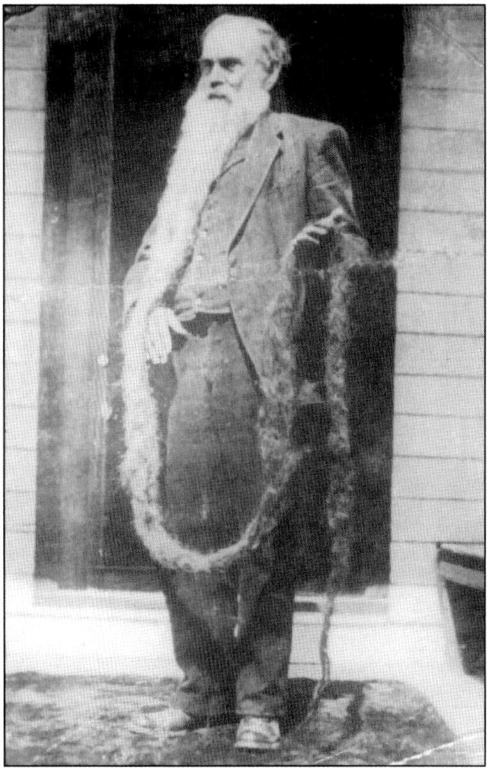

Frankford farmer Valentine Tapley (1831–1910) was related to many New Londoners. In 1860, he wagered never to shave again if Abraham Lincoln became president. He kept his word; his beard officially grew to 12 feet, 6 inches, and was reportedly 20 feet long when he died. His beard hairs were youthfully brown at the end but white at his chin. It was carried in a silk waist pouch. The photograph dates from 1900. (RCHS.)

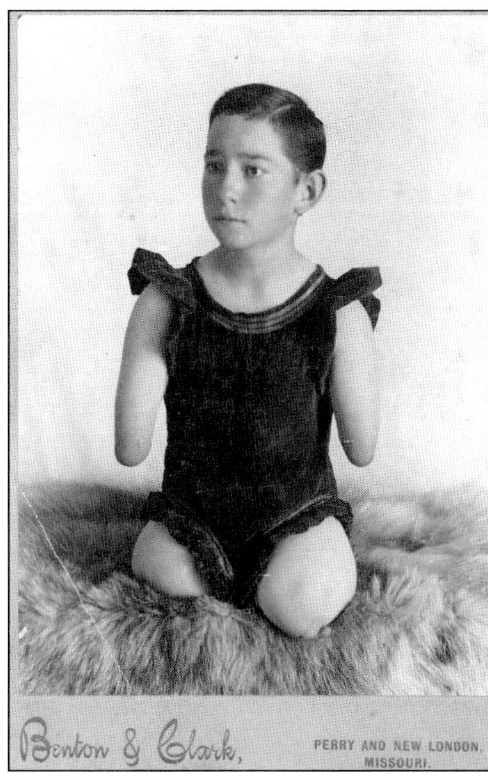

John Rodney Elzea was born handicapped in 1882 near Mexico, Missouri. His family later moved to New London where Rodney attended public school, drove a goat cart, and was fairly independent. Later billed as "Rex the Half Man," he worked quality sideshows, ate with a fork, wrote with Spenserian penmanship, played piano, and rolled his own cigarettes, flipping them to his hatband. He died of heart problems in 1936. (RCHS.)

Elijah Jameson (1833–1927) is enjoying biscuits and coffee near Butler Cave, northwest of New London. Jameson started with little, ventured to the California goldfields in 1850, and later acquired a 500-acre farm west of New London. In time, he became vice president of Ralls County Bank. Elijah was well liked and often seen in New London photographs. He broke his hip in 1927 and died soon after. (Archie Hayden.)

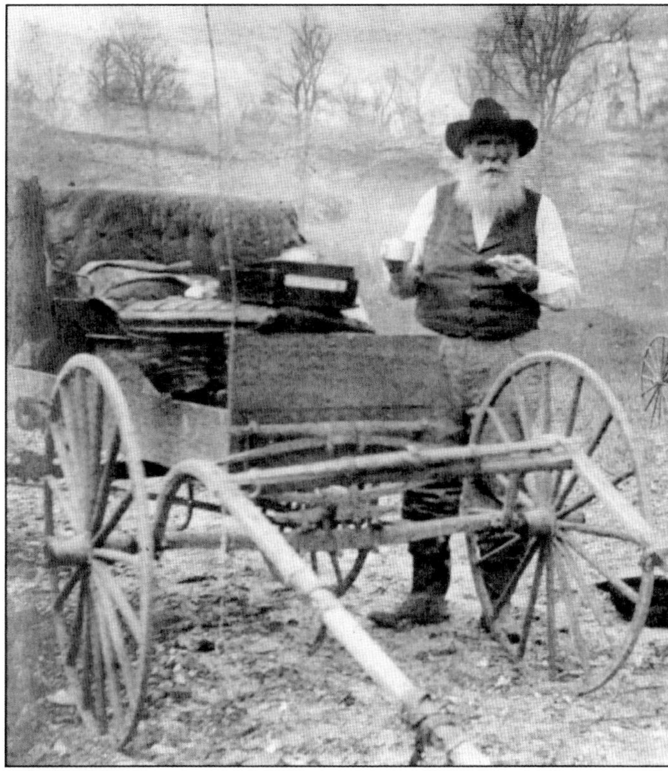

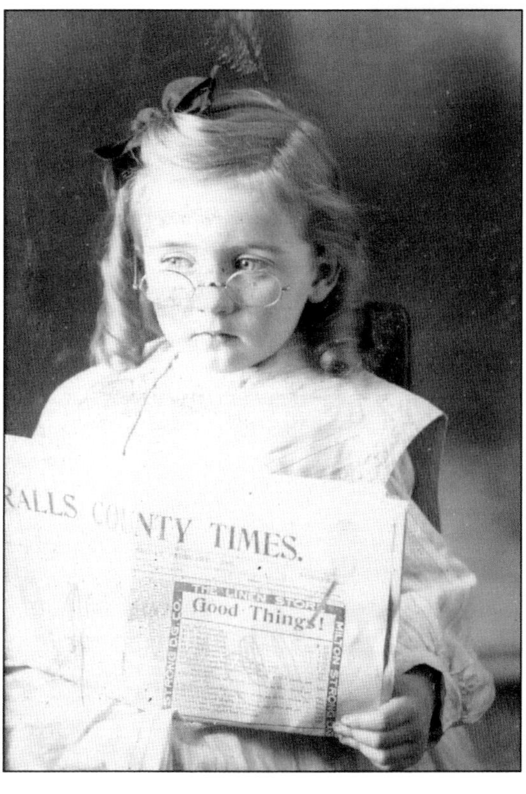

Little Lucille Martin is the five-year-old daughter of George and Susie (Jameson) Martin. George was telegrapher for the StL&HRR in New London. Lucy is reading the February 3, 1905, edition of the *Ralls County Times* where the big story is about the Dr. Taylor Jones Watson murder trial. Lucy's uncle John Porter Fisher was the co-editor of the *Times* and photographer of this image. (Archie Hayden.)

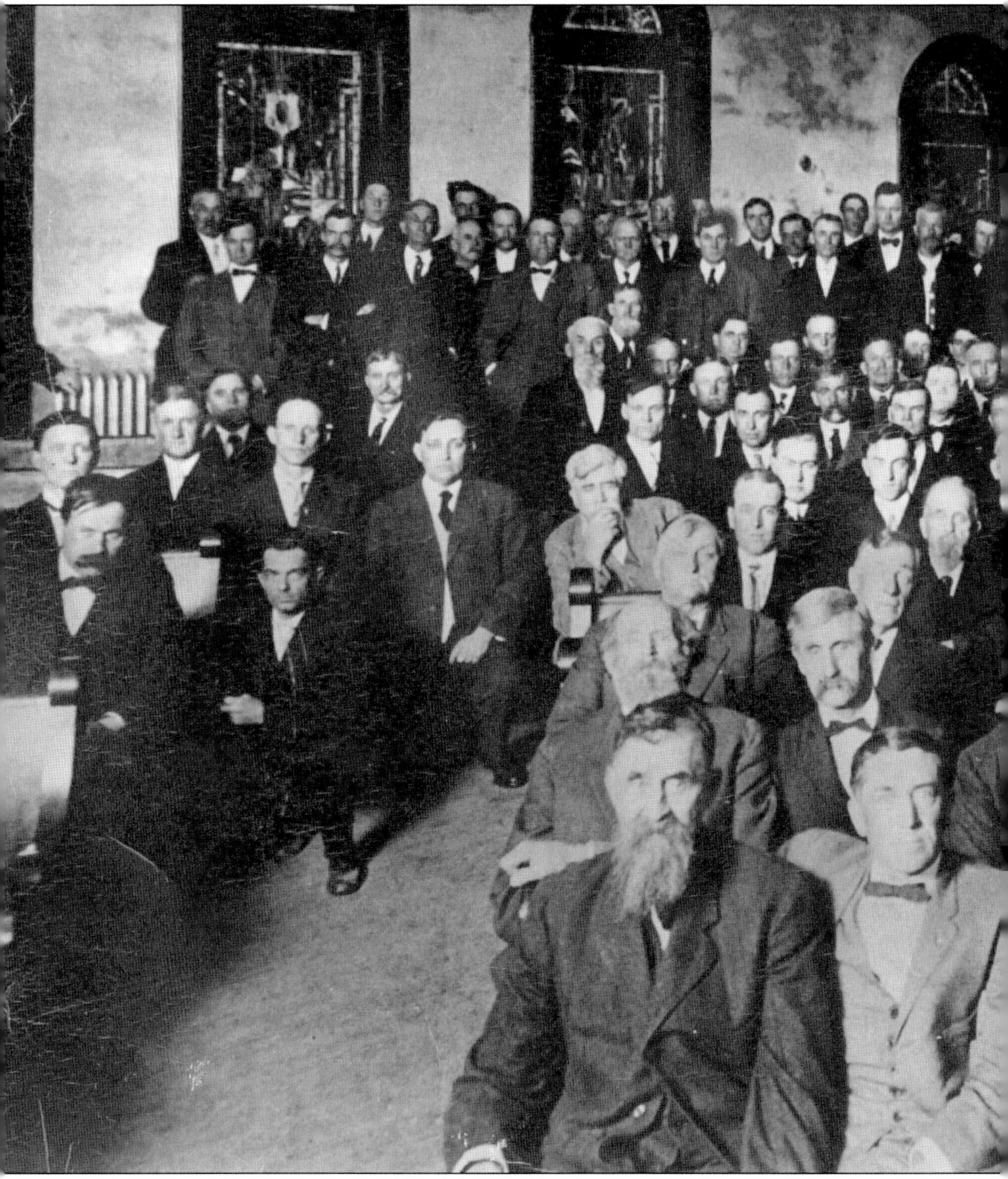

The New London Businessmen Bible Club paused for this photograph on March 21, 1912, at New London's First Christian Church. There are 118 men pictured, so it would be difficult to accurately list everyone, but many are early storekeepers, doctors, lawyers, and well-known citizens. In the first four rows are, from left to right, (first row) Jake Stout, Tom Carstarphen, Mack Stout, and Capt. Elijah Jameson; (second row) Enoch Matson, Jim Megown, John Will Rule, Sam Caldwell,

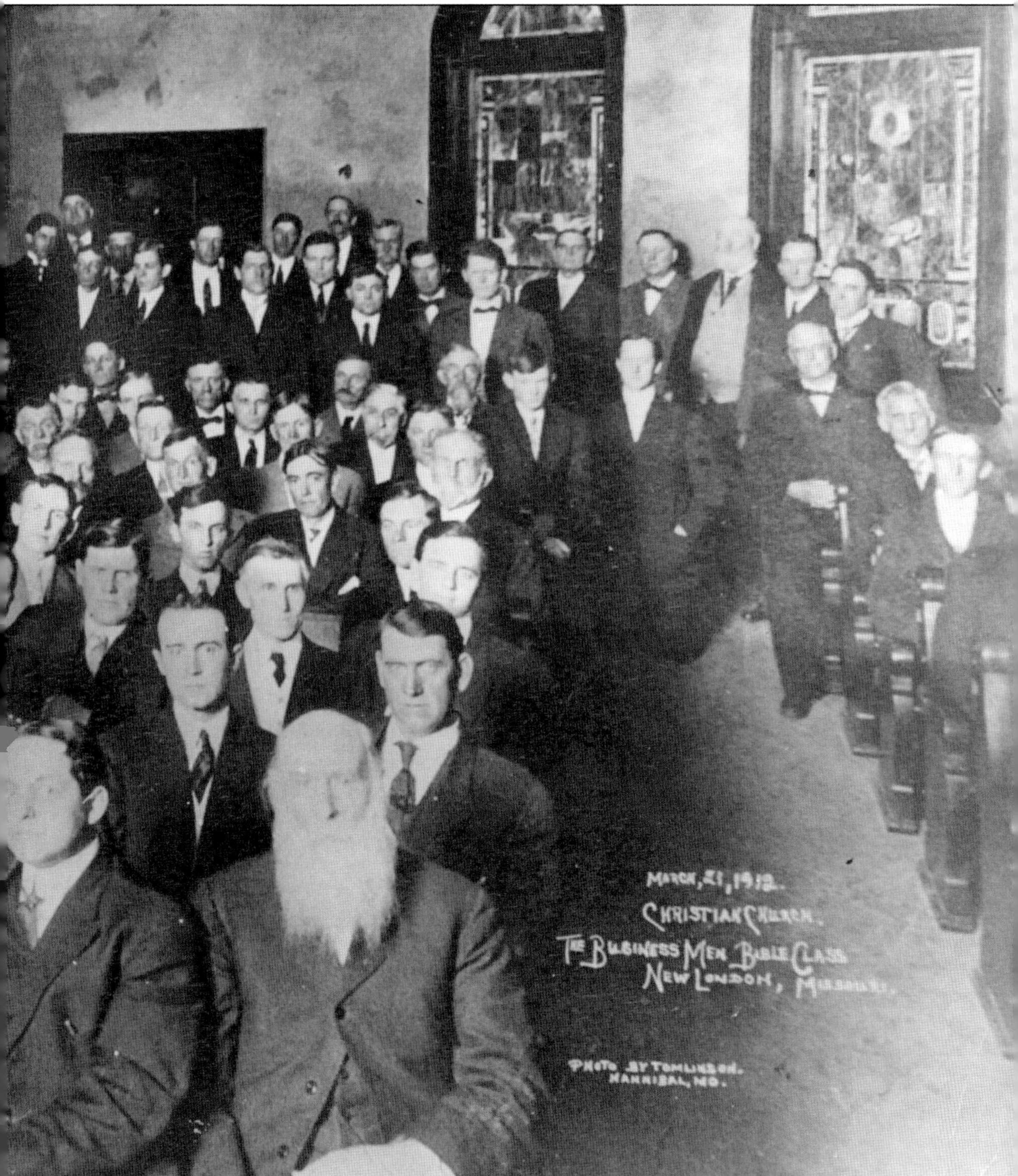

and Dr. Gay Bird Megown; (third row) John Crook, Tom Sykes, Harvey Piper, Arlie Lake, John Hendrix, and Sudduth Alexander; (fourth row) Guy Biggs, George Mayhall, Ed Conn, Harry Weaver, and Gene Carstarphen. Other notable men are Harry Briscoe, James O. Allison, John Wood, Dr. T.J. Downing, Drake Watson, Henry Indorf, and Dr. W.T. Waters. The church is new, and painting has not been completed. (New London First Christian.)

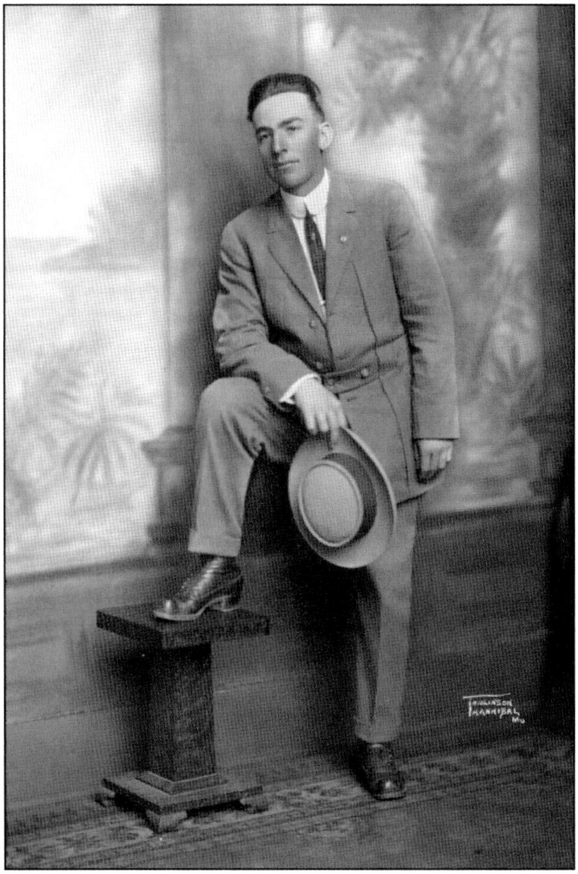

Here is a 1913 portrait of Charles C. Conn (1891–1987) of New London. Charles was a University of Missouri engineering graduate, taught country school, and became county highway engineer. From 1924 to 1946, he literally got "Ralls out of the Mud" by grading, widening, and graveling nearly all of the 845 miles of county roads, which was well before most Missouri counties. In retirement, he was known for his homemade holiday candy. (Mildred Serbin.)

The intersection of Fourth and Ralls Street in New London is seen here looking north in the 1910s. The courthouse is out of view on the left, but the Methodist church and the Ralls County Jail are in the background. The buggy driver is Allison Marion Evans (1888–1936), born in Madisonville to Thomas and Henrietta Evans. He was Ralls County collector at the time of his death from tuberculosis on September 18, 1936; his wife, Laura, succeeded him in office. (RCHS.)

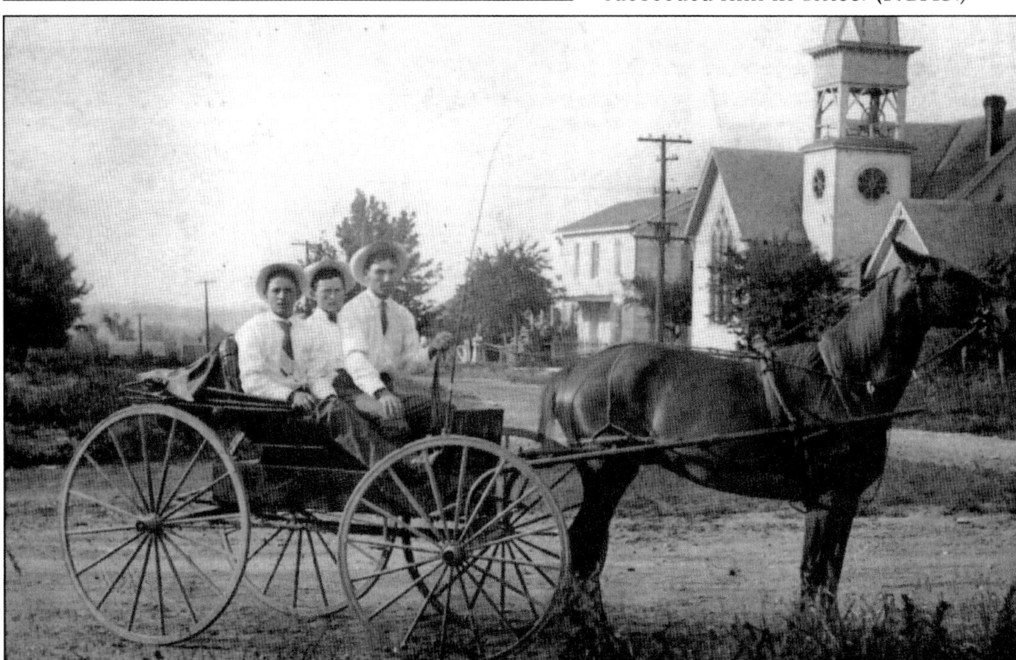

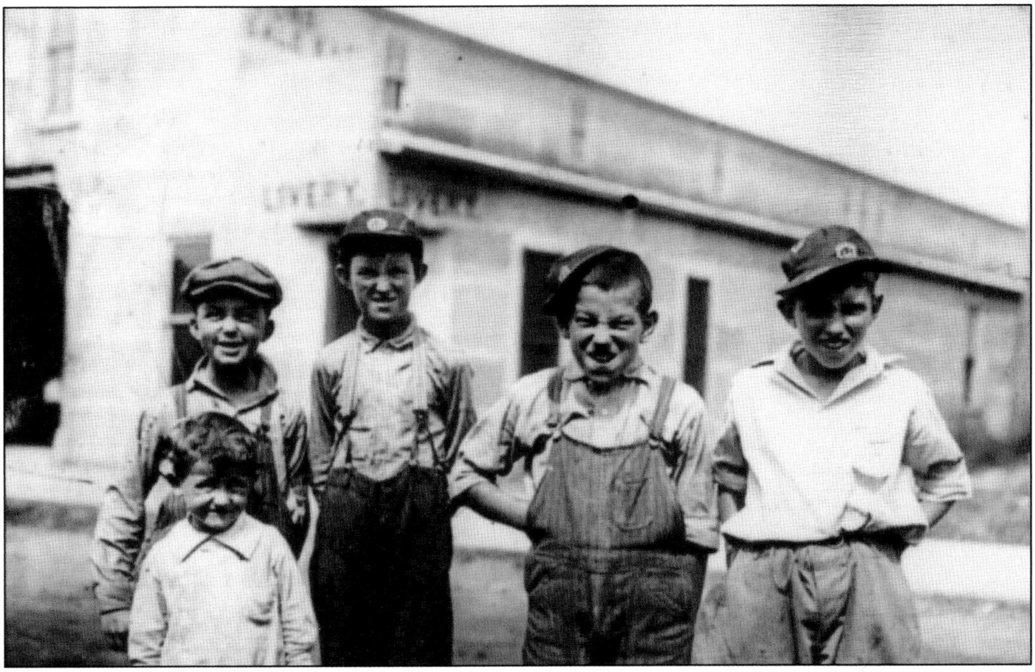

When viewing this captivating mid-1920s photograph, there are many old-fashioned adages that come to mind, such as "boys will be boys;" in this case, five unidentified Perry boys. There is also "better hope your face doesn't freeze like that." These boys are near the Perry Livery barn on Palmyra Street just north of the downtown area. (RCHS.)

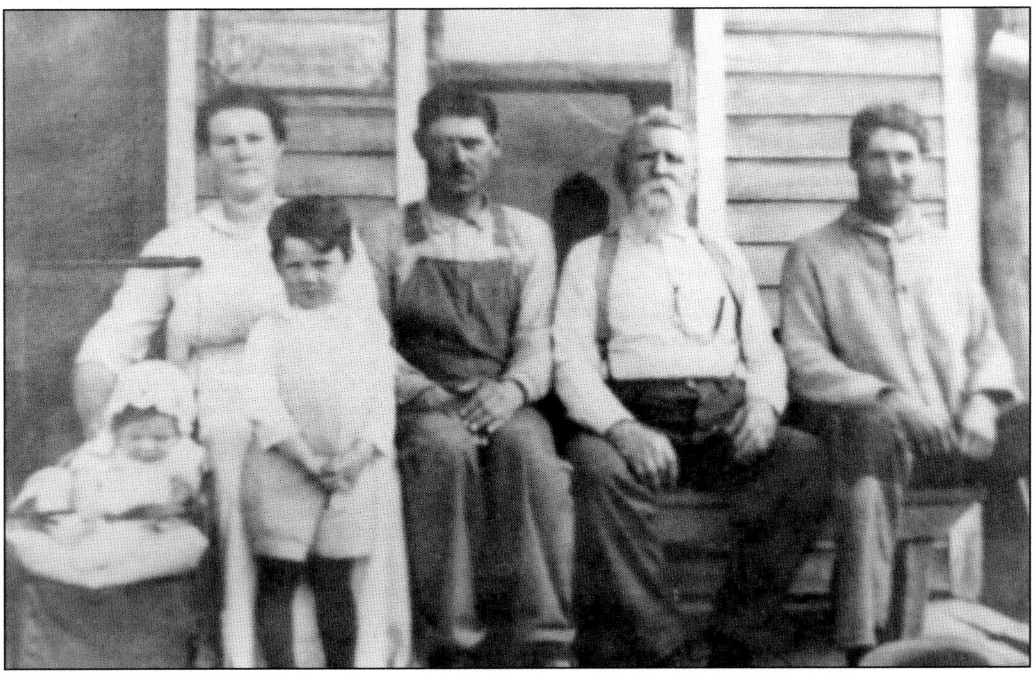

Shown in the 1920s, the Utterback family members are in front of their store in Greenlawn north of Perry. From left to right are Aubrey Lee Utterback, Alice Vera Adams Utterback, Maurice Adams Utterback, William Sutton Utterback, William Austin Utterback, and Jess Rosenstengle. (RCHS.)

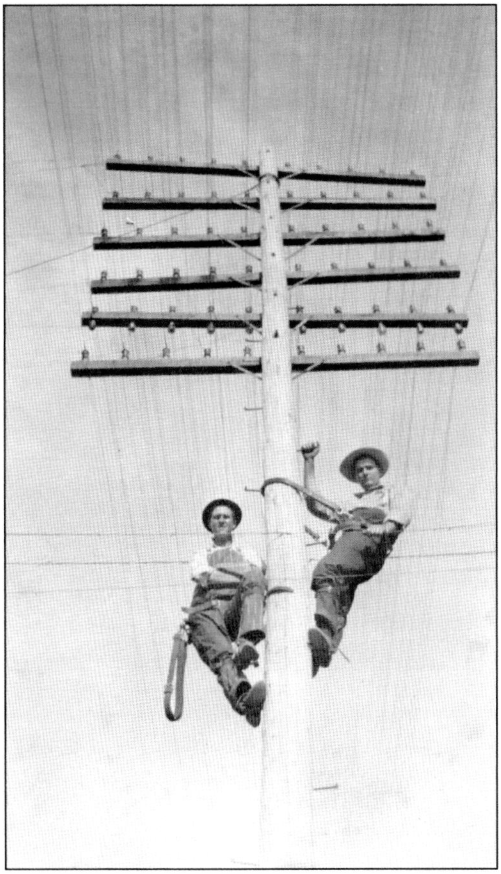

On the right is Lou Milton Dunfee (1881–1959) at work for the Perry Home Telephone Co. The photograph was taken on Palmyra Street down from the four-way. Dunfee was born in Bellaire, Ohio, and married Anna Catherine Stehle (1881–1966) on April 4, 1909. His in-laws owned the phone company. (Author.)

Below, standing on the road to Mineral Springs on the Ralls-Pike County line north of Frankford in 1927 are, from left to right, Roberta Blackwell, Mary K. Degroff, Lucy Glascock, Evelyn Glascock, Dorothy Nett, and Hilda Krigbaum. (Liz Gingry.)

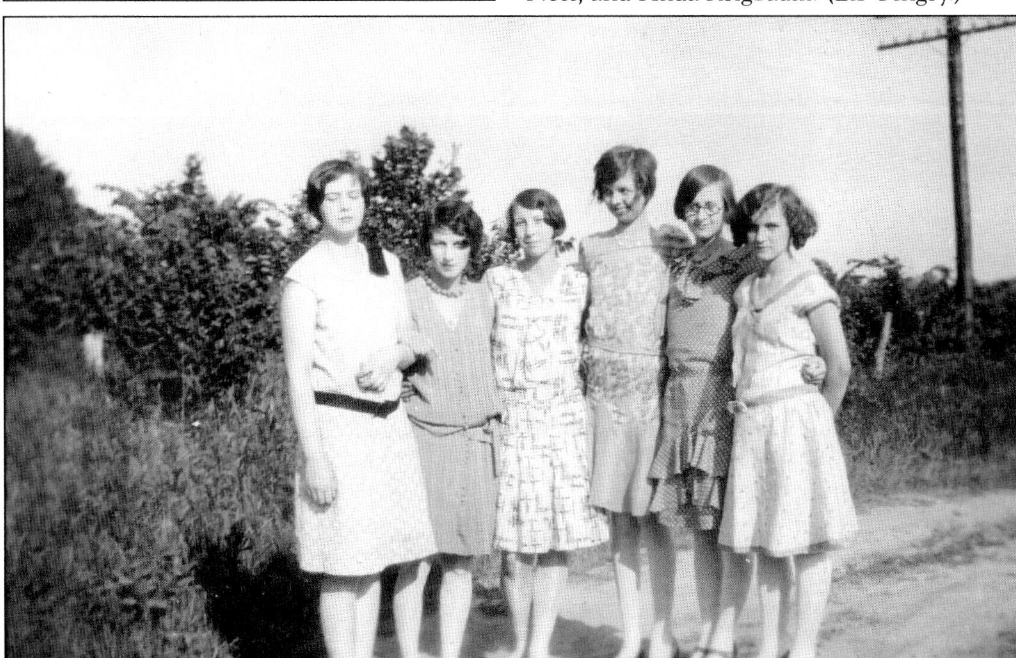

Owendale was a flagstop siding west of New London on the StL&HRR Perry Branchline consisting of two stock pens. The Frankford section crew stopped to visit Eugene "Pete" Strode, who lived here in 1932. The men standing are unidentified. Roy Tanner, section foreman, is seated next to the young Pete Strode, who became a railroad man and post commander of Hannibal's Emmett J. Shields American Legion No. 55. (Mary Frances Strode Quinlin.)

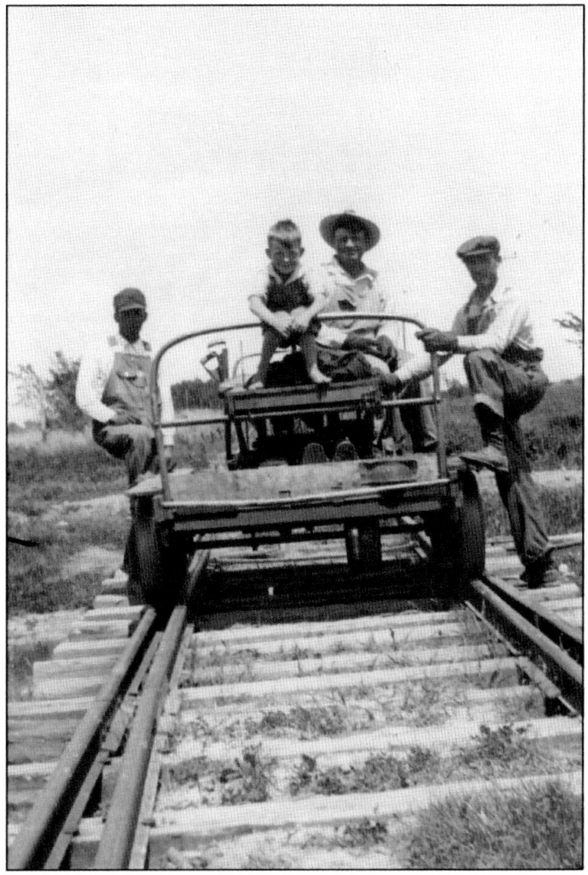

Below, Rev. John W. Golden (1891–1959), "The Old Ridge Runner," poses with his mother, Caroline, around 1930. He pastored many rural Ralls and Marion County Christian churches and "retired" to Troy, Missouri, preaching in Lincoln County. He often preached at six small churches a week. In his career, he baptized 1,350 souls, performed 3,341 weddings, and hosted 4,569 radio programs. He conducted 5,042 funerals, including five services the week he died. (RCHS.)

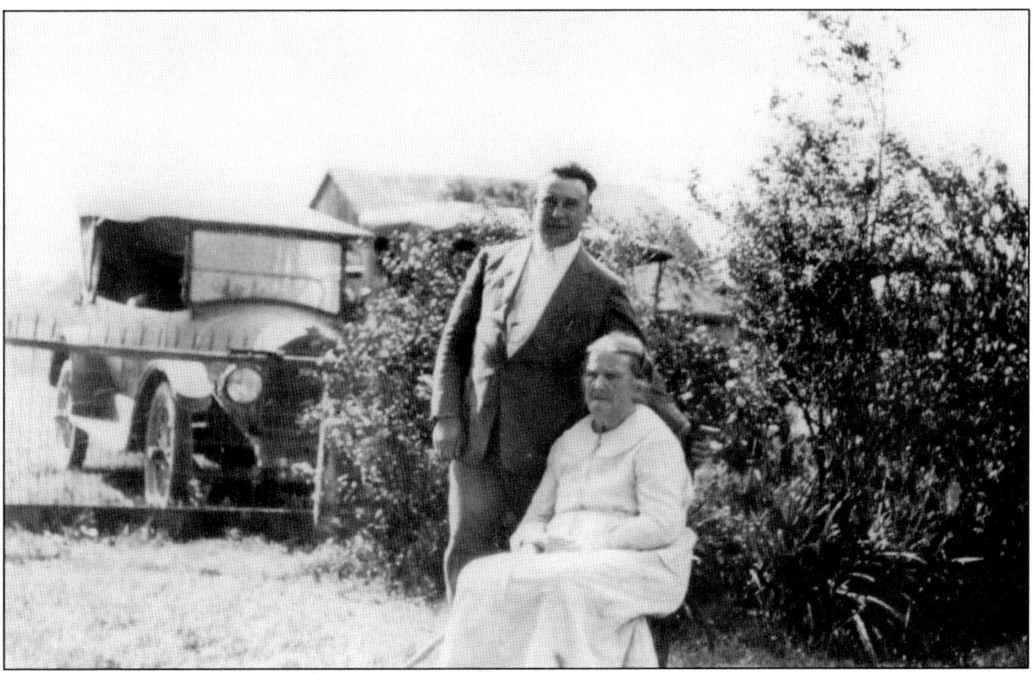

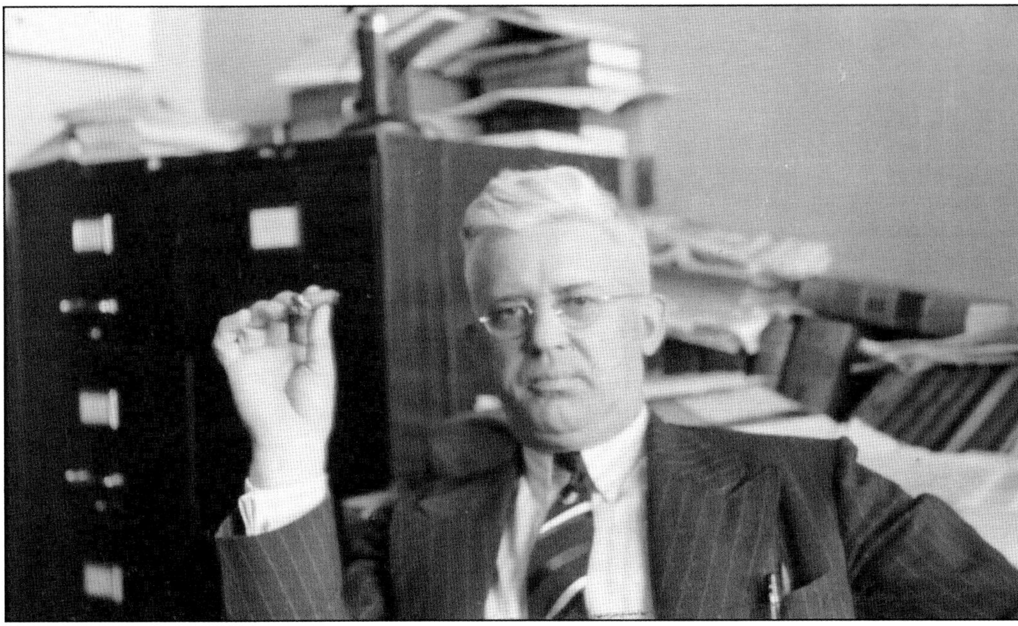

Murray Drake Watson (1887–1951) was a 1907 law graduate of the University of Missouri, a New London lawyer, and in 1917 became Democratic speaker of the Missouri House. In 1923, he wrote a complaint published in the *Ralls County Record* alleging the tax assessment on the Atlas Cement plant was too low and caused an undue tax burden on Ralls County farmers and landowners. (Liz Gingry.)

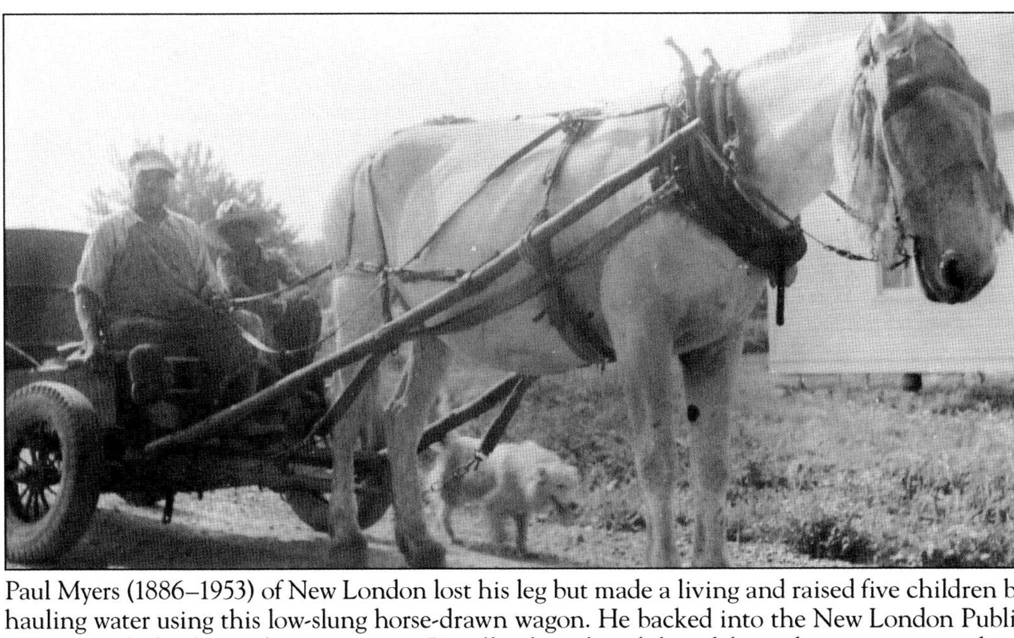

Paul Myers (1886–1953) of New London lost his leg but made a living and raised five children by hauling water using this low-slung horse-drawn wagon. He backed into the New London Public Spring, used a bucket to dip water into a 50-gallon barrel, and then delivered to customers without wells, dipping the water out again. He charged 25¢ a barrel in 1940. (Frances Hays.)

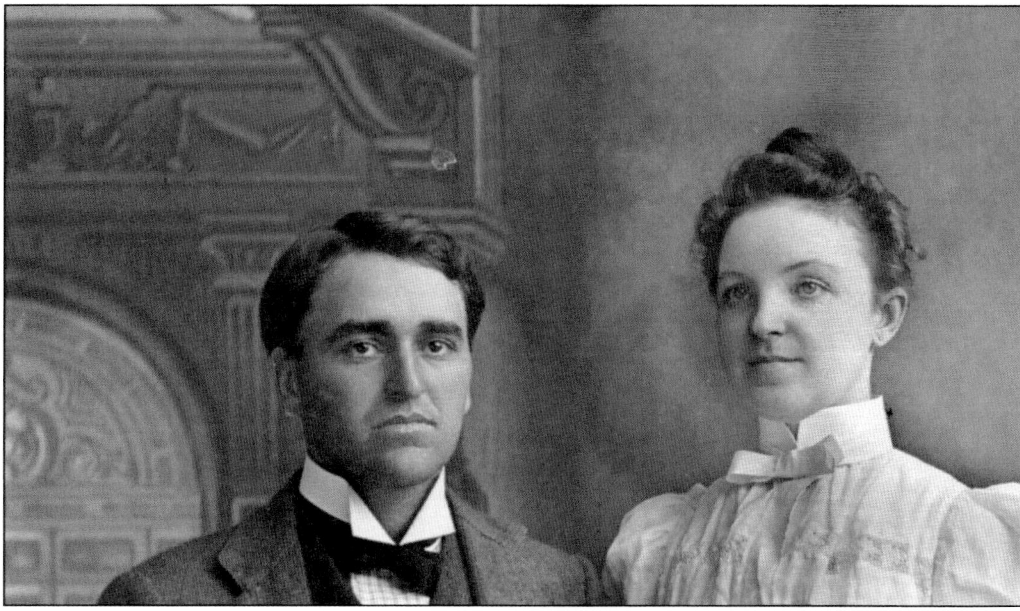

These photographs show Dr. Tom and Olivia Waters at different stages of life. Above is their 1896 wedding photograph, and at right is a late-1940s "brownie" snapshot from a trip to his Kentucky medical school alma mater. Dr. Tom delivered over 1,000 babies and was the first white doctor to vaccinate black children at New London's Douglass School. Most people recall him as a kind, happy man, who cared for everyone's needs especially when they needed it most. Olivia Waters enjoyed flowers and raising prizewinning poultry for the Ralls County Fairs. Her father was Samuel Watson; their ancestors were French families escaping Huguenot religious persecution in the 1600s. (Both, author.)

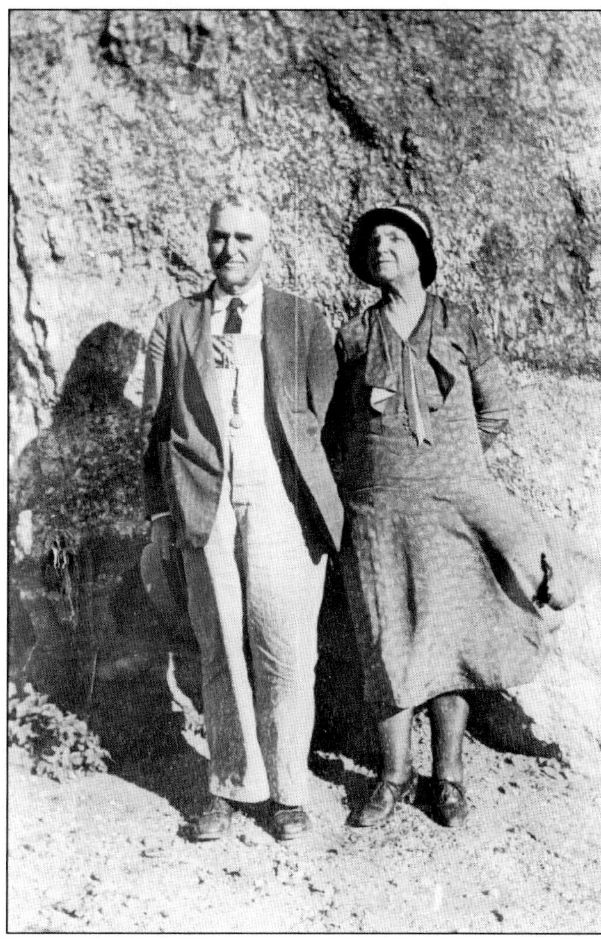

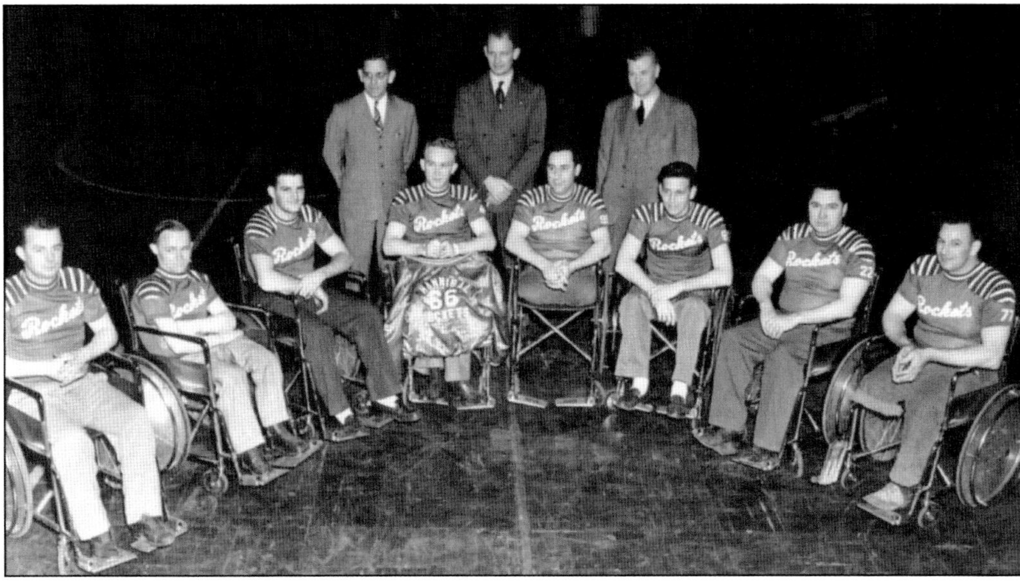

Pictured are members of the Hannibal Rockets basketball team at the Admiral Coontz Armory in the early 1950s. From left to right are (first row) Gordon Shinn, Dean Snow, Bill Delaporte, Bill Elsner, Bill Hohner, Del Willis, Verdan Harris, and Bill Gingry; (second row) Bill Broaddus, Archie Craig, and George Dalton. J. Lyle "Bill" Gingry of New London lost his leg in Italy during World War II. He later became Ralls County circuit clerk and recorder. (Liz Gingry.)

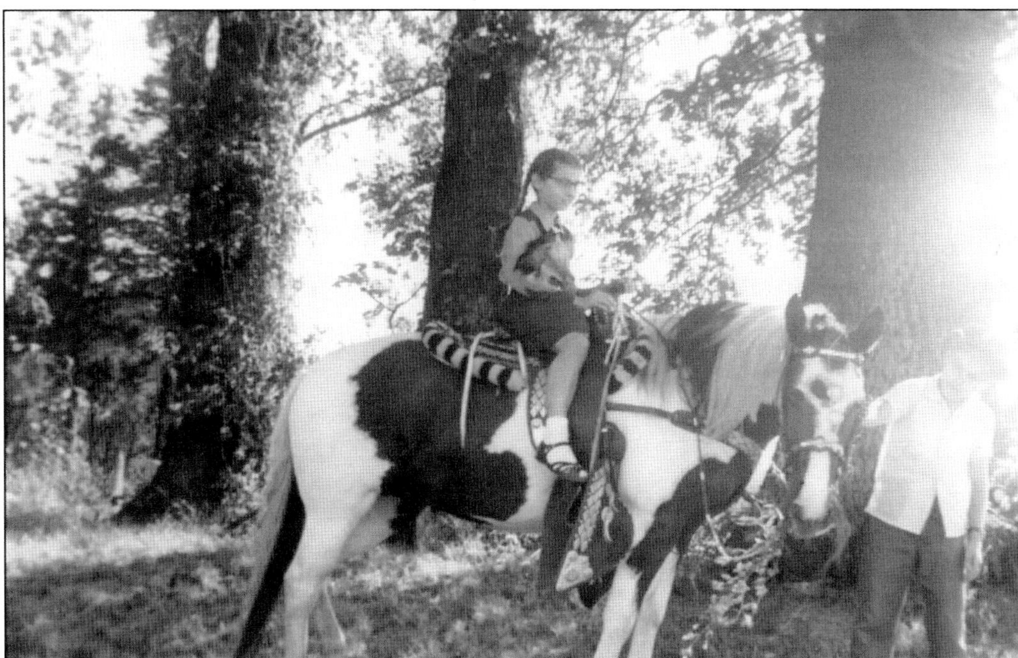

Tri-State baby boomers recognize Cactus Jim (right) as a television legend. In 1953, Richard "Dick" Moore ran audio for KHQA-7 TV; they asked him to host a children's show sponsored by Prairie Farms Milk until 1970, when it closed on WGEM-10. Janie Gingry is atop Dick's horse Lady in 1955. The author appeared on the *Cactus Jim* show twice. Dick lives in El Paso, Illinois, and has a Facebook page. (Liz Gingry.)

Four

Readin', Writin', and Savin' Souls

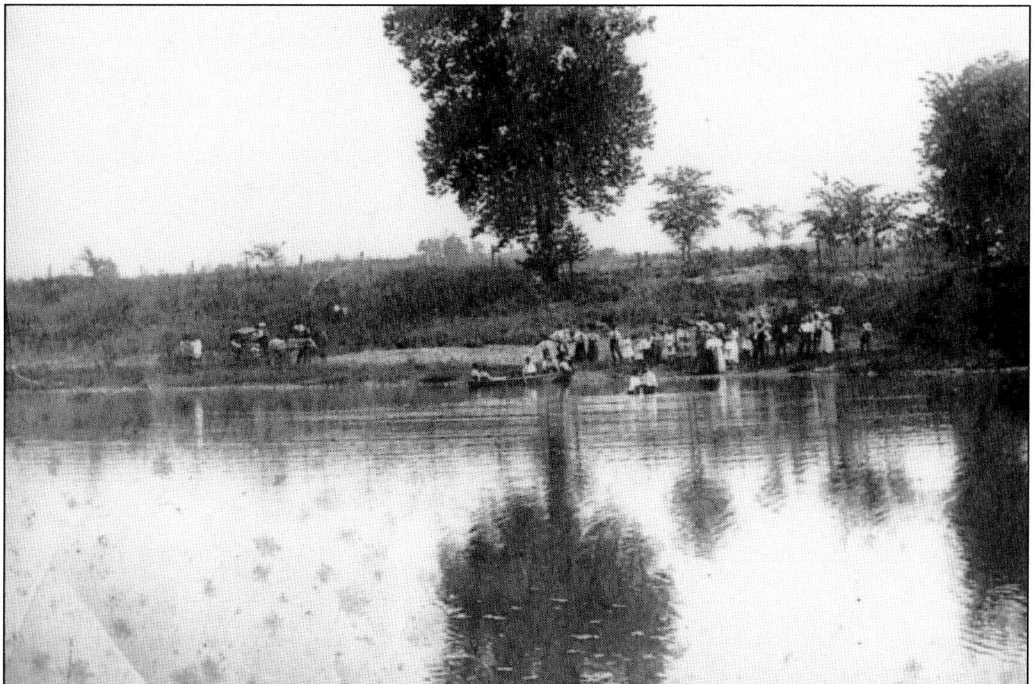

Here is a good old-fashioned mass baptism underway in the Salt River at an unknown location in Ralls County in the 1900s. More than likely, this is near a bridge or one of many low-water crossings. Occasionally, some people still request a genuine river dunking instead of a sanctuary baptismal. (RCHS.)

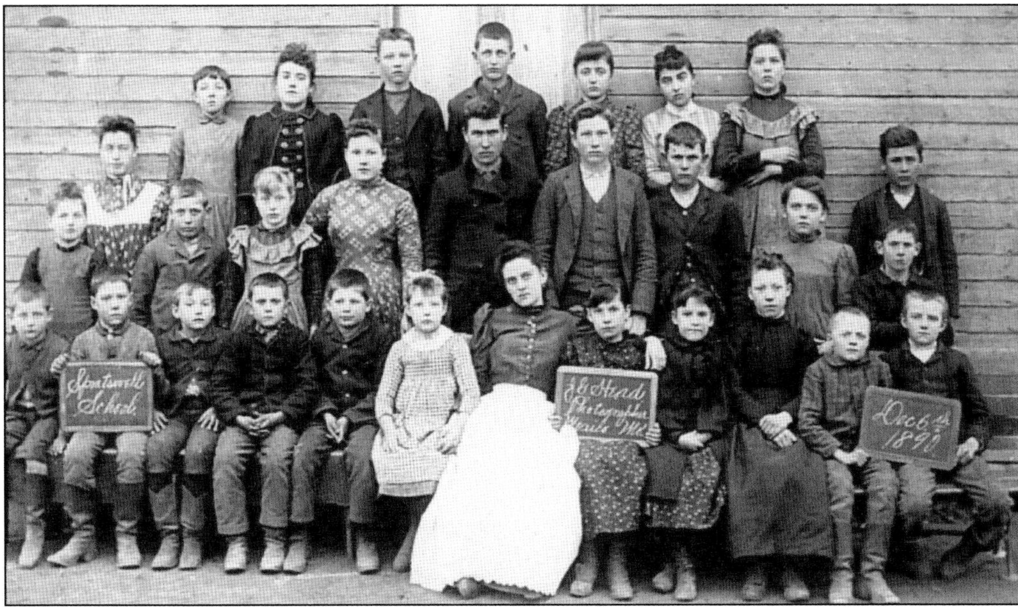

This December 6, 1890, photograph is of the Spratswell School west of Lick Creek, named for John S. Spratswell. When it needed replacement, the Moore families built a new school named Piddletown. Mary Moore Jackson coined the name. When asked for a name, she replied, "Why not Piddletown? The Moores just piddle around anyway." (RCHS.)

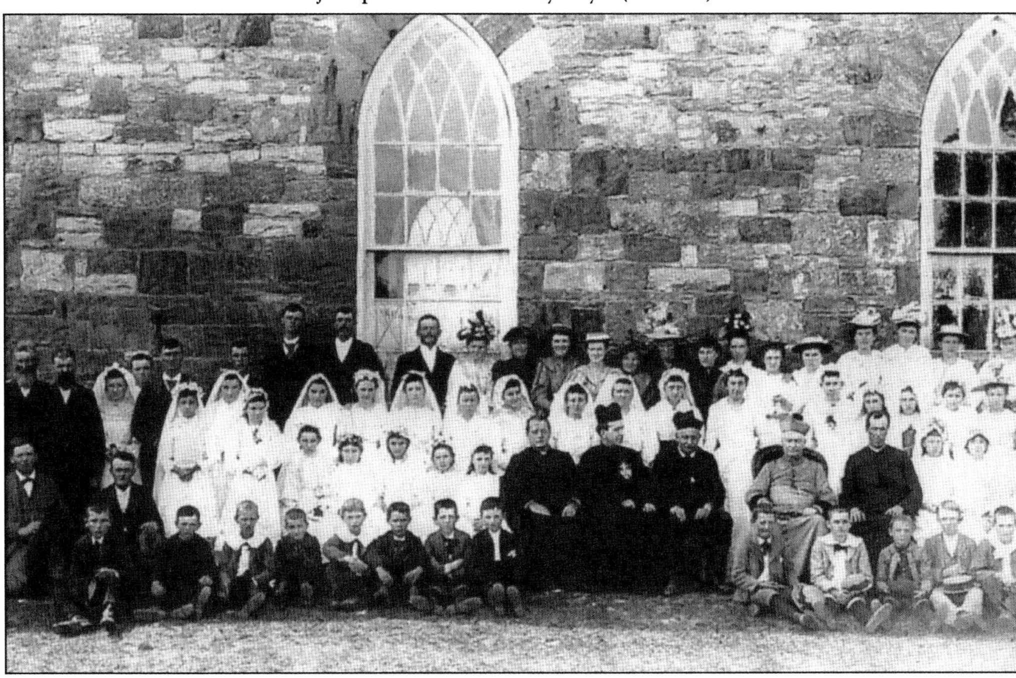

An 1890s church group poses at historic St. Paul Church, located west of Center. The church was built in 1859 and was listed in the National Register of Historic Places in 1969. The cemetery dates to 1819, when Thomas Whittington was interred. Revolutionary War veteran Ignatius Greenwell died in 1847 and is buried here also. This area was known as Leake's Station before the church was erected. (RCHS.)

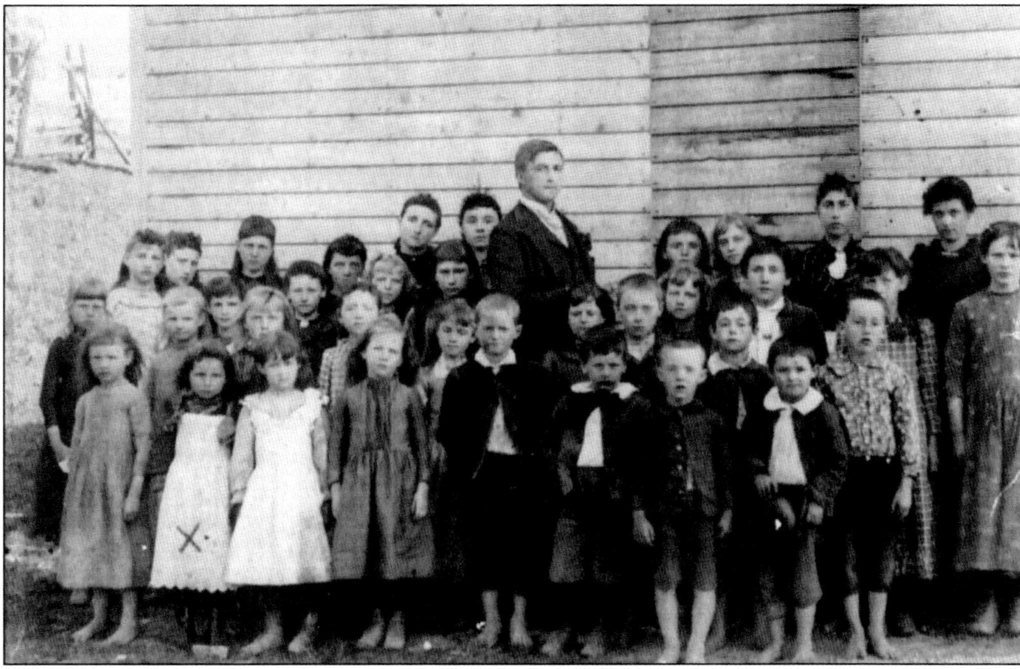

Spalding School No. 12 children and their teacher are shown in 1891. In later years, Spalding consolidated with Rensselaer School. (RCHS.)

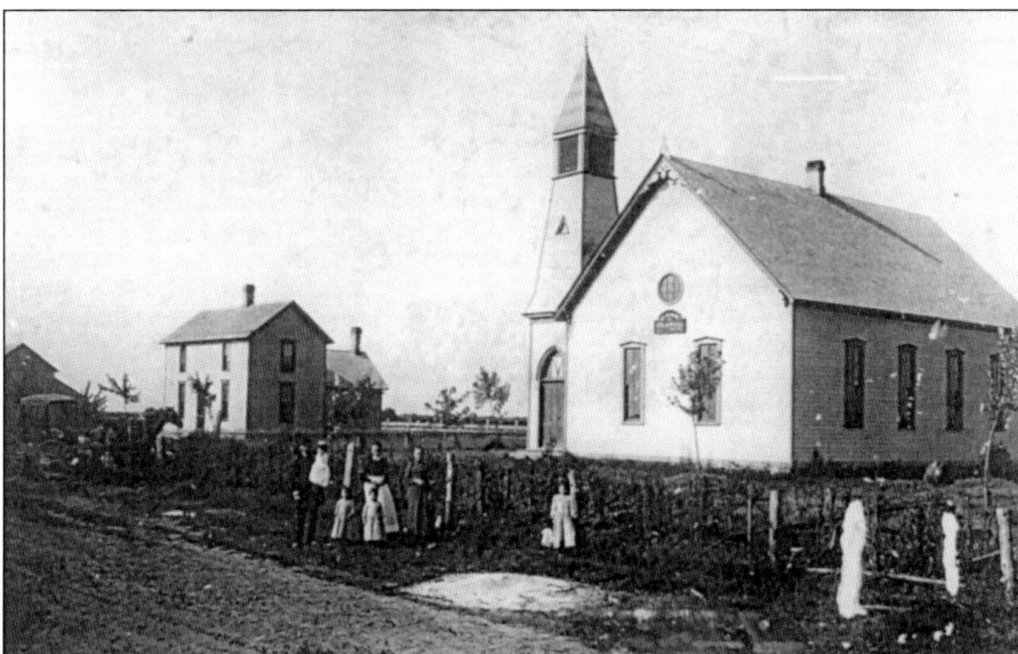

Fern Chapel Methodist Church, shown around 1895, was built around 1888 with land donated by William and Lucillin Wood, east of Perry. A burial ground was already established prior to the church, which was named for 14-year-old daughter Fern Wood who died October 30, 1887. In 1957, the building was carefully restored under the leadership of Joe Meissert and Charles Hawkinson. (RCHS.)

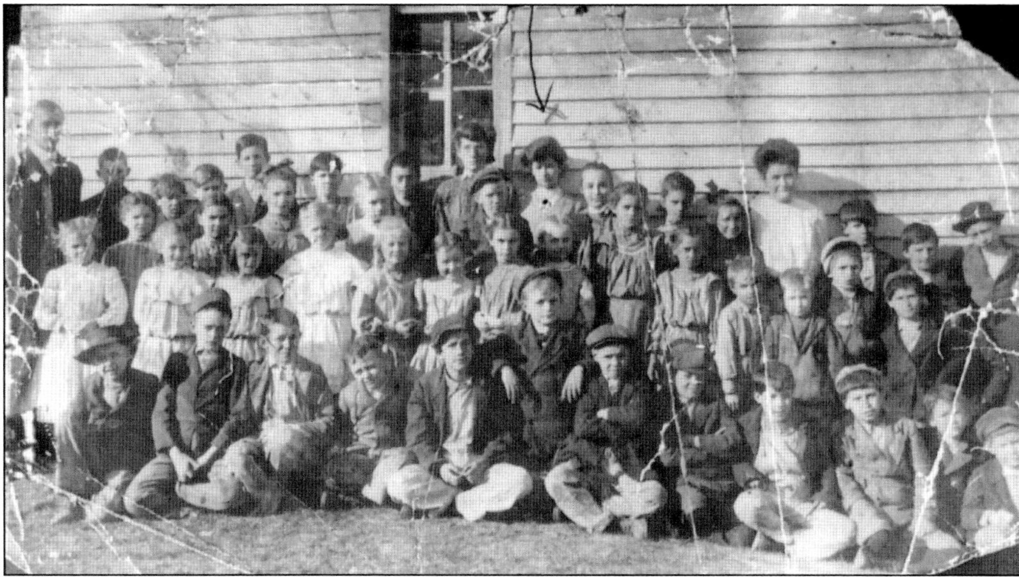

Here is an early-1900s Saverton No. 18 class. A note on the back says, "Jesse Calvert, right of window." This school burned in 1933, so school was held in the Saverton Methodist Church until a new building was completed north across the road from the previous. When it closed in 1959, it reverted to the Fisher family, who donated it for use as a community center. (David Polc.)

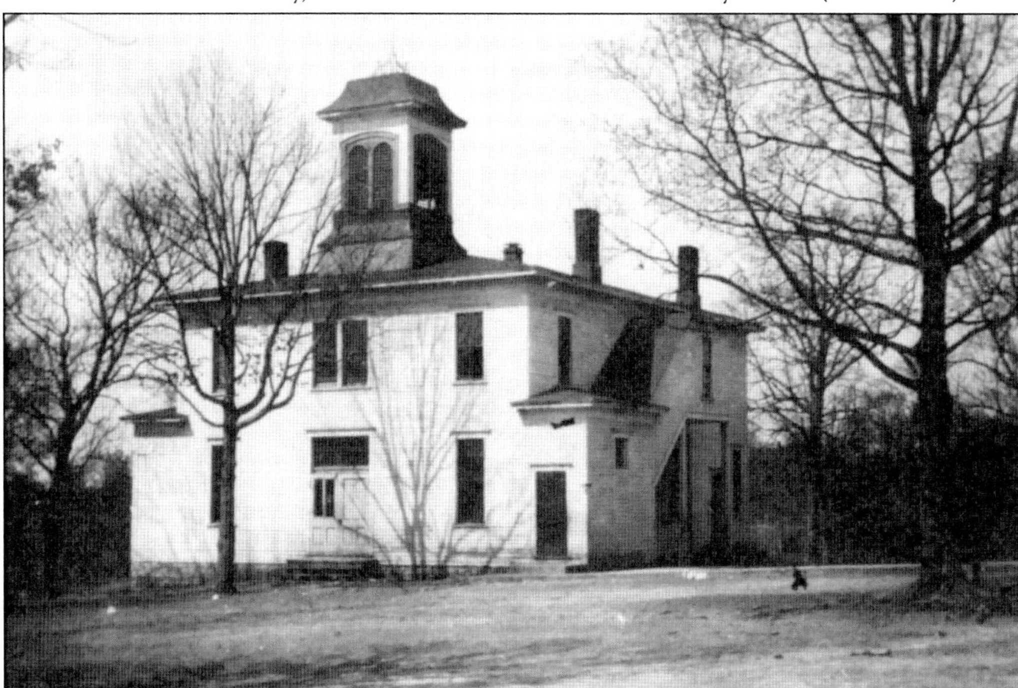

A school and dormitory built in 1885 on the north side of Perry was offered to Prof. French Strother for private schooling, which became the Strother Institute. If Strother stayed six years, the building and eight acres would become his. After taking possession, he traded it for property in Mexico, Missouri, where he built a new institute. The buildings were then used until 1914 as the Perry Grade and High School. (Author.)

This is a c. 1905 real-photo postcard of first Olivet Christian Church of Center, Missouri. Built in 1873 north of town at the Olivet Cemetery site, the congregation decided to have it moved by A.M. Leatherman in 1890 to Hawkins and Foster Streets for $400. On August 13, 1912, it was struck by lightning and burned. The present 1914 brick building was patterned in reverse after the Elsberry Christian Church. (David Polc.)

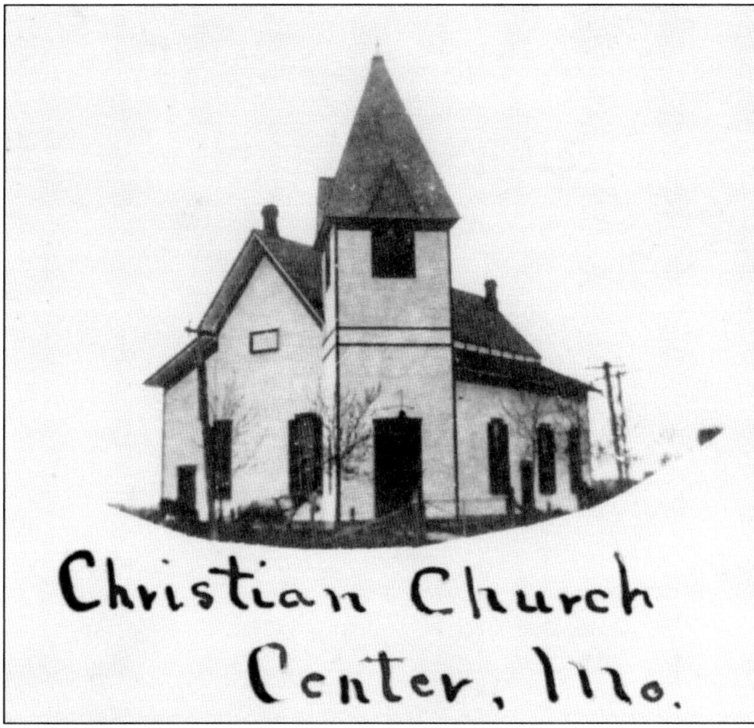

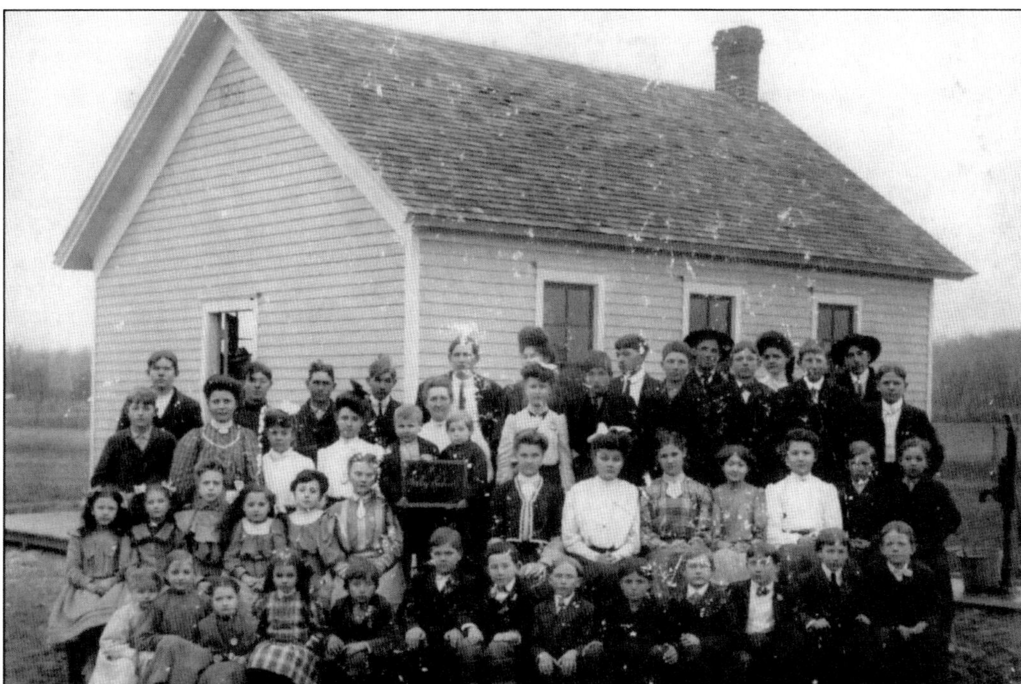

This early-1900s photograph shows a group of Seely School No. 52 students in southern Ralls County. The school was built in 1896, closed in the 1950s, and reverted to then-owner Mary Nell (Conn) Liter (1906–2002). It was razed in the late 2000s. Spencer Creek runs behind, along the trees. (RCHS.)

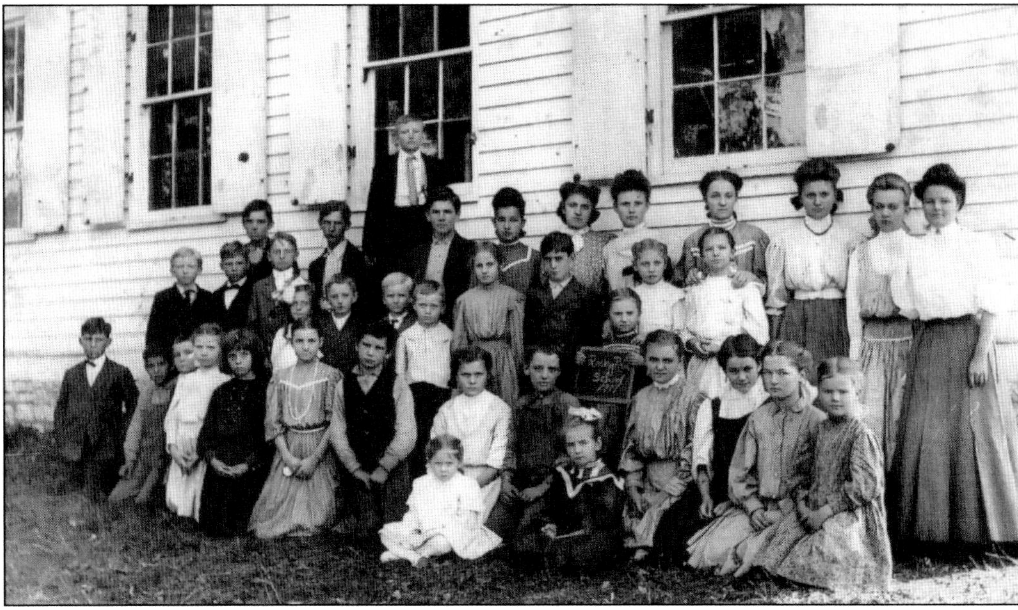

This photograph of Rocky Point No. 36 School is dated 1907. This school is south of New London on the east side of US Highway 61. Most of the country schools began closing in 1956 with the consolidation into the Ralls R-VI District. But for many years later, the school building served as a community center. It was recently sold to a private owner. (RCHS.)

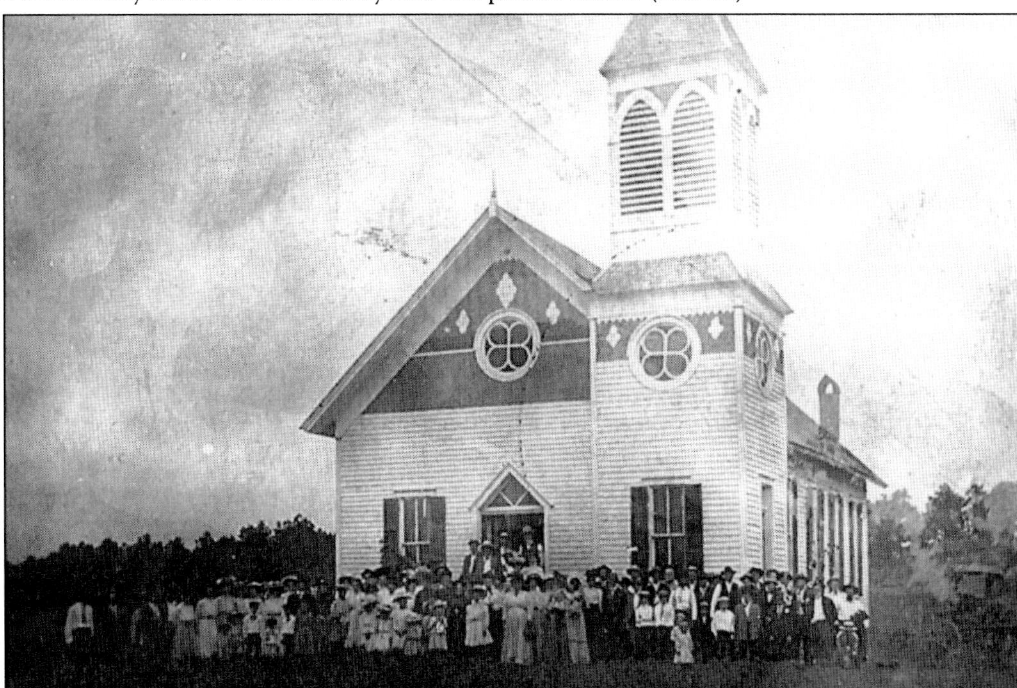

This 1900s photograph is of the Oakland Baptist Church near Joanna, Missouri. This 1891 frame Victorian-influenced building was 40 by 60 feet and could seat up to 250 souls. Rev. J.B. Frisbe was its first pastor. As the Cannon Dam construction began this church was torn down, the cemetery was moved, and a new church was built about a mile north. (RCHS.)

This photograph of New London's 1874 St. Joseph Catholic Church is from the late Phil Conn's collection. It is an unusual view of a man installing a downspout on a long-gone two-story home in the 600 block of Main. This perspective details the landscape, or lack thereof, at Seventh Street, the former tall steeple on St. Joe's, and the gazebo in front of the home on the southwest corner. (RCHS.)

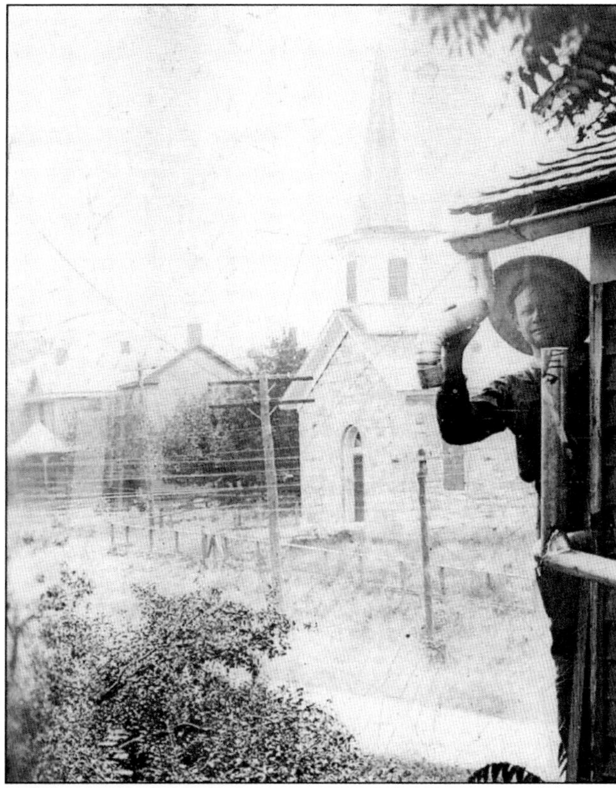

Gatson School No. 47 students are pictured in 1911. The school was located east of Greenlawn on the east-west road. Note the children are still barefoot. Children often would not get shoes until very late fall, when it became cold. Even then, shoes had to last until spring. A person only had shoes year-round if he or she worked. (RCHS.)

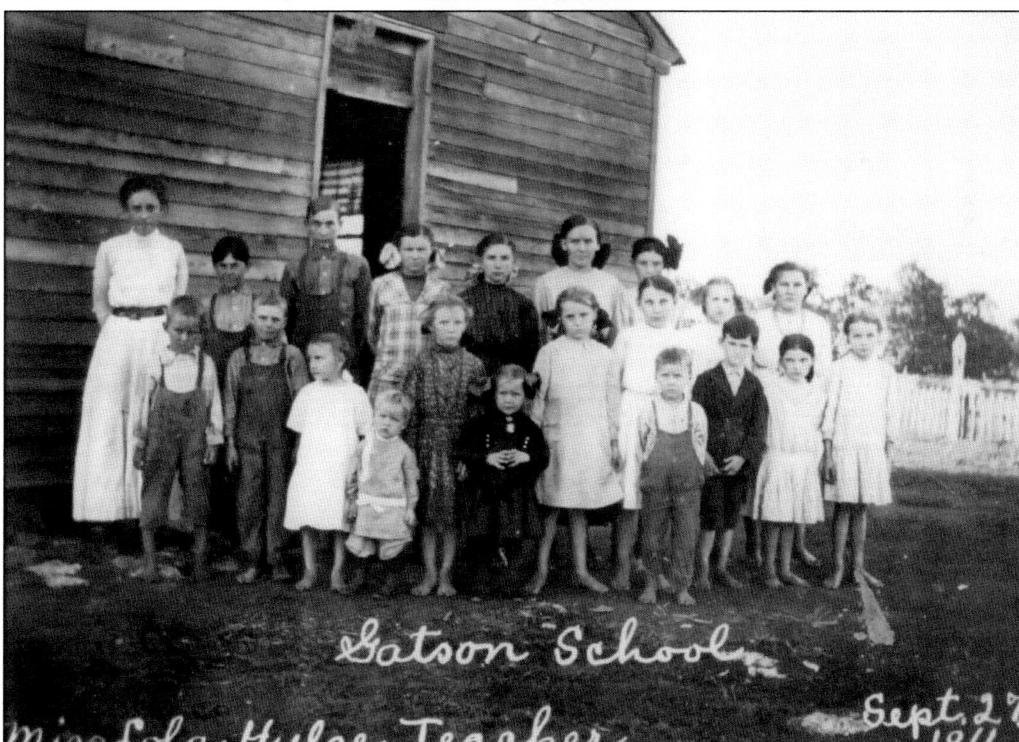

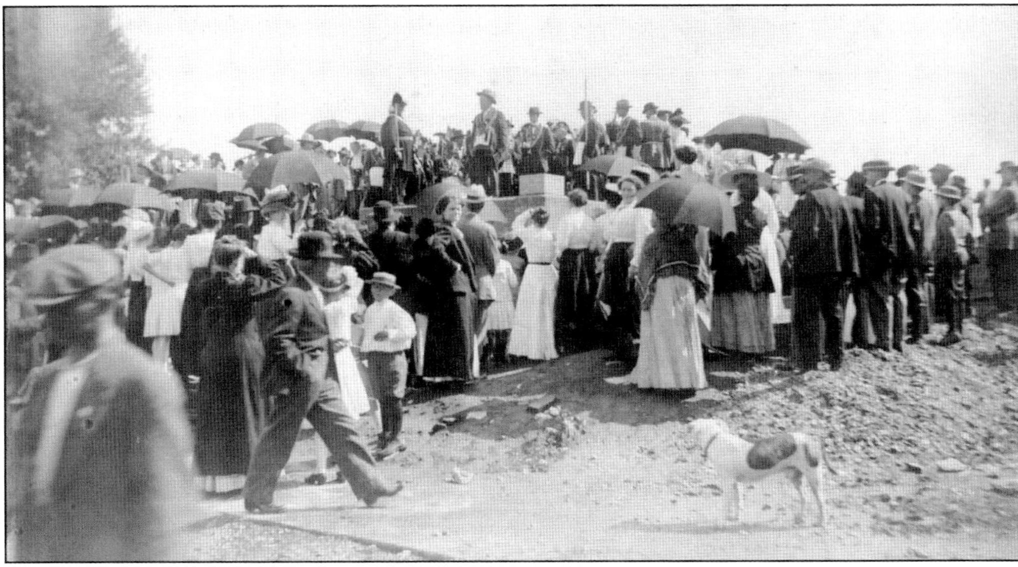

In the fall of 1911, the congregation of New London First Christian laid the cornerstone for its third building at the same location. The previous was lost to fire spread from a neighbor's shed. Church history indicates that Dr. W.T. Waters was building chairman. In the photograph, local Masons are present, and so is a dog. The new Akron-type building was capable of seating 300 people, similar to Perry Christian Church. (Archie Hayden.)

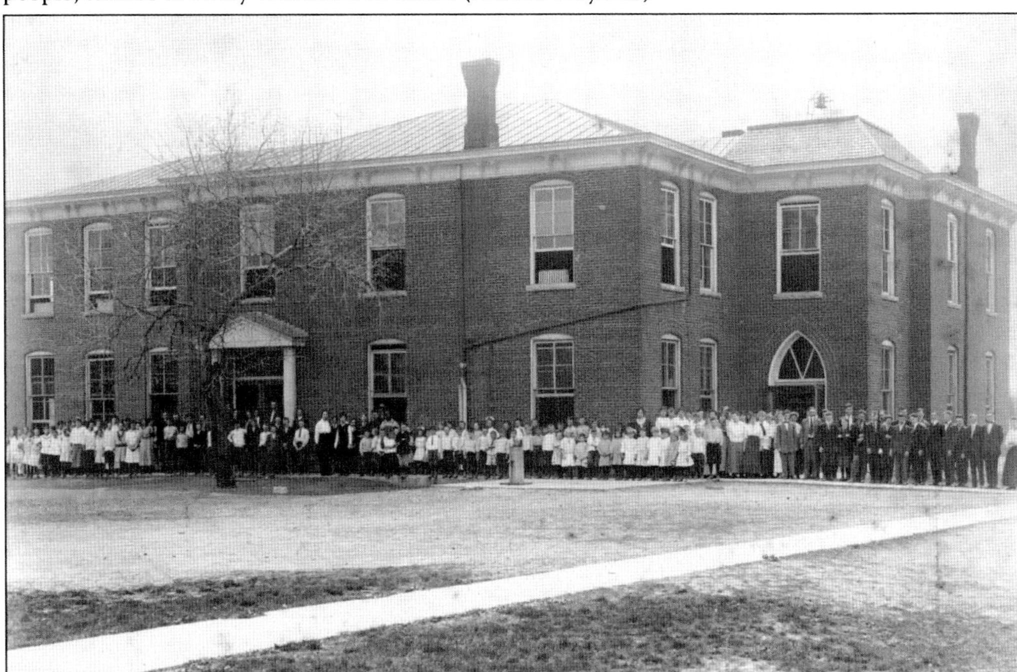

Shown around 1912–1913, this brick building served New London School No. 23 at Fourth and College Streets and was erected in 1892. The last seniors graduated in 1959. A new school was built in 1954 on South Main Street, and area country schools were consolidated into the Ralls R-VI District. The building was occupied by Cerf Bros. Bag and Tarp and slowly demolished for a new plant on this location. Cerf Bros. Bag and Tarp closed in 2008. (Liz Gingry.)

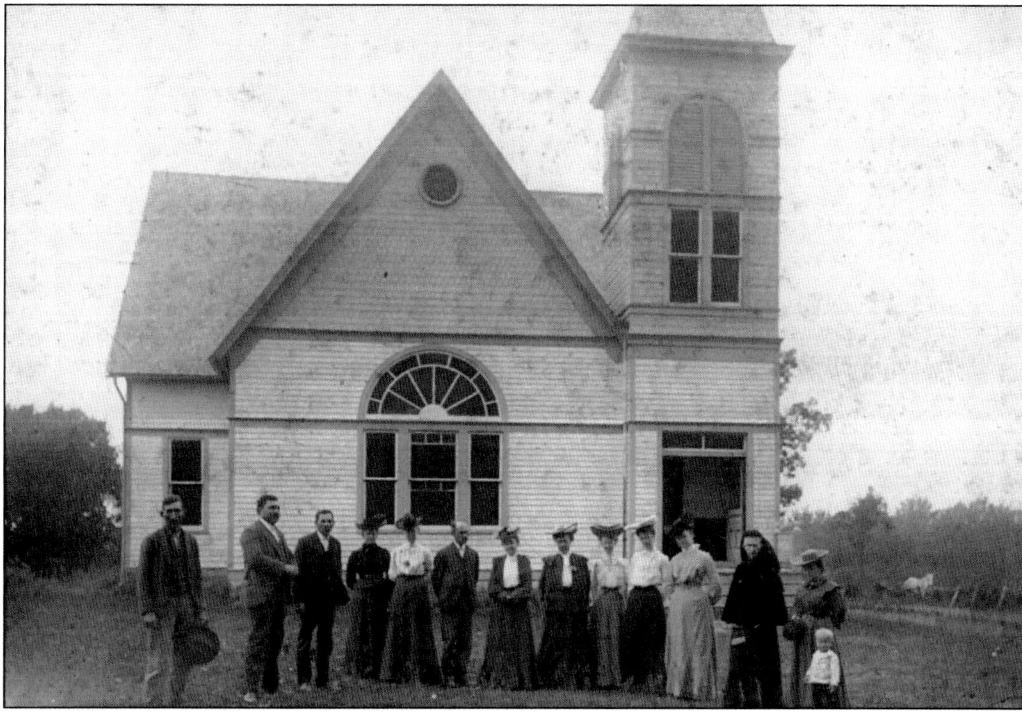

Salem Baptist Church is located southwest of New London on the old east-west road before Highway 19. Salem Church is the oldest Ralls Baptist organization, having started in 1832. This fourth building is classic American Gothic architecture and cost $2,500 to construct in 1898. It burned in May 1929. Nancy Jeffries Epperson, the first white child born in New London, was an early member of Salem. (RCHS.)

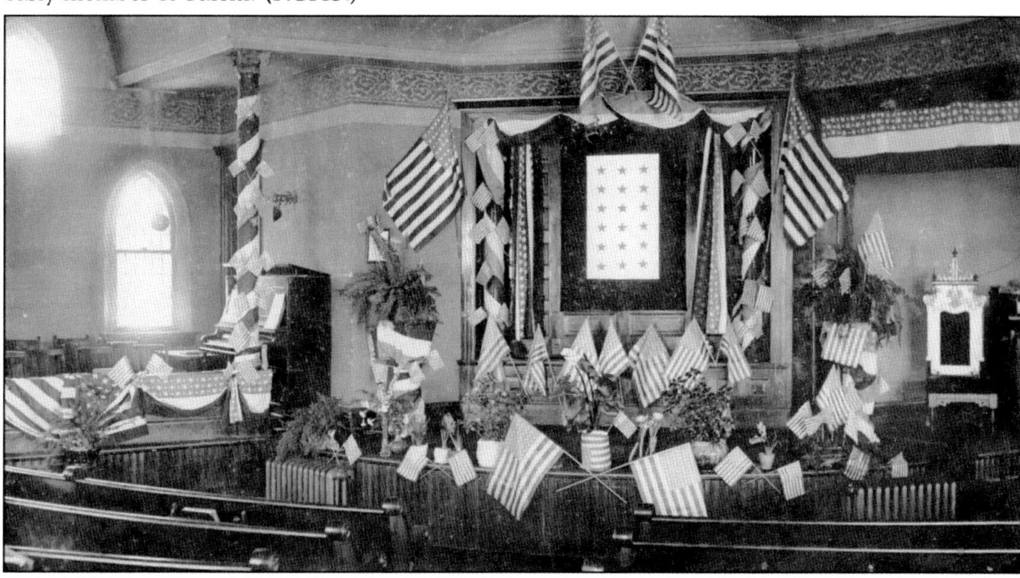

Minnie Stehle photographed this 1918 interior view of Perry Christian Church. The auditorium is decorated in a patriotic theme readied for a prayer service to remember World War I servicemen. The banner with 18 gold stars indicates the number of Perry men sent out in the service of America. In days past, nearly everyone would have attended. (Author.)

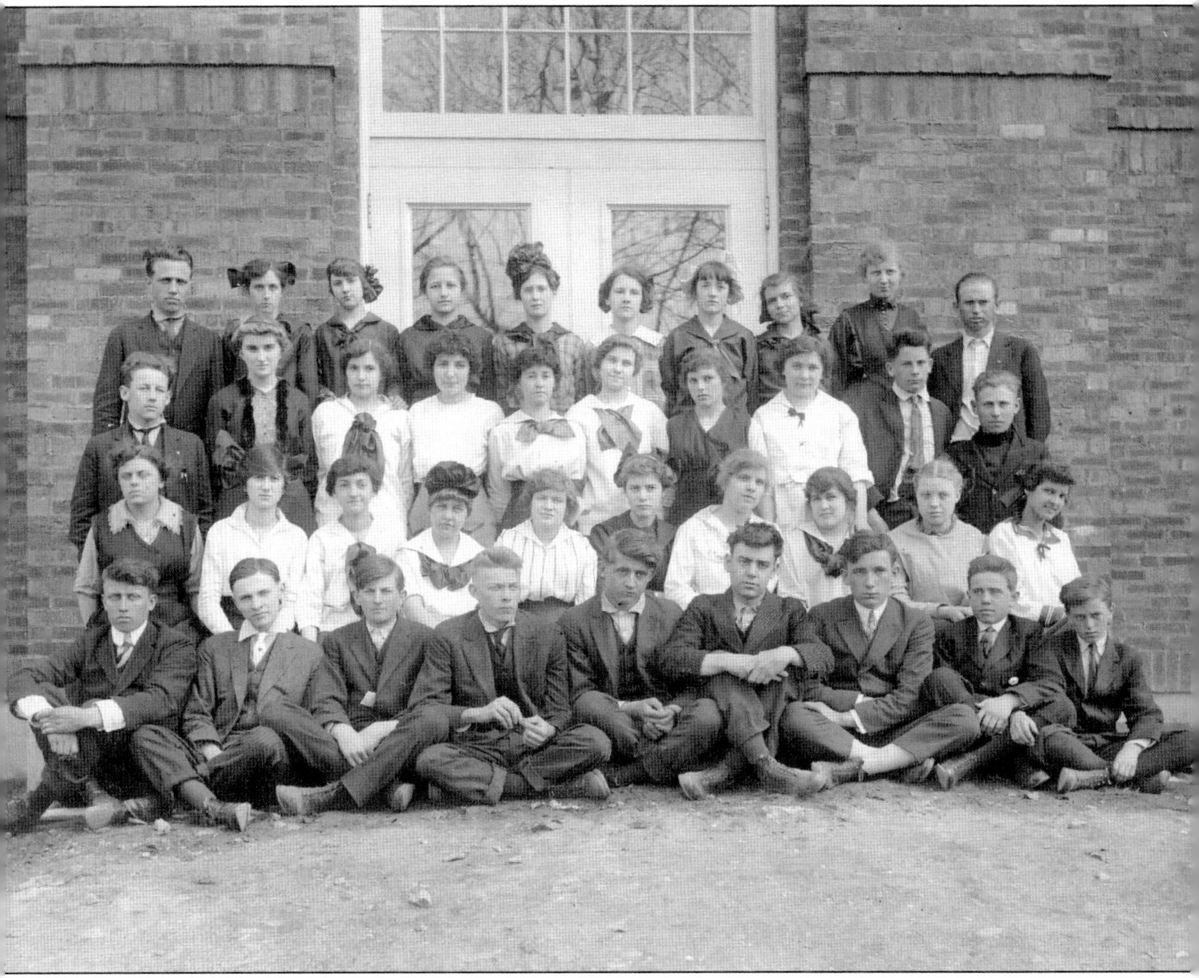

The Perry Philomethian Literary Society is shown in 1915–1916 at the new Perry High School No. 57. From left to right are (first row) Joe Smelsor, Melville Barr, Dewey Moriss, George Judy, Henry Moore, Edwin Coil, Harold Woods, Harold Mitchell, and Curtiss Johnson; (second row) Lucille Davis, Camille Smith, Janetta Cowherd, Ruth Mitchell, Gladys Rosalle, Artemesia Coil, Mabel Anderson, Mary Elliott, Hazel Nichols, and Josephine Ward; (third row) Keith Tibbles, Mary Alice Morris, Lorena Hoar, Ida Grimes, teacher Frankie Westfall, Anna Bea Smith, Nina Smith, Adelle Wasson, Willie Wasson, and Herman Utterback; (fourth row) Irene Logerman, Irene Carter, Jewell Smith, Jaunita Cole, Margaret Westfall, Florence Cole, Ruth Elliott, Nina Jenks, and Willie Leake. (Ben Akers.)

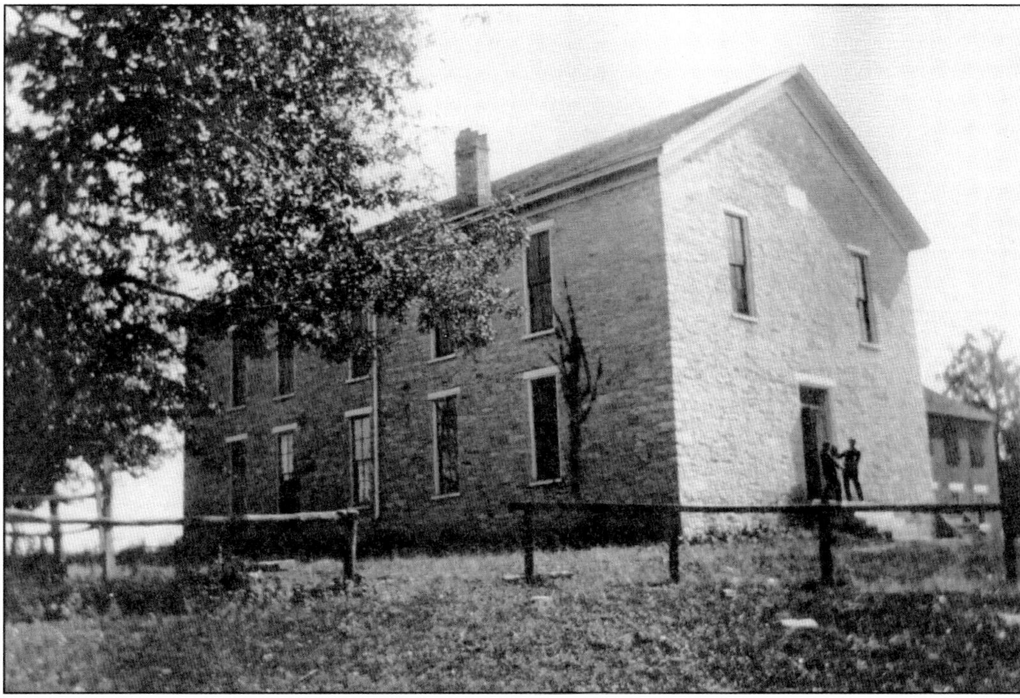

This 1919 postcard shows Big Creek Church, Rensselaer, Missouri, organized in 1834. Church members first met in homes or in the Big Creek schoolhouse. By 1850, a frame building stood by the present cemetery when the congregation established Van Rensselaer Academy, and a two-story brick building was constructed. In 1866, this stone structure was built to house the church and academy, which closed in 1915. The previous building became the black school. (David Polc.)

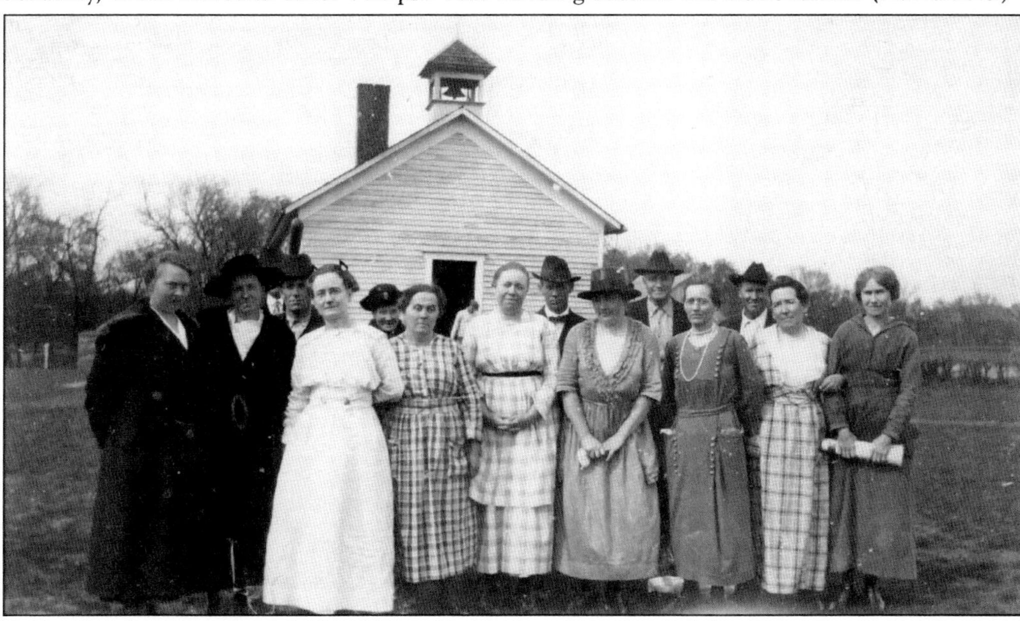

A small group of unidentified residents has gathered in front of the West Hartford School No. 56 in the 1920s. West Hartford was located at a junction north of Hutchison, east of Perry, and south of Noonan. (RCHS.)

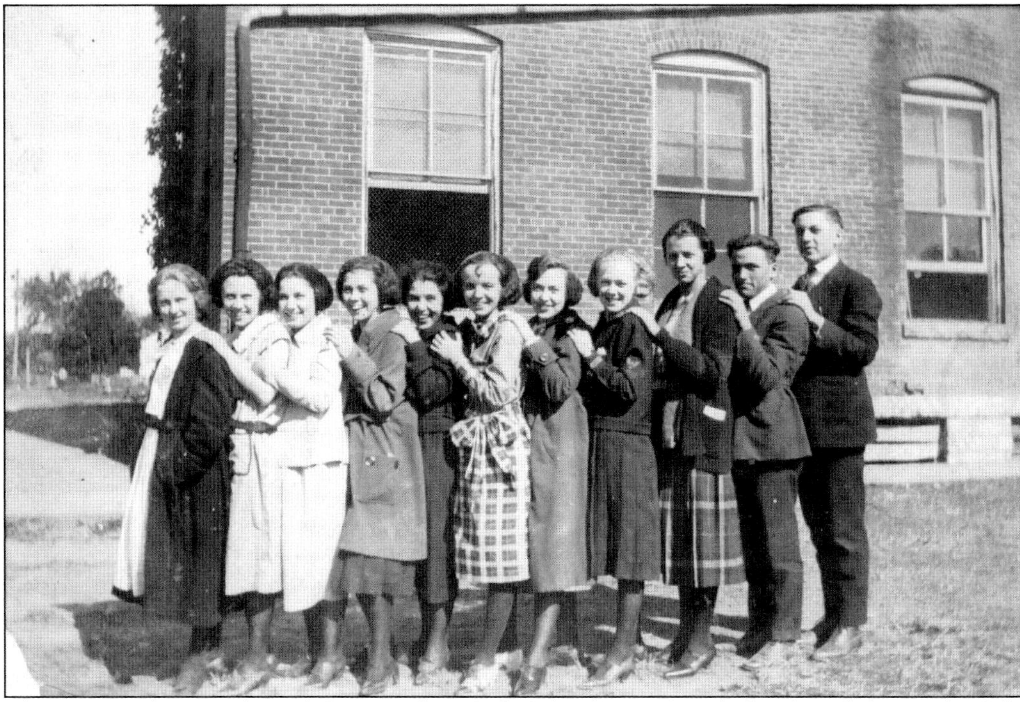

The 1922 graduating class of New London High School No. 23 includes, from left to right, Julia Strode, Anna Mae Bowles, Lottie Kennedy, Etta Mae Callison, Carolyn Brown, Ruth Hulse, Emily McCune, Mary Sayre, Mary Elliott, Julian Johnson, and Roi Wood. (Liz Gingry.)

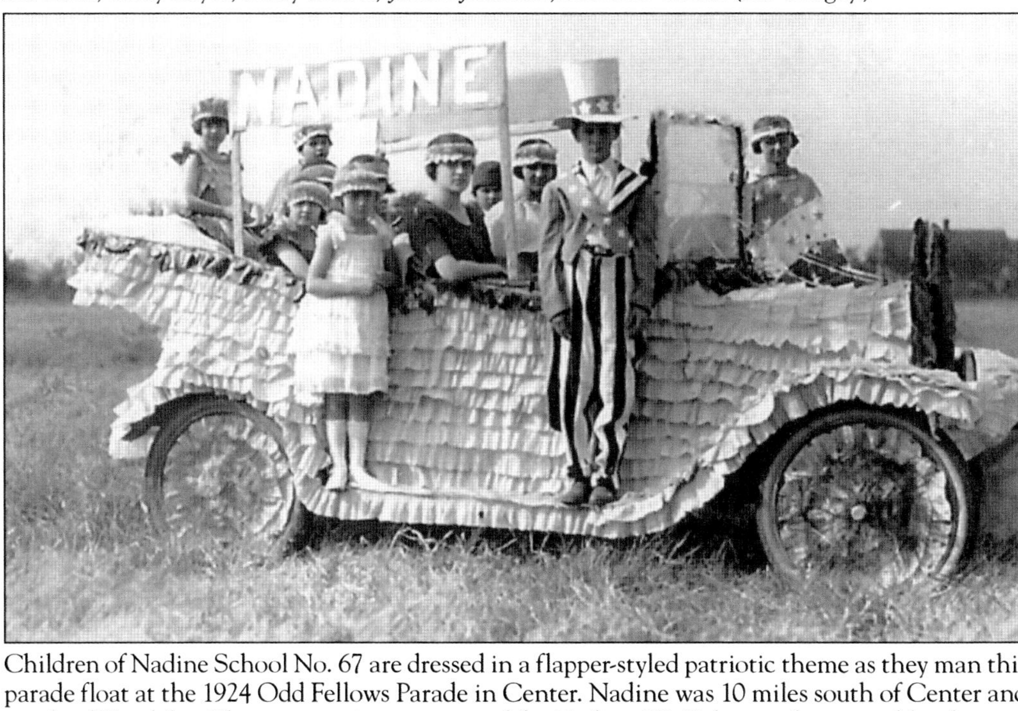

Children of Nadine School No. 67 are dressed in a flapper-styled patriotic theme as they man this parade float at the 1924 Odd Fellows Parade in Center. Nadine was 10 miles south of Center and north of Vandalia. The community was named for Nadine W. Colvert, who owned land across from the post office. (RCHS.)

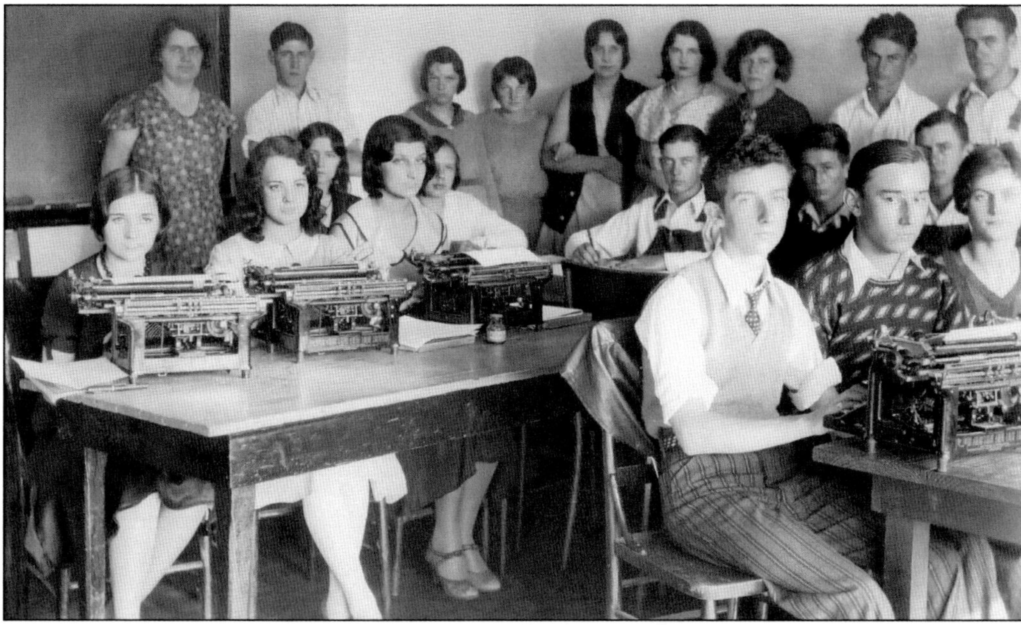

Unidentified students of Center High School No. 40 are seen in this typing class in the 1930s. (Author.)

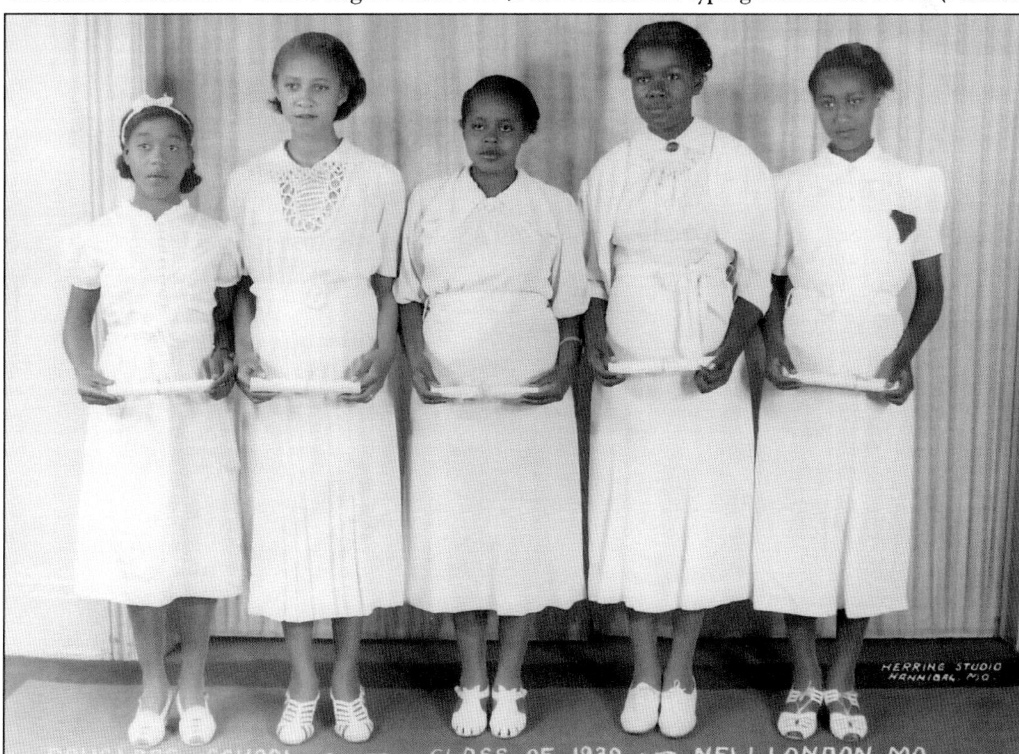

These five young ladies are 1938 graduates of New London's Douglass School. They have completed eighth grade; to continue their education, students took the Short Line's motor coaches to Lindell Avenue and then walked to Hannibal's Douglass High School on Willow Street. When the St. Louis & Hannibal was abandoned in 1944, black students took a bus to Douglass. (Author.)

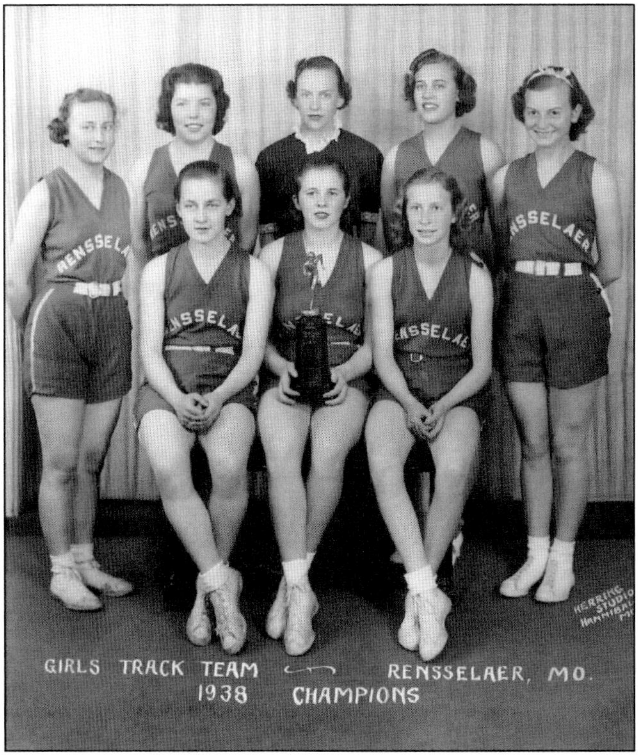

At left are the 1938 girls track champions of Rensselaer High School No. 5. These young ladies are unidentified. (Author.)

The Ladies' Aid Society of Dr. Martin Luther Slovak Lutheran Church, Ilasco, Missouri, is pictured below. Members are, from left to right, (first row) Mary Rajt, Susan Bozalka Tretiak, Suzana Miskovsky Viglasky, Eva Gvolik Valach, and Susan Besina; (second row) Susan Tretiak, Juda Ukrop, Susan Valach Vajda, Mary Mikula, Mary Bozalka Krudy, Anna Valach, Anna Zivicky Polc, and Helen Viglasky; (third row) Margaret Valach, Mildred Bozalka, Wilma Viglasky, and Mary Valach. They helped purchase school items and made altar linens. (Author.)

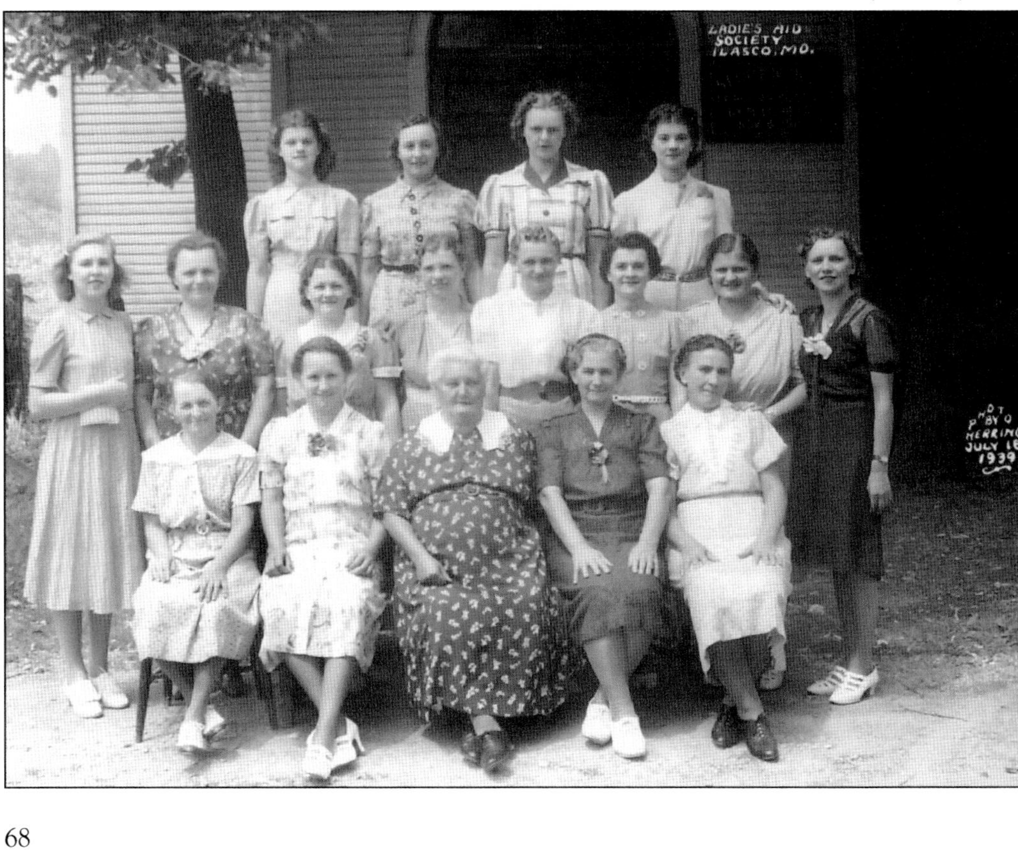

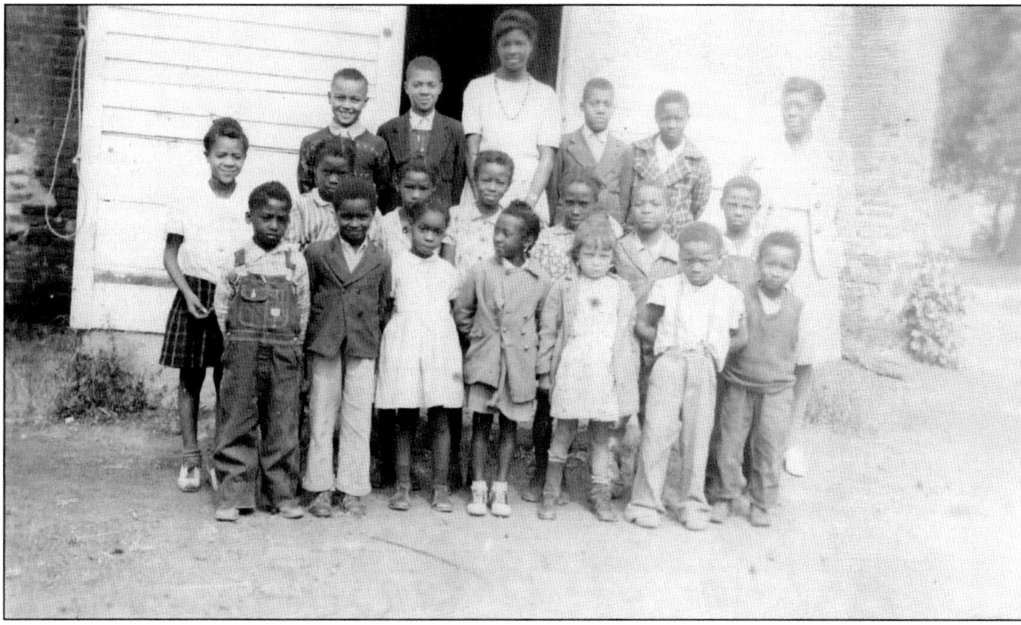

Big Creek Colored School No. 5 in Rensselaer is shown in 1948–1949. Jane A. Terrill was the teacher; the children are unidentified. This class met in the former Van Rensselaer Academy, built in 1850. This building still survives under the care of Big Creek Church. (David Polc.)

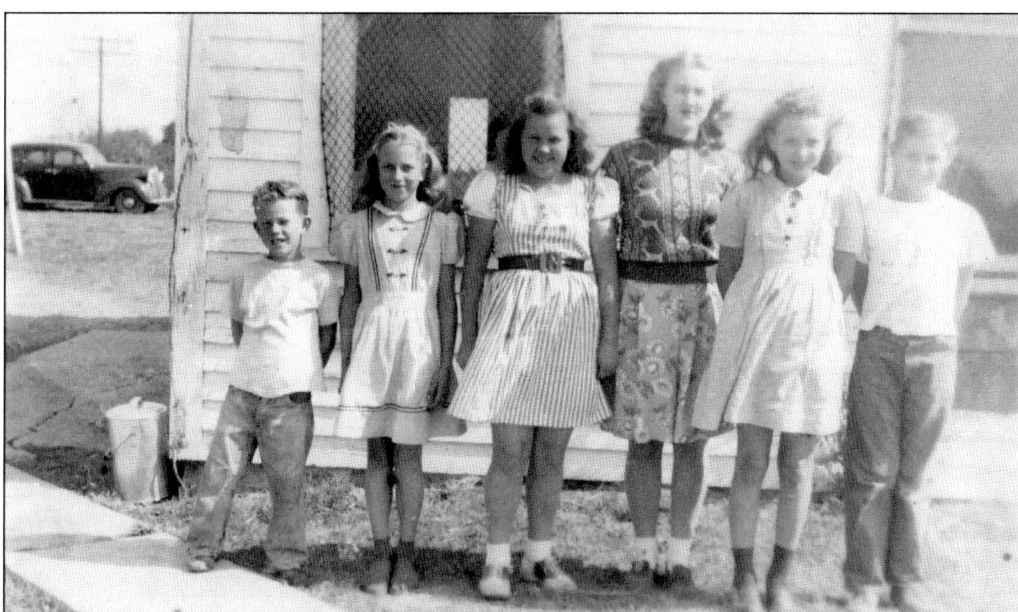

Huntington School No. 6 is pictured in 1948–1949. From left to right are John Bunn, Janice Ogle, Pat Schulse, teacher Betty Shulse, Helen Watkins, and Bernie Bunn. A 1904 map shows the school one block northeast of the MK&T Railroad tracks. (David Polc.)

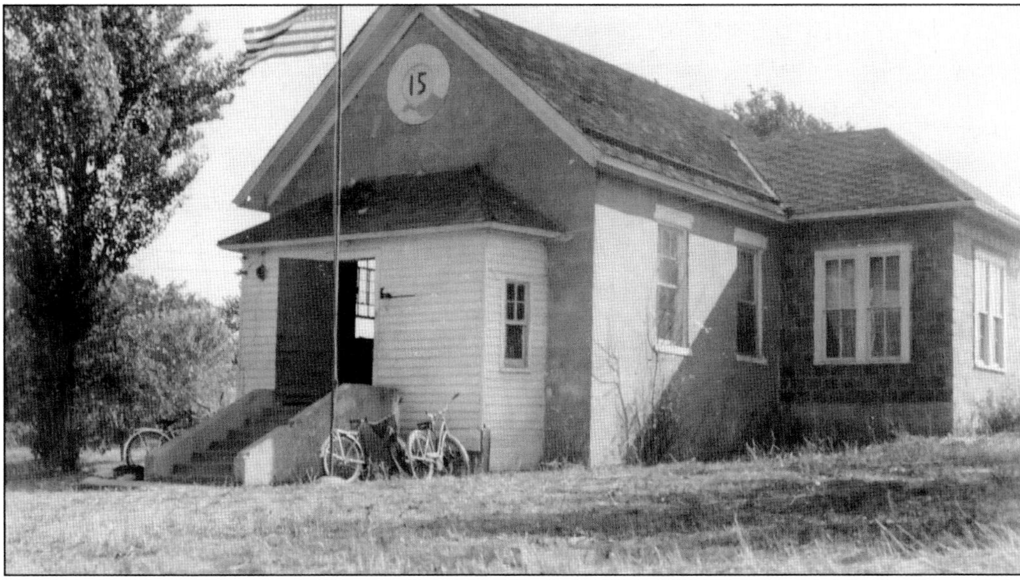

Ocean Wave School No. 15 was located on the east side of New London Gravel Road, three miles south of Hannibal. Elizabeth Kane was the teacher in 1948, and enumeration records show an enrollment of 50 children. When built, this school was the first to be heated by a cast-iron wood-burning stove. The name molded into the stove was "Ocean Wave" and was a source of community pride. (David Polc.)

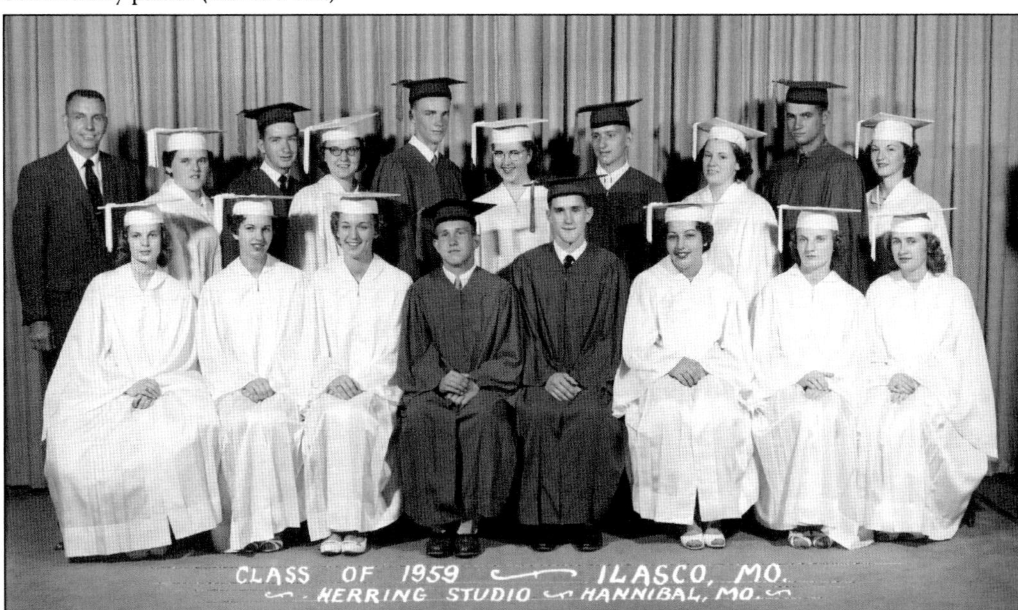

Members of the class of 1959 were the final graduates for Ilasco High School No. 1. They are, from left to right, (first row) Marsha Bechtold, Linda Novel, Ferol Northcutt, Wayne Haden, Leonard Rosenkrans, Lorna Ledbetter, Sue Stewart, and Dorothy Glascock; (second row) Supt. Cleo White, Dorothy Grisham, David Smith, Ruth Oaks, Earnest Sanders, Mary Johnson, Harry Rosenkrans, Carolyn Marks, Larry Arthaud, and Mary Gould; Robert Williams was absent. Cleo White started as clerk with Ilasco in 1922. (Author.)

Five
Rules, Regulations, and Civilization

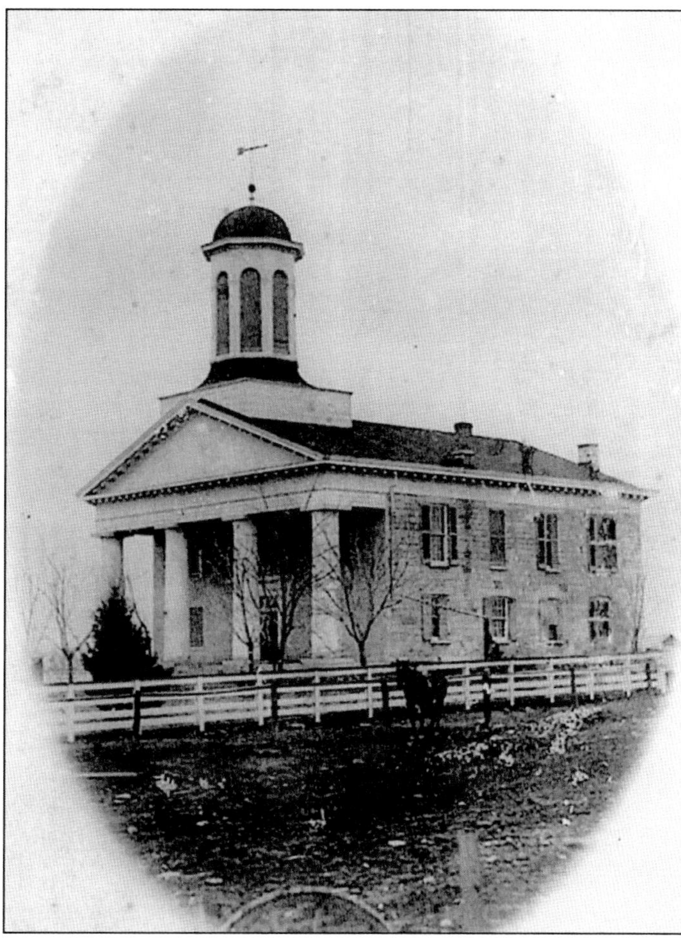

Here is an early image of the Ralls County Courthouse in the 1870s. It is the county's third courthouse and the second one built on the New London Public Square, replacing a two-story brick structure used from 1835 to 1858. The first was a two-level 24-by-18-foot log structure at Fourth and Clay Streets built in 1822. Today, this building is one of the oldest courthouses in continuous use west of the Mississippi River. (RCHS.)

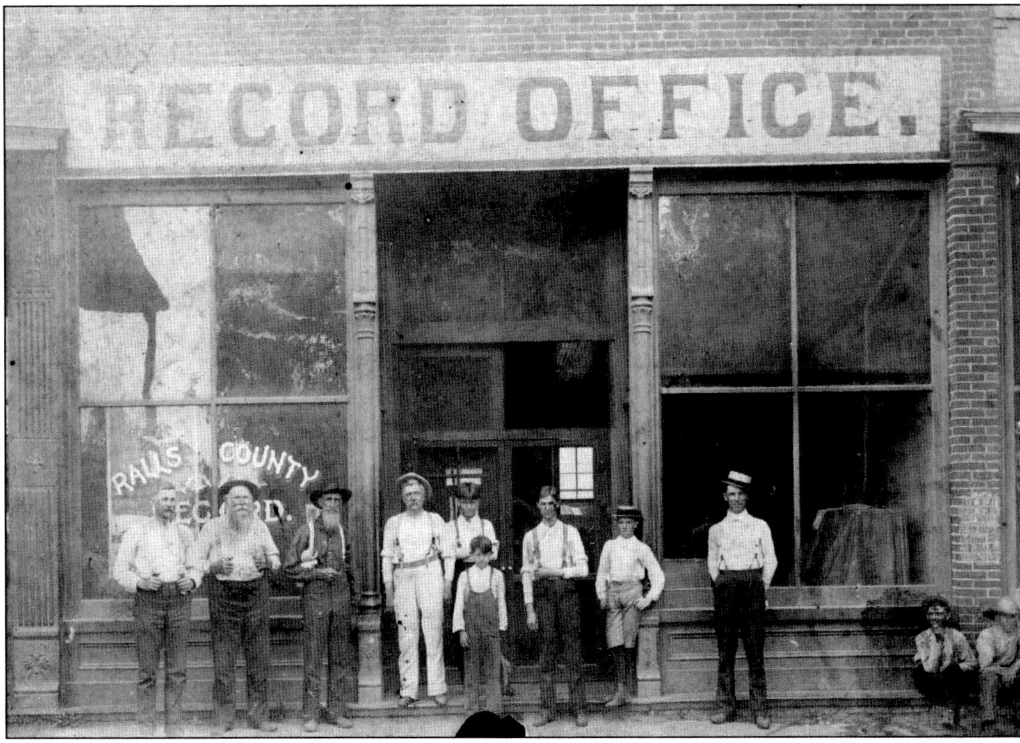

Shown about 1895, the office of the *Ralls County Record* is on the west side of the mid-400 block of Main Street. Most of the men in this photograph are New London newspapermen. From left to right are possibly Guilford Harris, George Washington Jameson, Clay "Men" Mayhall, Joe Burnett, three unidentified, ? Fisher, John P. Fisher, and two unidentified. Joe Burnett purchased the newspaper from Clay Mayhall for $3,500 in 1895. (Steve Chou.)

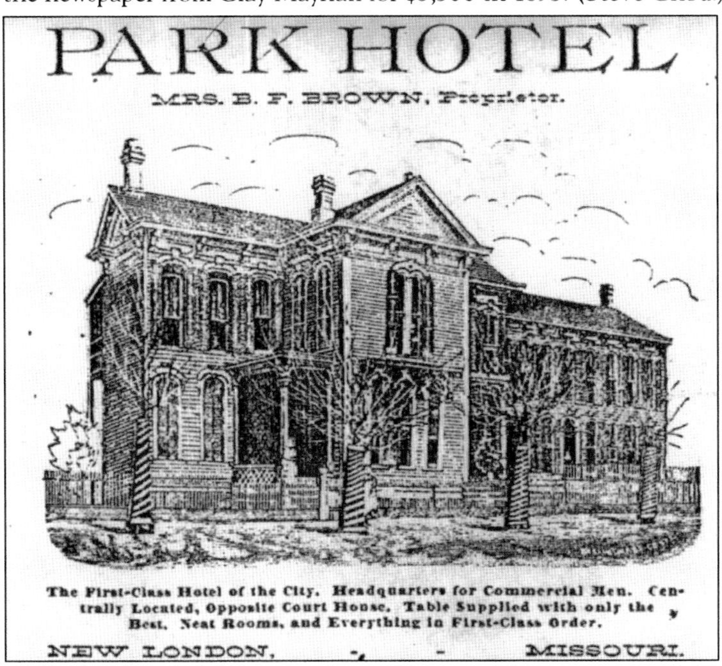

Here is an advertisement for New London's Park Hotel, located on Fourth Street, south, across from the Ralls County Courthouse. The brick structure provided top accommodations in its day. It burned to the ground June 8, 1916, as did nearly every building adjoining it. (RCHS.)

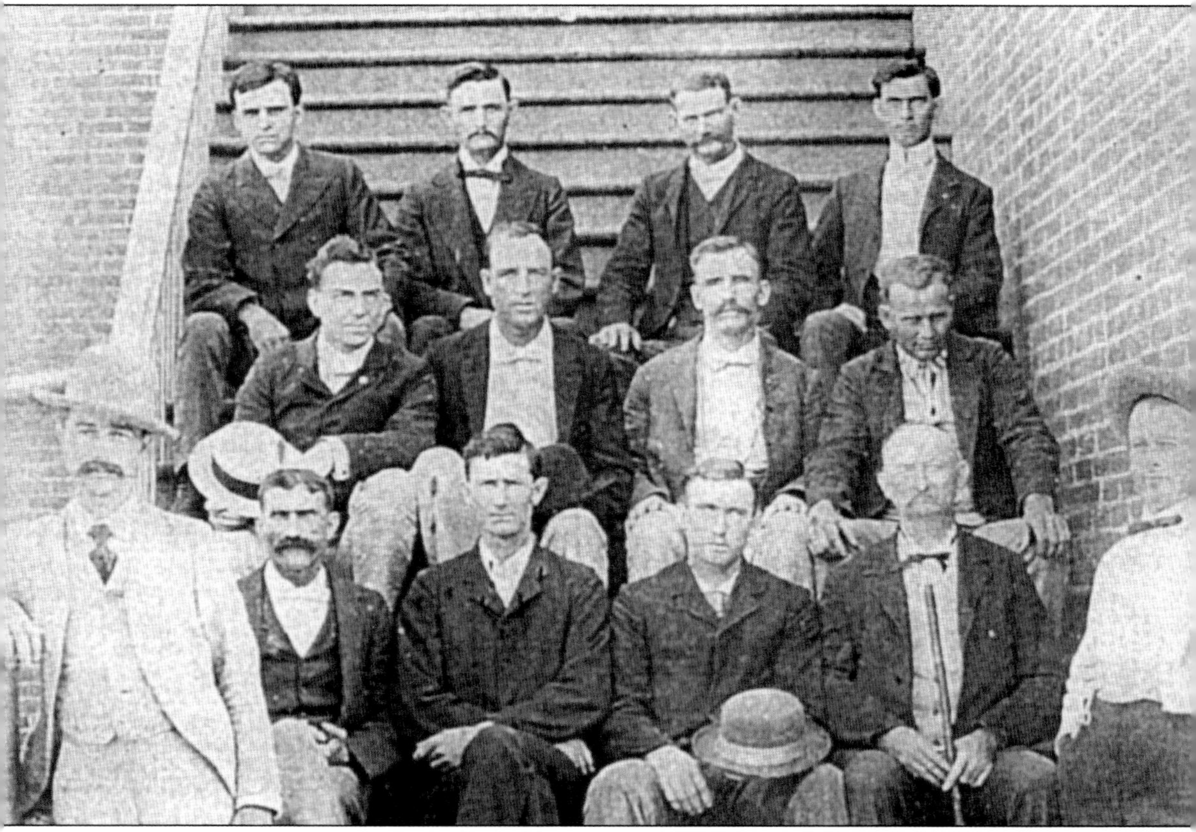

Jurors for the July 1900 Alex Jester murder trial pose on the steps of the Park Hotel. Jester, 80 years old, was charged with the 1871 death of 19-year-old Gilbert Gates, who disappeared near Middle Grove, Missouri. Both were traveling together, and Gates was never seen again. Jester was captured with a watch, ring, and antelope skin coat belonging to Gates and jailed in Mexico, Missouri, only to escape before trial. Gilbert's brother John W. Gates, Consolidated Steel and Wire owner, found Jester living as a minister in Oklahoma Territory in 1900. Jester asserted that Gates sold the items and that he had left him alive and well, while witnesses claimed Jester dumped young Gates's body in ice-covered Allen Creek. The three-week trial drew national press but ended with a verdict of acquittal. Jester reportedly made a deathbed admission of guilt in August 1904. (RCHS.)

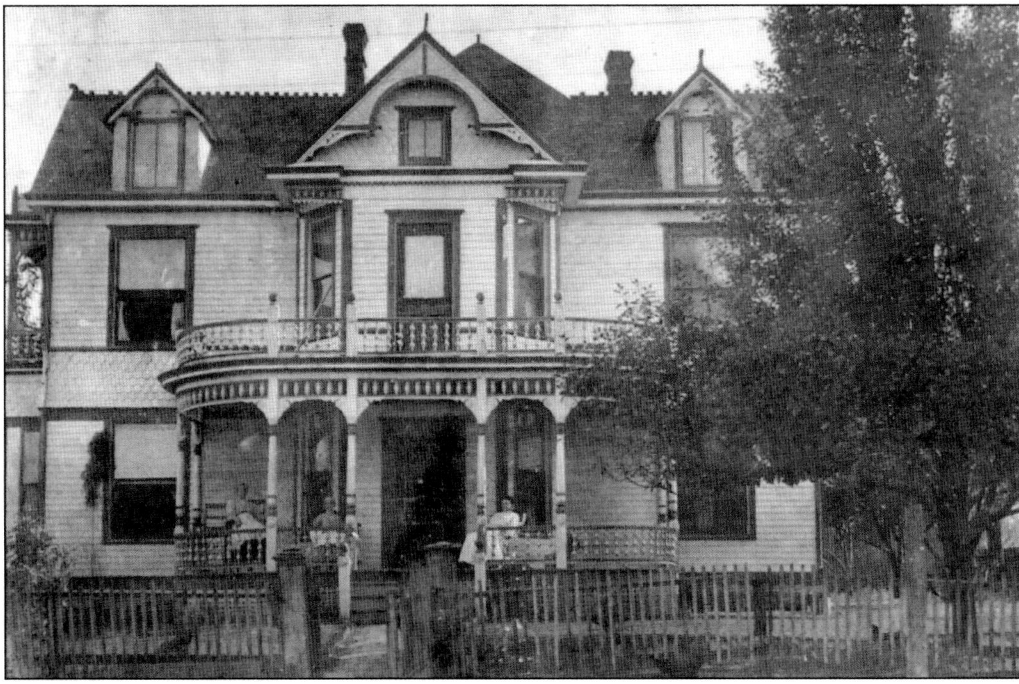

Here is the George Washington and Ella Jameson house at Seventh and West Streets, New London, around 1905. This delicate 1892 Victorian featured family rooms downstairs, small bedrooms upstairs, two sets of pocket doors, fluted heart pine trim, wainscoting, gingerbread embellishments, and a summer kitchen on the back. Summer kitchens reduced fire risks to the main house. Jameson was the mayor of New London and Ralls County sheriff. (Archie Hayden.)

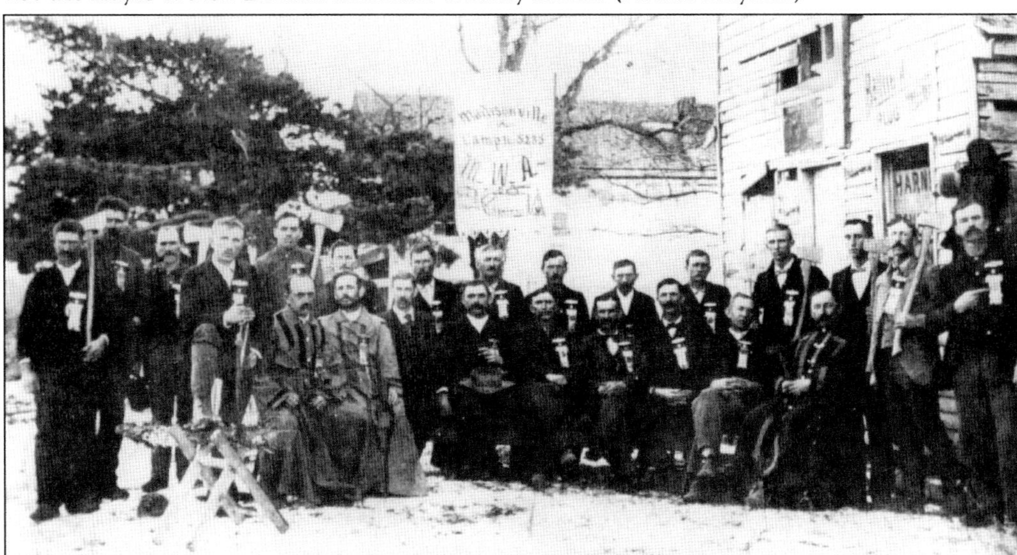

Here is a group photograph of the Madisonville Modern Woodmen of America Camp No. 5235. New London had an MWA camp as well. Today, the Modern Woodmen is the third largest fraternal benefit society in the world, providing insurance and scholarships to members, performing tree plantings, directing youth programs, and assisting with disaster relief. Joseph Cullen Root founded the group in 1883. (RCHS.)

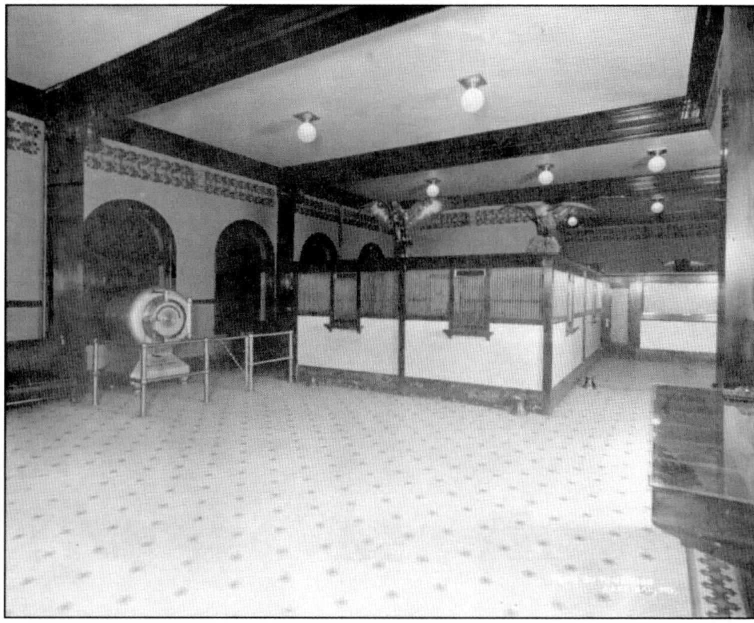

Herb Tomlinson of Hannibal shot this interior view of the new Peoples Bank of Perry in 1912. The lobby is richly adorned with patterned subway tiles, ornate wall borders, coffered ceiling, sculpted eagles, and brass cuspidors. In 1930, this bank and Perry State Bank merged to become the only banks in Ralls County to survive the Great Depression. (Author.)

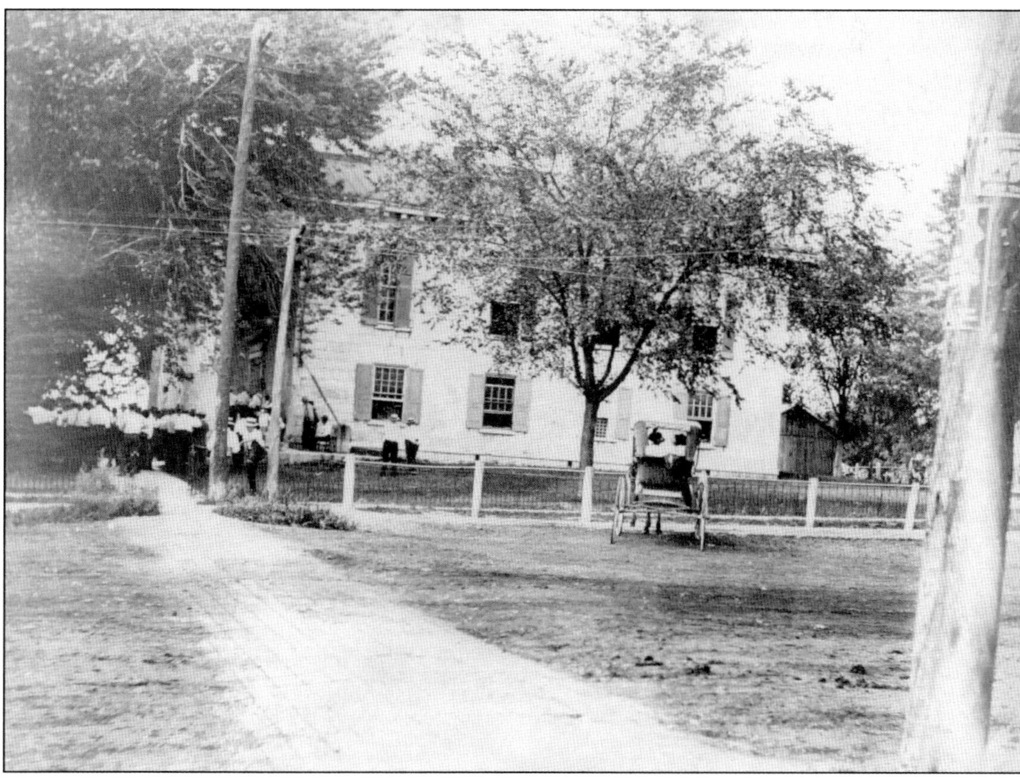

Based on summer attire, size, and location of gathering, this is a 1912 August primary crowd waiting for election returns. The county clerk counts the votes, comes to the front veranda, and writes them on a large blackboard for all to see. This process is a Ralls tradition and occurs following municipal and general elections. Note the granitoid sidewalk across Fourth Street. (Archie Hayden.)

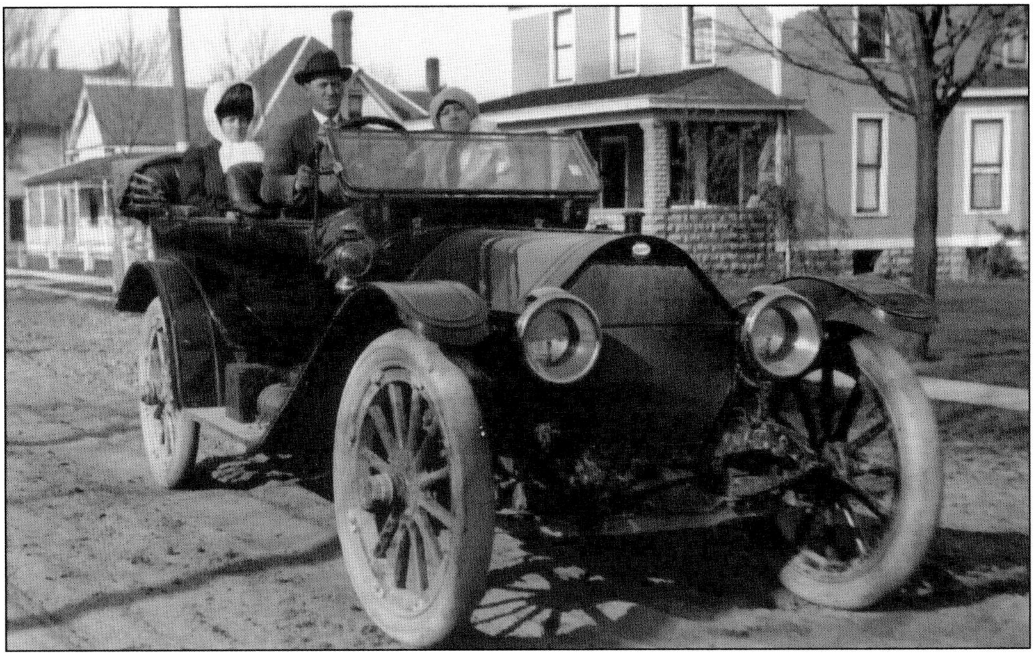

From left to right, Ivy (Spratswell) Waterston, David E. Waterston, and their daughter Margaret are enjoying a ride in their 1913 Overland Model 69 automobile near the 300 block of East Salling Street in Perry. David was a Perry banker. Margaret married Dyas White in 1918. (RCHS.)

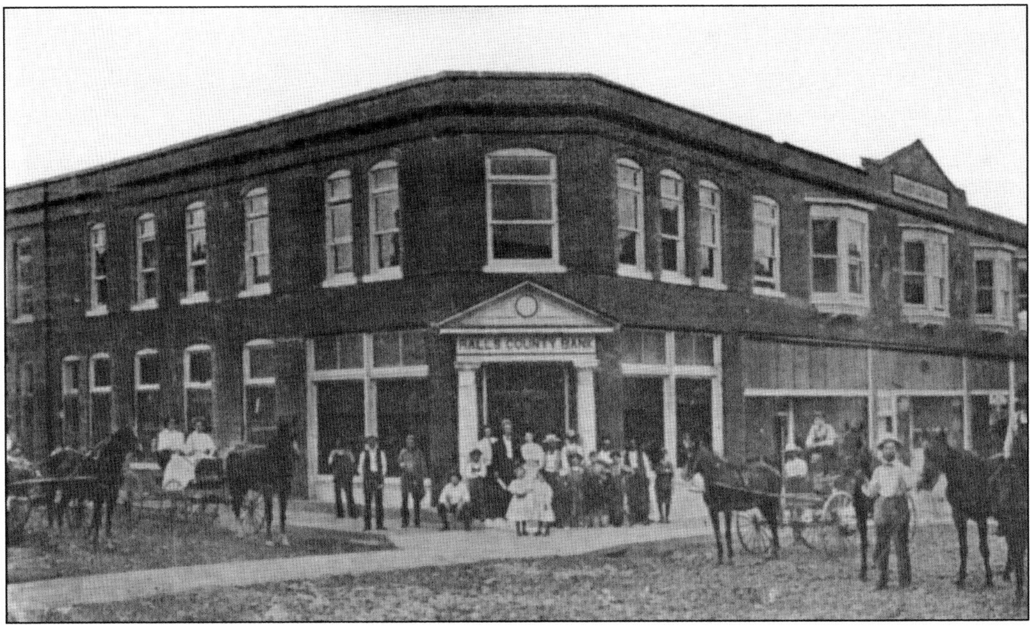

Here is a postcard view of Ralls County State Bank at Fourth and Main Streets around 1910. The street is still dirt, and the granitoid crossing and Kennedy-Indorf grocery to the right are visible. The bank remained here until 1994, when a new facility was built at Fifth and Main Streets. The *Ralls County Herald-Enterprise* is located here today. (Author.)

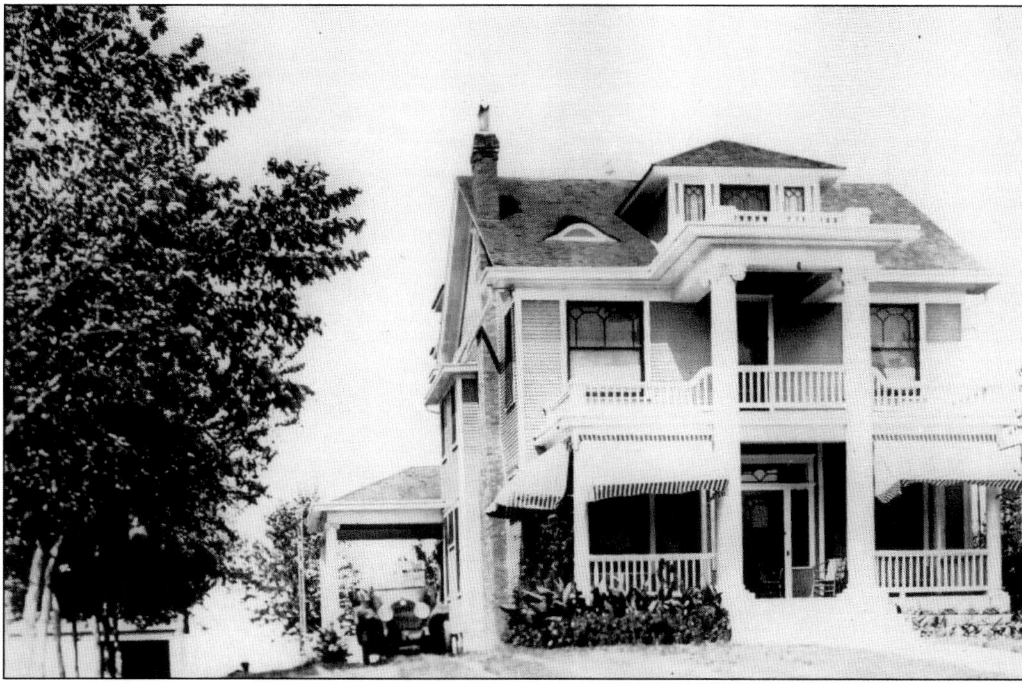

As Perry and Ralls County grew, many businessmen prospered, building architecturally significant homes for themselves and their children. Many still stand today, including this one in Perry. James and Alameda Neville built this beautiful home for their daughter Sammie Lou when she married Gill Richards in 1905. (RCHS.)

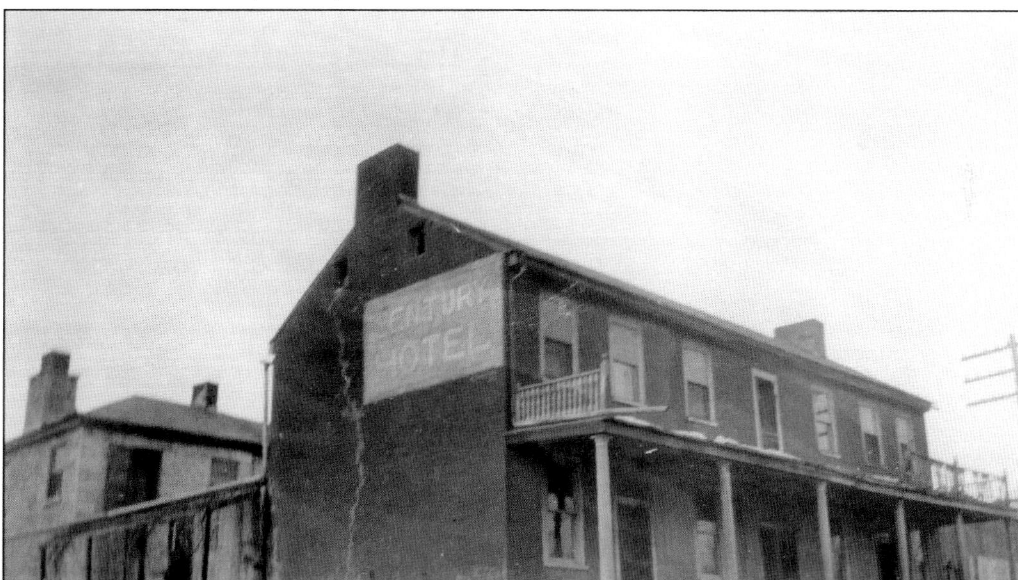

Century Hotel, shown around 1920, was located in the mid-500 block of Main Street, New London. Built in 1819 of logs on the stage road, it was owned by Richard Jones. In 1829, this brick structure was named Caldwell's Tavern. Politicians, like Thomas Hart Benton, spoke here, social events were hosted, local surgeons dissected transient cadavers on Tuesday evenings to perfect their skills, and lawyer Charles Rouse was assassinated on October 6, 1829, on the porch. (RCHS.)

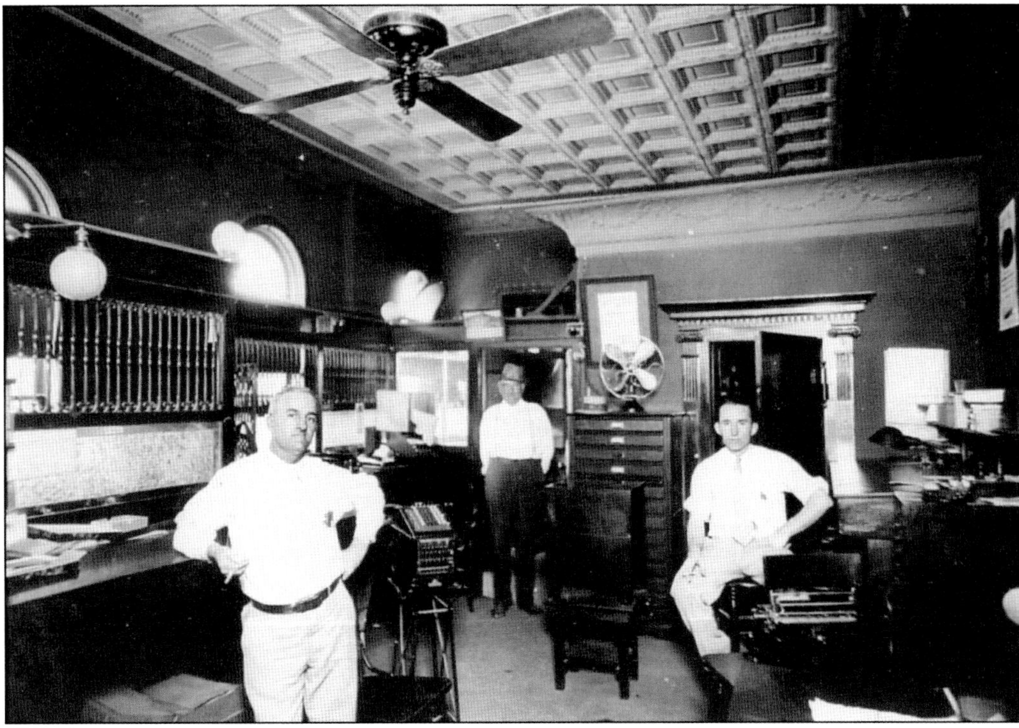

Here is an interior view of the Peoples Bank of Center; the date is unknown. The bank was erected at North Public and Hawkins Streets near the railroad crossing. From left to right are president William E. Floweree, unidentified, and Arthur Carter, seated. During the Depression, F&M Bank took over in 1932. Later, this location served as the Ralls County Library until it was demolished in 2003 to make way for a new library building. (David Polc.)

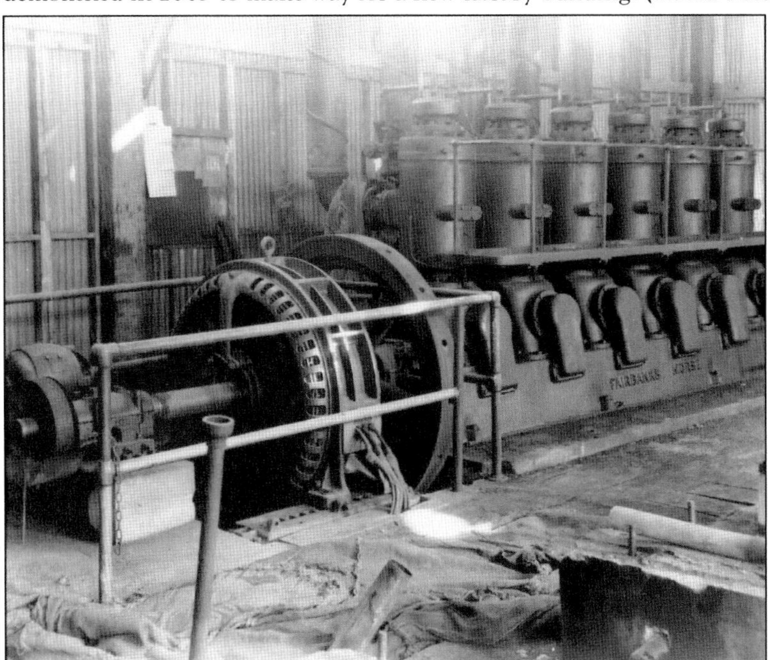

As part of Depression-era Works Progress Administration projects, the Mississippi River Lock and Dam No. 22 was completed at Saverton in 1938. The W.C. Johnson Machinery Co. of St. Louis installed this Fairbanks-Morse diesel, which provided power for operating lock gates and pumps. Hermann Herring took this photograph for the US Army Corps of Engineers on October 29, 1936. (Author.)

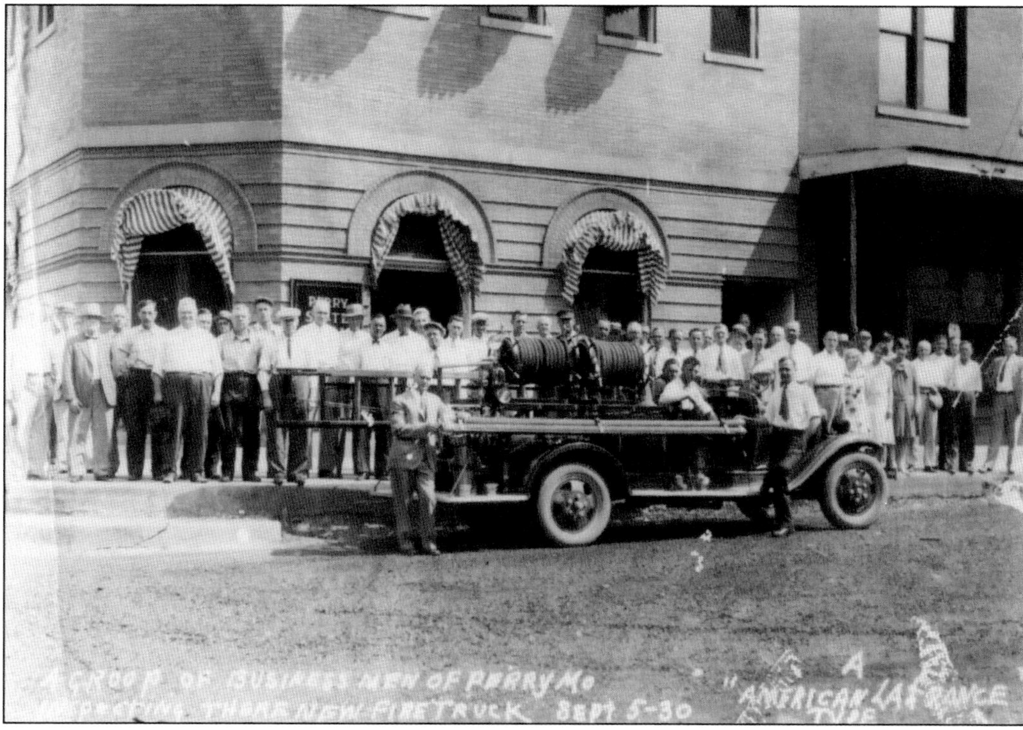

Businessmen of Perry are lined up on Main Street proudly showing off their latest acquisition, a 1930 American LaFrance ladder and hose fire truck. Sam Gill is standing at the rear of the truck. The photographer obviously misspelled the word "Groop" in the caption. (RCHS.)

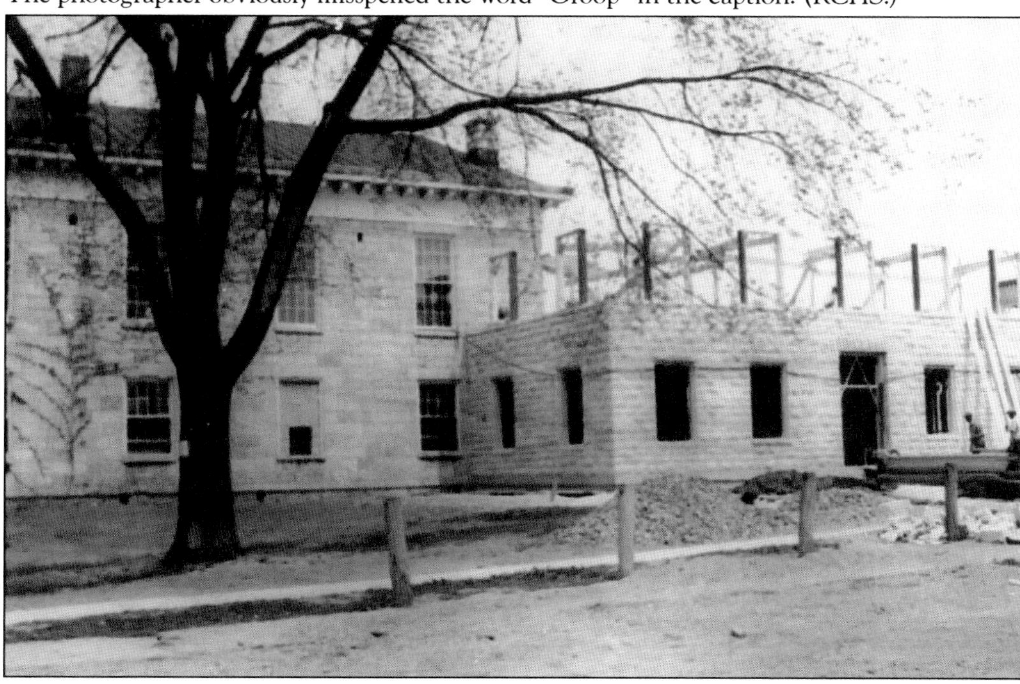

Construction is well underway on the much-needed courthouse annex in 1936. The second-story window frames are in place awaiting masonry work. (RCHS.)

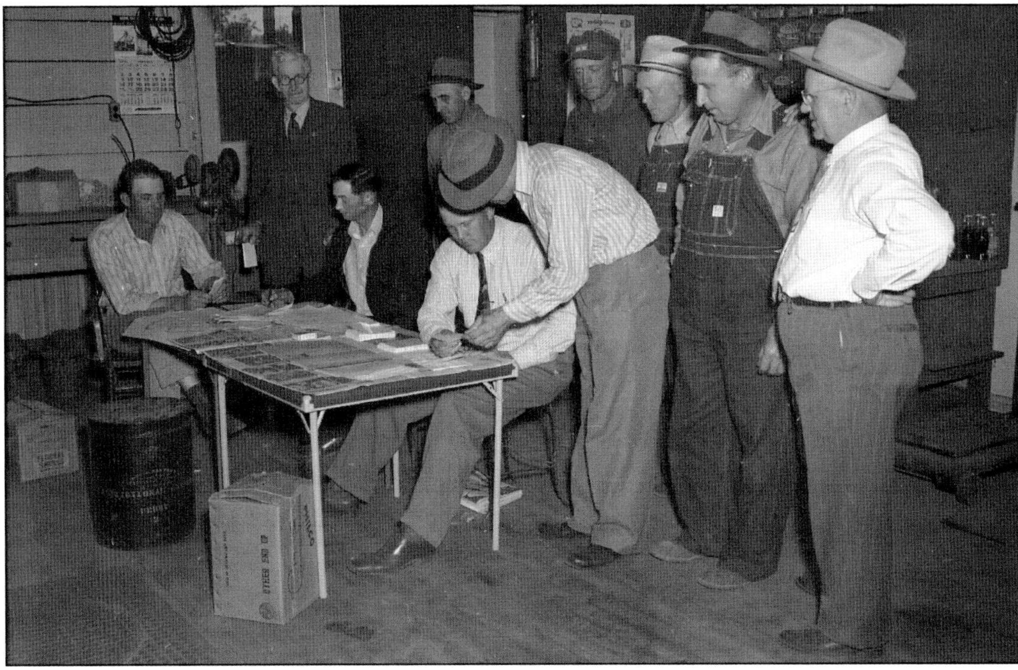

Unlike bigger cities, a small-town election is often an enjoyable civic experience, as seen here in January 1949. Besides exercising one's constitutional rights, people are able to catch up with one another. The men are, from left to right, (sitting) Jack English, Wilson Leake, and unidentified; (standing) unidentified, Ernest Deckerd, Levi Walton, Preston Yager, Jesse Poage Sr., and unidentified. The man leaning over the table is unidentified. (Author.)

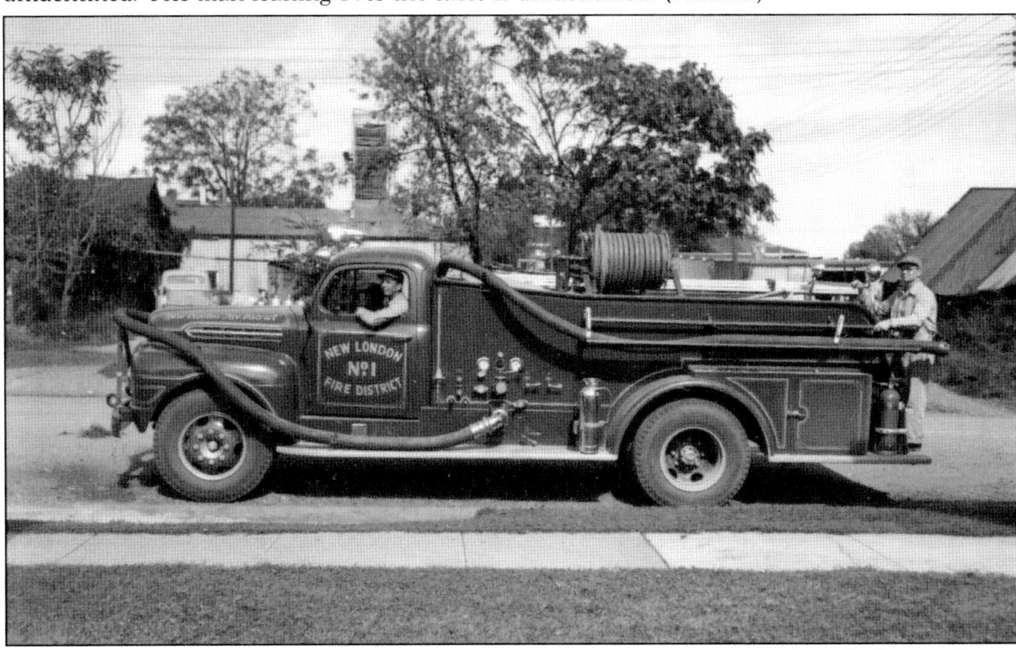

New London's new fire truck is seen at Fifth Street Fire Station behind the telephone office in June 1954. The driver is Jim Sam Silvey, and young Kenny Silvey, barely visible, is inside wearing a ball cap. An unidentified fire department member is on the back. (Author.)

Six

Wildlife, Caves, and Resources

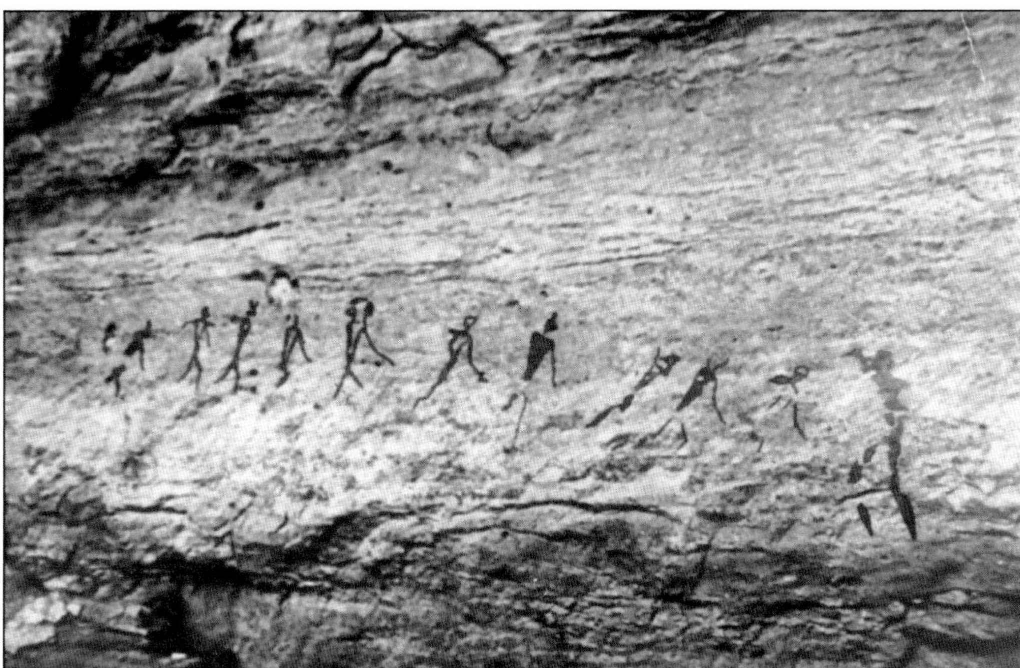

Dee West took this undated photograph of the Indian rock paintings on the southern bluffs above the Salt River, located near the former Cincinnati settlement. They are documented prior to 1836 and have been the source of speculation since white men arrived in Ralls County. Though greatly faded and inaccessible for close viewing, they remain a priceless cultural resource left by early inhabitants. (RCHS.)

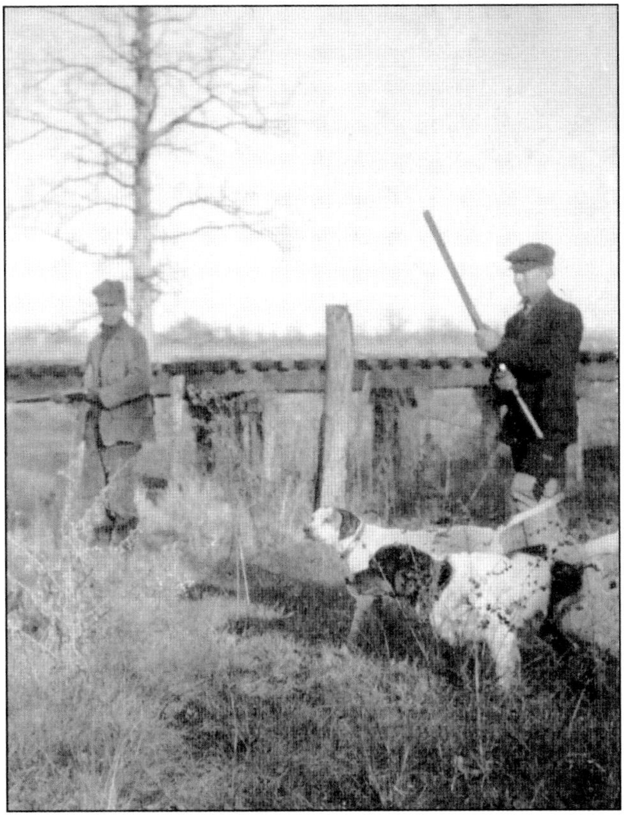

George Martin and an unidentified man of the John Fisher hunting party hope to bag some quail. Fisher's dog Vick, shown in the foreground, is along to do some pointing. This c. 1906 view looks west near the St. Louis & Hannibal's Plum Creek wooden pile trestle, close to the Yeager flag stop at the Ralls-Pike County line. (Archie Hayden.)

Telephones finally arrived in New London in 1889 for the offices of the *Times*, a doctor, and a lawyer. But then came centralized service, owned by Cleve Christian. He sold it, and ownership was passed to the Raffenbergers, Alfred Matson, Samuel Caldwell, and finally Henry and Richard Glascock. John Ramage owned a rural phone service. Below is the New London switchboard around 1906, found in a two-story building between Fourth and Fifth Streets on Main Street. (Steve Chou.)

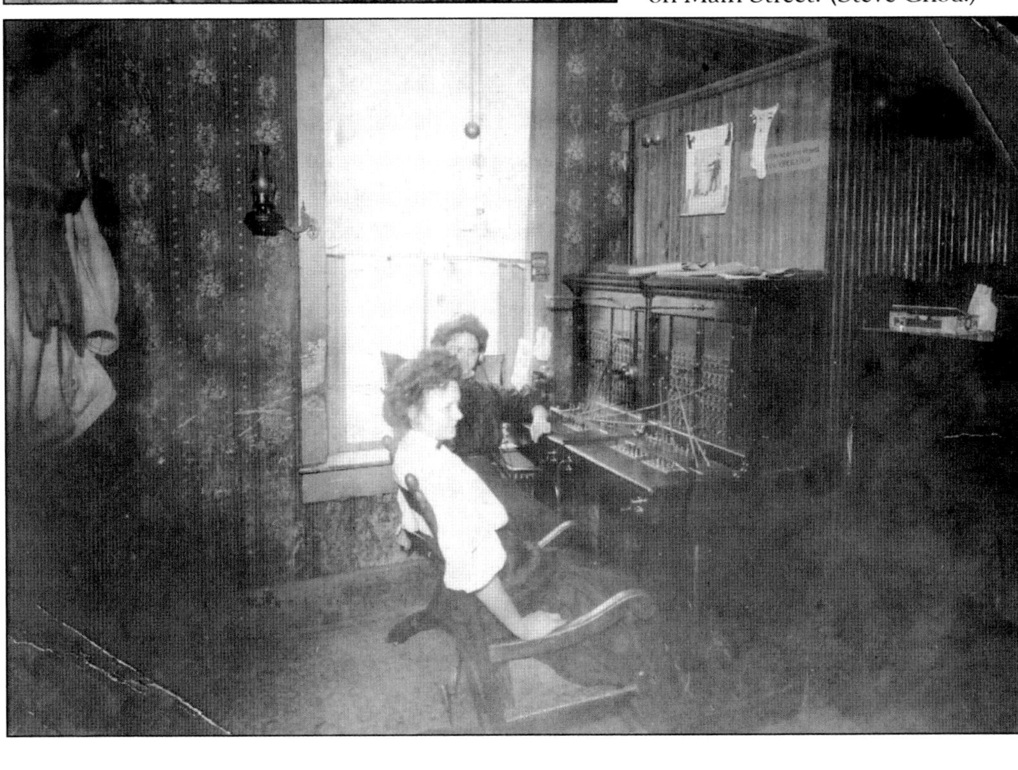

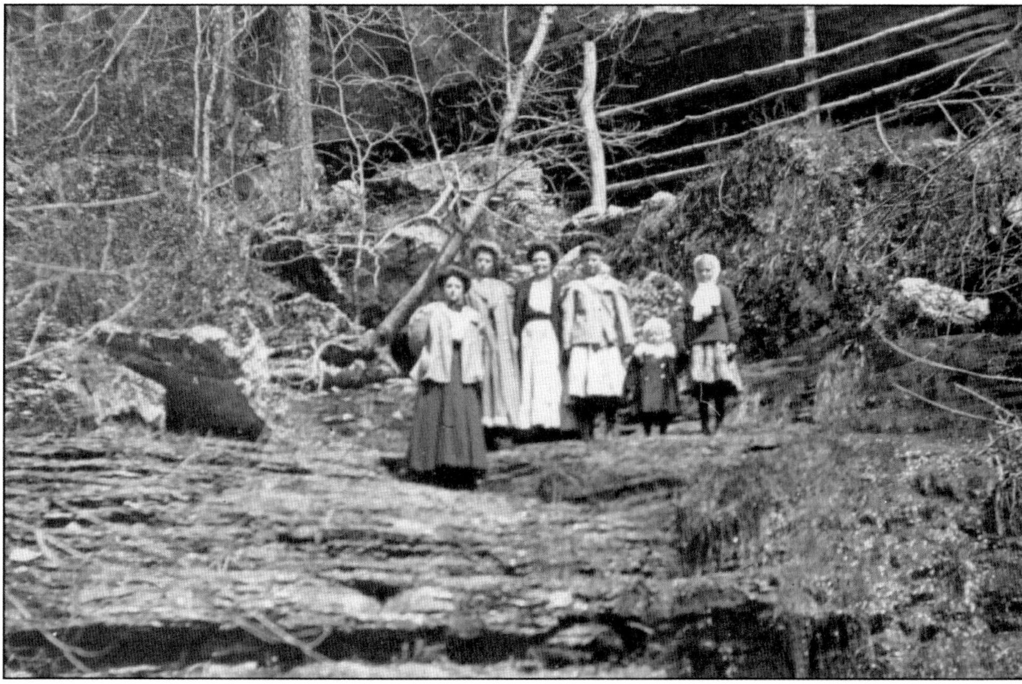

Ralls County boasts numerous caves, such as LeBaume, Fisher, Ogle, and Griffin Hollow, and many contribute saline springs or flow to the Salt River. The Fisher family poses in 1908 at Butler Cave, northwest of New London. Zora is at lower left, and the small girl is her daughter Mildred. Fisher Cave has an 85-by-135-foot interior chamber with a ceiling height of 25 feet and a large water pool. (Archie Hayden.)

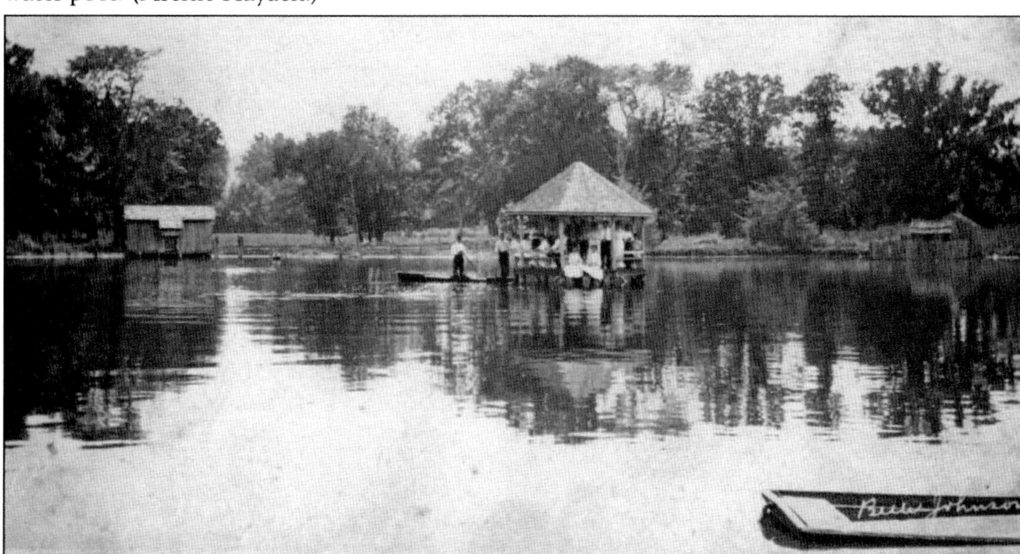

Louis Bouvet, an early settler searching for salt-making opportunities, settled the future Spalding Springs but had operations at Hannibal's Bay de Charles, which was where Indians killed him around 1820. Robert Spalding bought Bouvet's property at a courthouse sale, developed the springs into a lake, and added a hotel, cottages, and dance hall. Spalding Springs was a popular vacation destination by train and then car into the 1930s. (David Polc.)

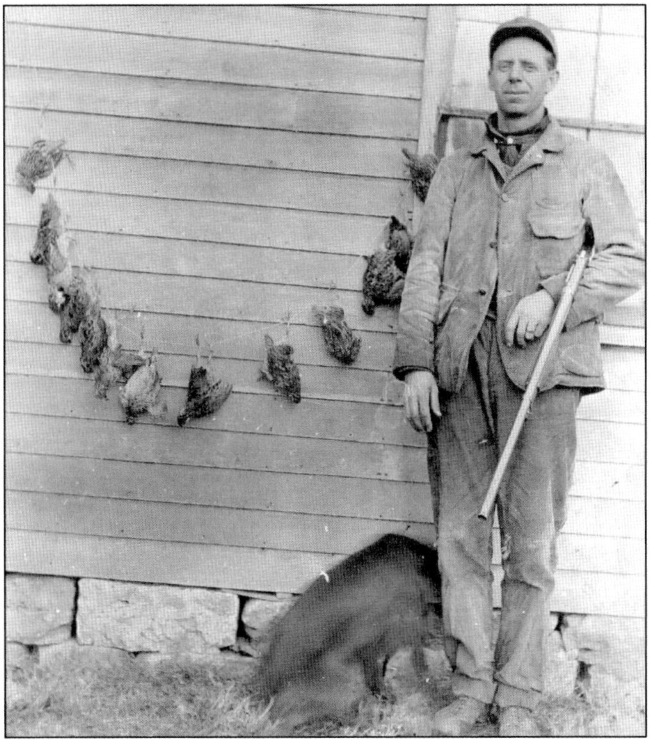

Ralls County is blessed with bountiful wildlife opportunities, with several species of fish, white tail deer, and turkey drawing people from far away. In days of old, wildlife was a necessary food staple. John Porter Fisher of New London shows off his day's effort hunting quail around 1910, but his dog is a little camera shy. (Archie Hayden.)

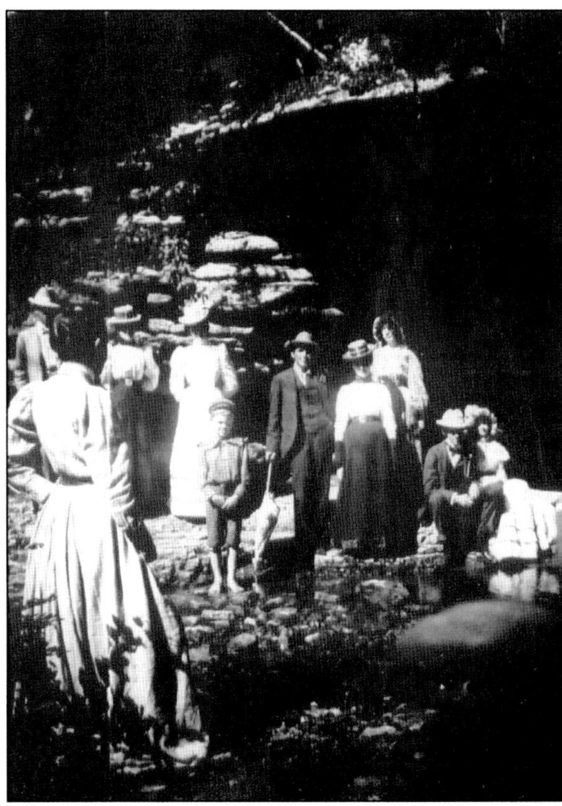

An unidentified family poses at Buford Cave west of New London in the 1910s. This cave is along Turkey Creek and named for early landowner James Buford. (RCHS.)

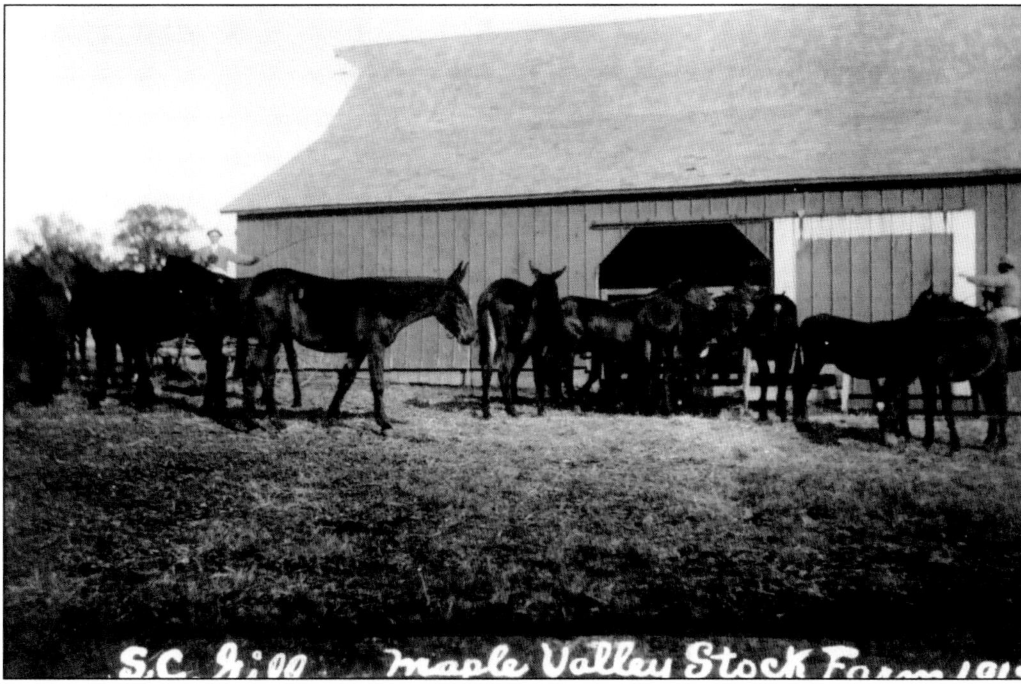

Samuel "Sam" Criswell Gill, son of Thomas Gill, had a quality livestock farm and was a Perry banker living on Salling Street. Early on, he was partners in the mercantile business with Marion Richards. Here are mules on his Maple Valley Farm. Gill, standing with whip in hand, was also owner of the Maple Valley Coal Company around 1912. (RCHS.)

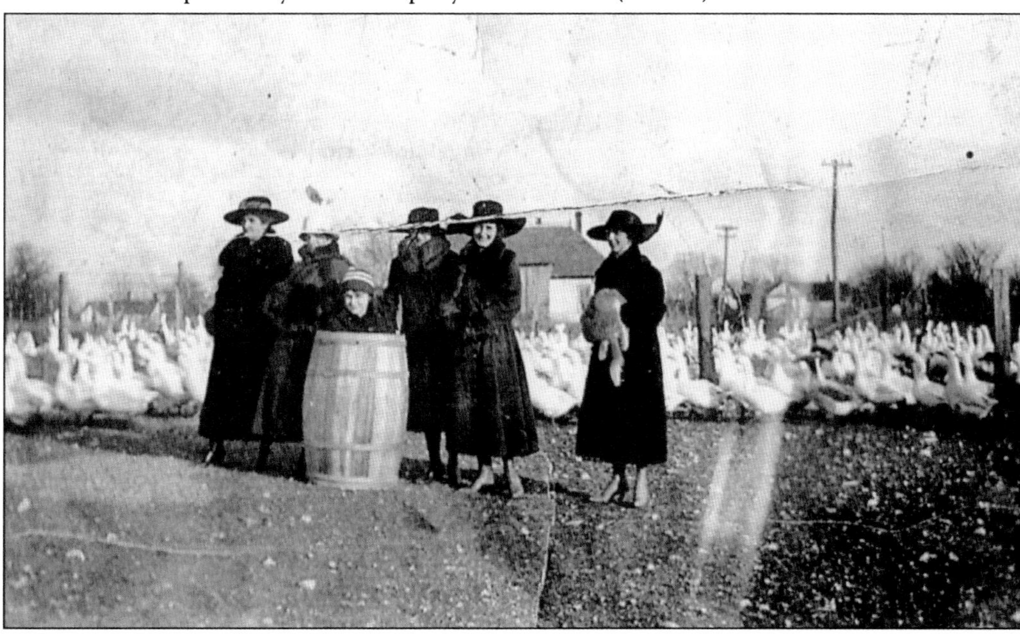

Ralls County Mercantile, Center, Missouri, had poultry and egg operations in Perry as well. Many of their dressed and frozen products were shipped under the Blossom brand name to New York City in four days by the Short Line. From left to right are Nora Keithley, Jewell Buchanan, Susie Myers, Lurine Bailey, Bess Henderson, and Florence Bailey. (RCHS.)

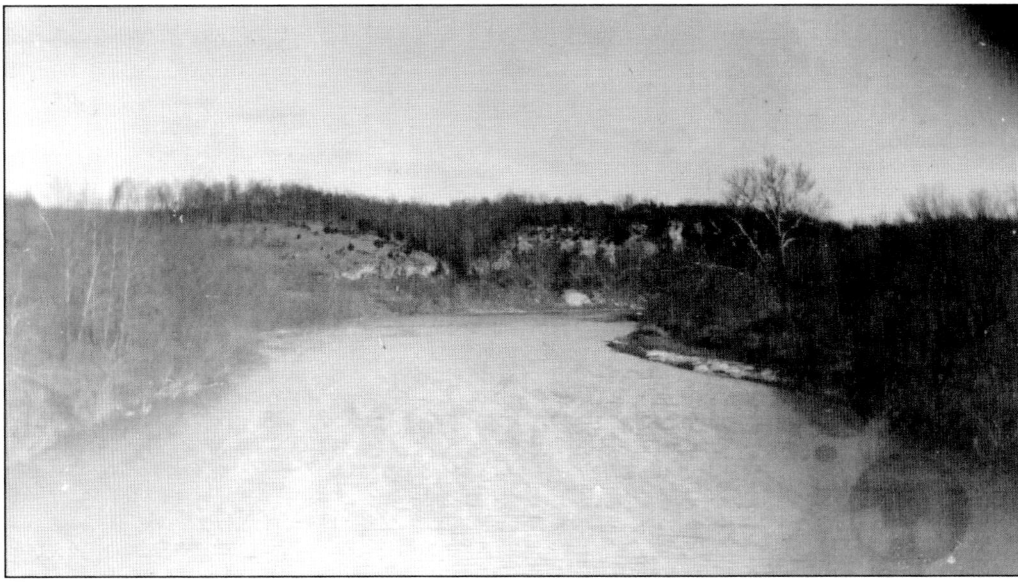

One of the biggest natural resources of Ralls County is of course the Salt River. Here is a real-photo postcard looking north from the Organ Ferry Bridge, dated about 1920. Future bridges will be built at the sharp bend mid-picture. (David Polc.)

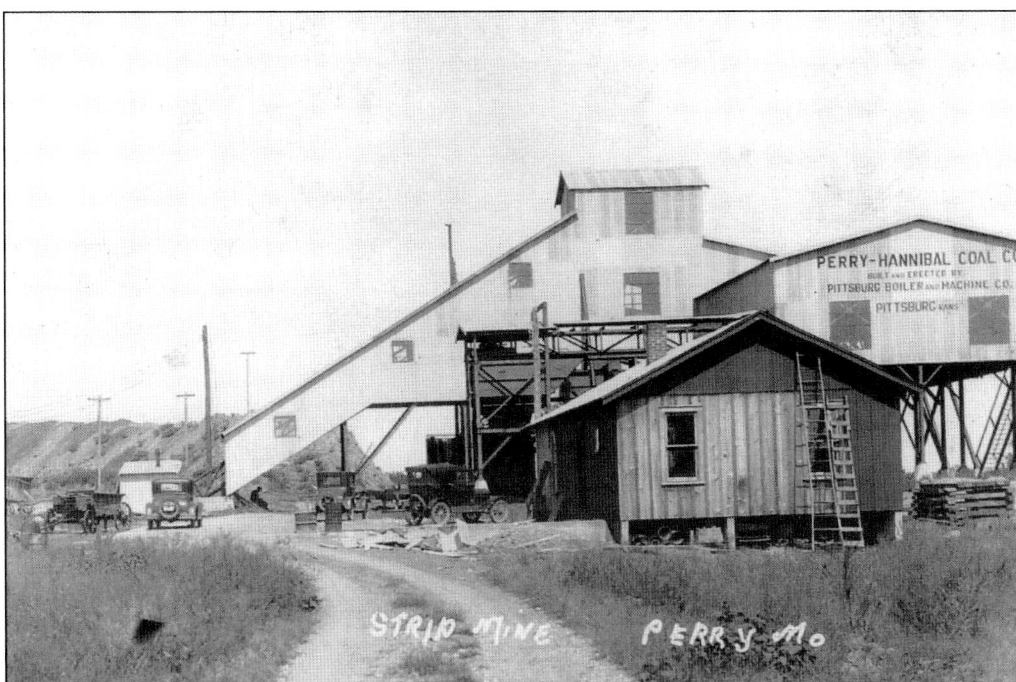

This is a mid-1920s view of the Perry-Hannibal Coal Co. northeast of Perry, co-owned by John Ringling, J.M. Carey, and S.C. Gill. Carey was president of Madison Square Garden and owned Virginia coal mines. The St. Louis & Hannibal Branchline was constructed because of the abundance of coal and livestock around Perry. Geologists estimate 144 million tons of coal remain around Perry today. (RCHS.)

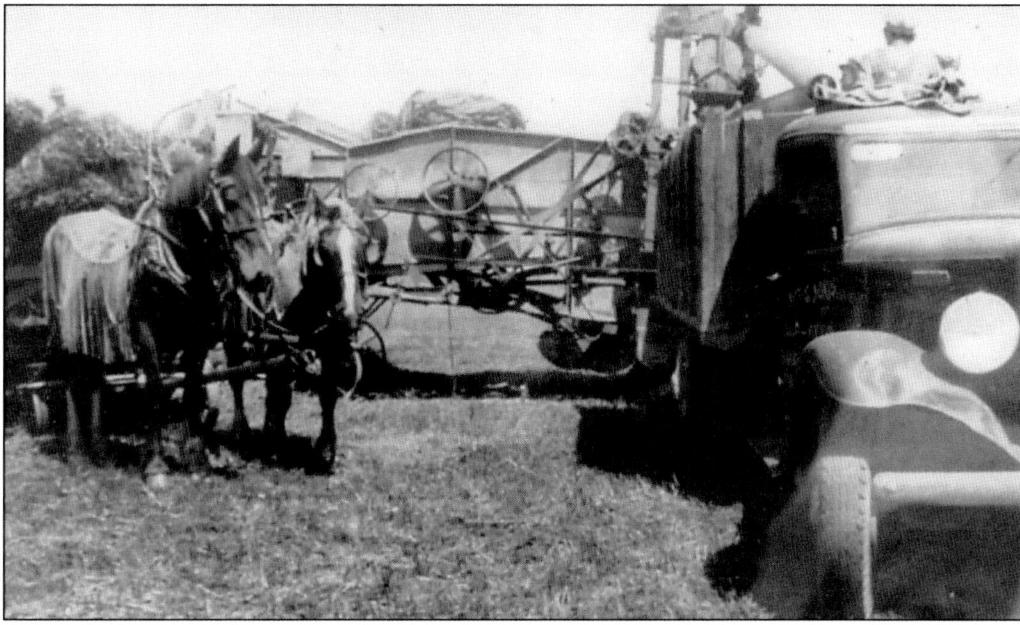

Yet another valuable resource of Ralls County is the abundant farmland and pastures. Early settlers and merchants heavily relied on the efforts of farmers, like the Shulse family. While agricultural mechanization was available, old methods, like horse-drawn hay wagons, were still used for threshing in 1936. (RCHS.)

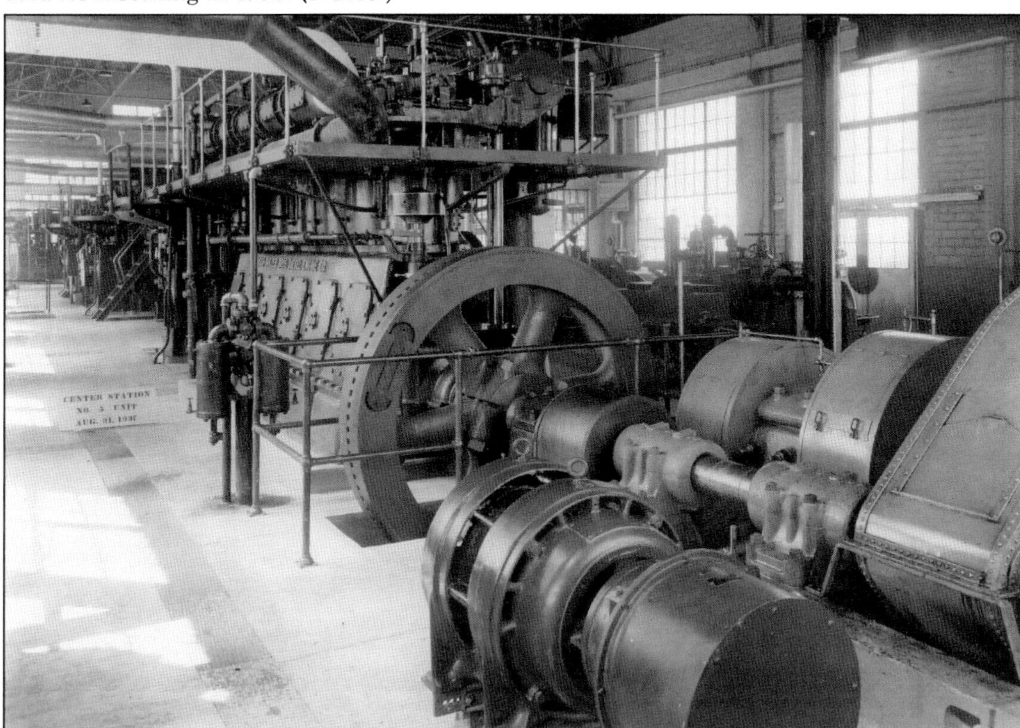

This photograph, dated August 31, 1937, is an interior view of the Texas Empire Pipeline Pump Station south of Center, Missouri. (Author.)

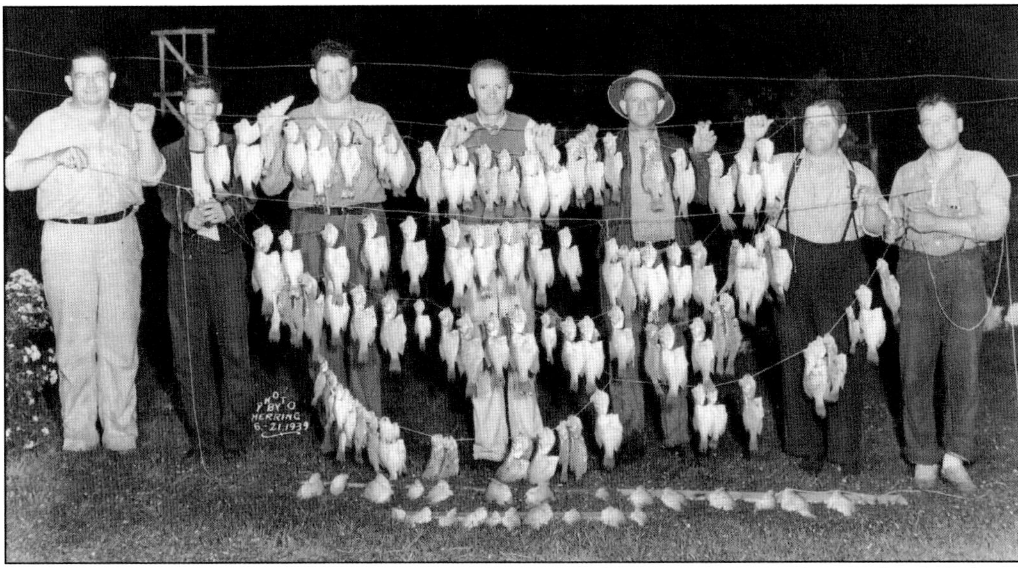

It looks like Mike O' Donnell of Oakwood and his buddies are going to have a big fish fry in their future with this string of 125 fish. Pictured on June 21, 1939, are, from left to right, Mike O' Donnell, mortician; young Pete Schambacher; Ben Phillips, policeman; Pat Mabery, barber; Deacon Burch; Ross Johnson; and Pete Schambacher, policeman. (Author.)

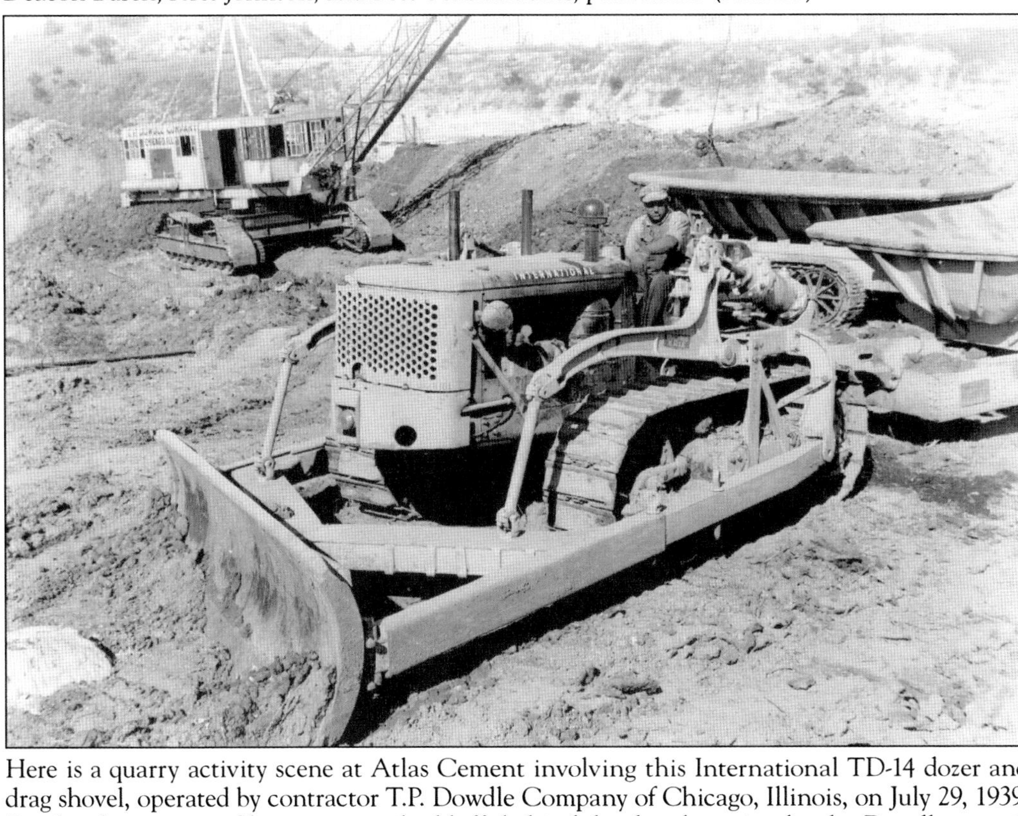

Here is a quarry activity scene at Atlas Cement involving this International TD-14 dozer and drag shovel, operated by contractor T.P. Dowdle Company of Chicago, Illinois, on July 29, 1939. Besides the mining of limestone in the bluffs behind, land reclamation by the Dowdle crew is underway. (Author.)

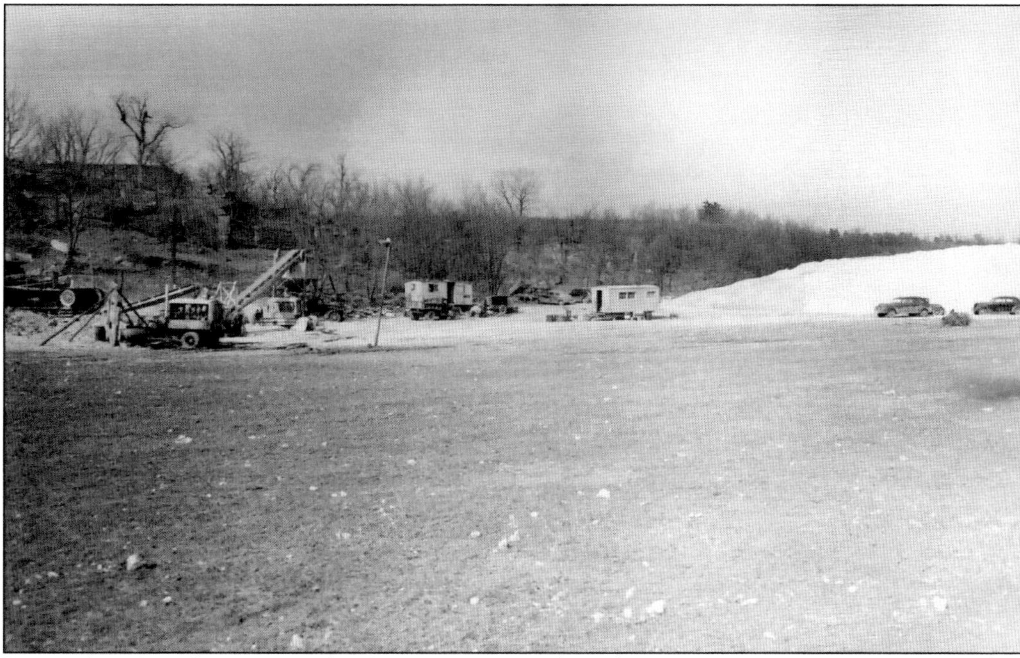

Pictured on March 11, 1942, the Concrete Materials and Construction Company just north of Salt River near New London was a source of sand, gravel, and limestone until being closed for decades. In 2008, it reopened as a natural sport park for sanctioned truck rock crawling and jeep trails, such as RRock and SheRock events. The quarry became active in 2011 with removal of limestone once again. (Author.)

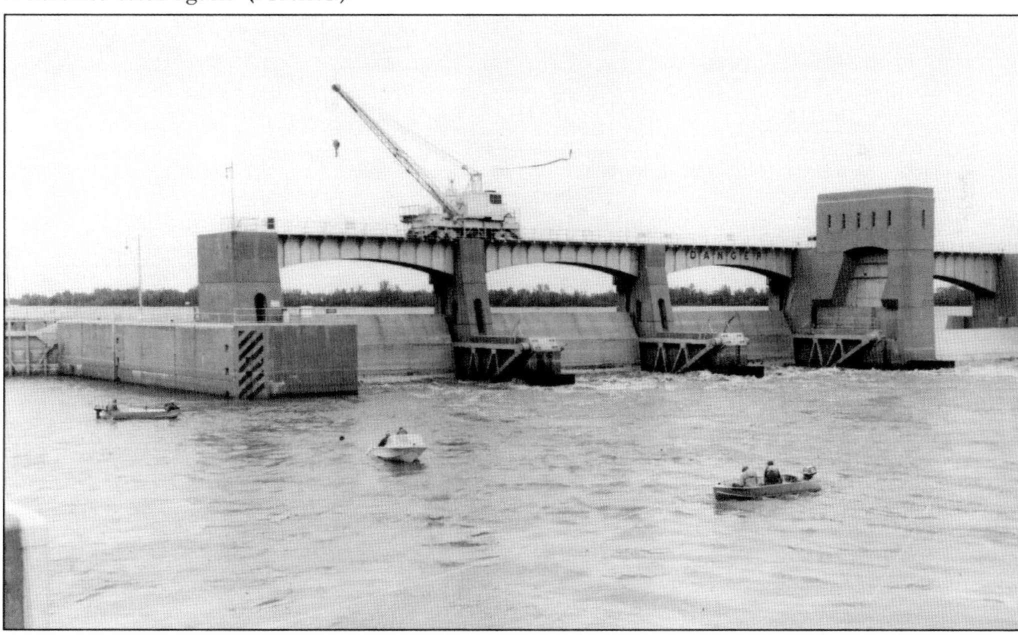

The Lock and Dam No. 22 at Saverton are part of a system of locks that help maintain river channel levels for efficient shipping of cargos, flood control, and the operation of pleasure craft on the Mississippi River. The locks are overseen by the US Army Corps of Engineers. (Hannibal Chamber of Commerce.)

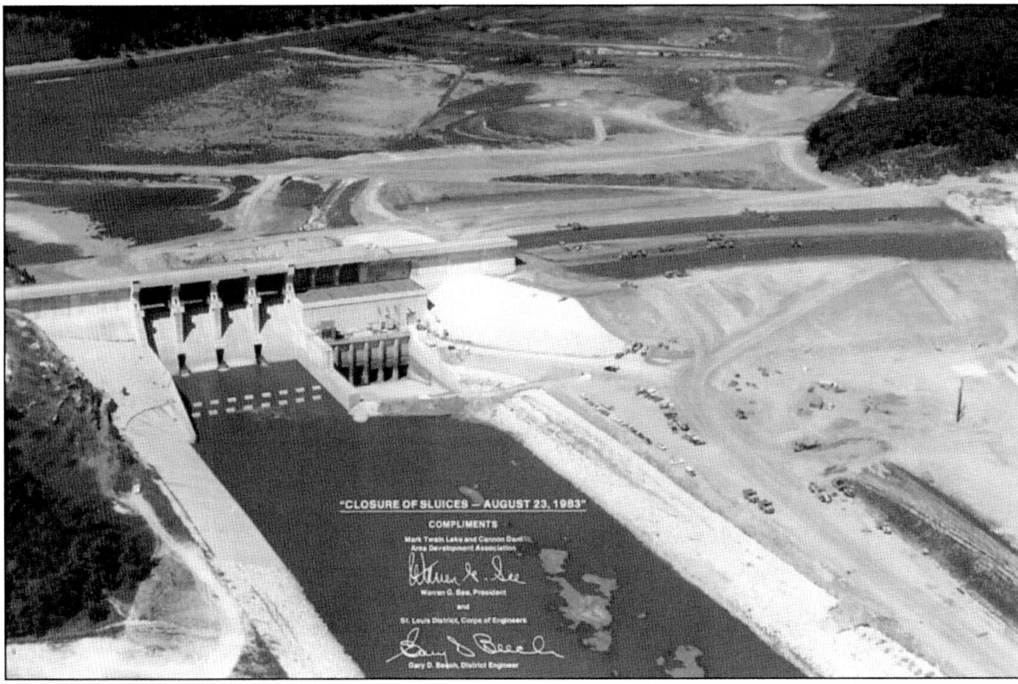

The US Army Corps of Engineers had this aerial photograph taken of the Clarence Cannon Dam sluice gate closure on August 23, 1983. The north levee and road is not yet completed for the new Route J. (RCHS.)

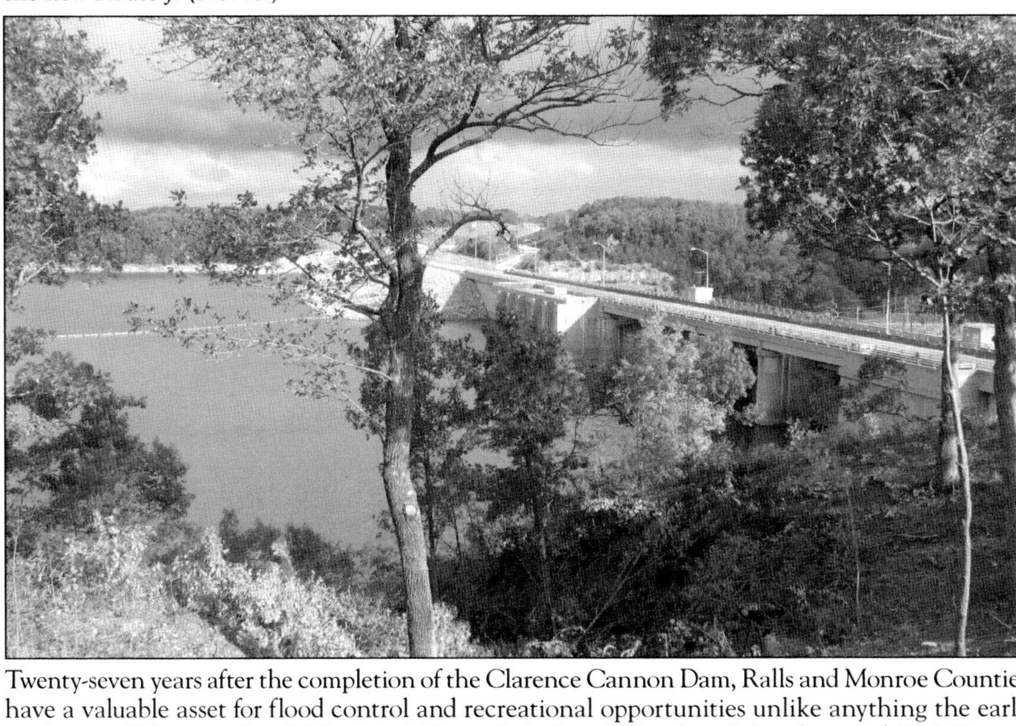

Twenty-seven years after the completion of the Clarence Cannon Dam, Ralls and Monroe Counties have a valuable asset for flood control and recreational opportunities unlike anything the early settlers could have realized. The Mark Twain Lake has 285 miles of shoreline and 18,600 acres of surface area, and the actual park encompasses 55,000 acres. (Author.)

Seven
FIRES, FLOODS, AND ACCIDENTS

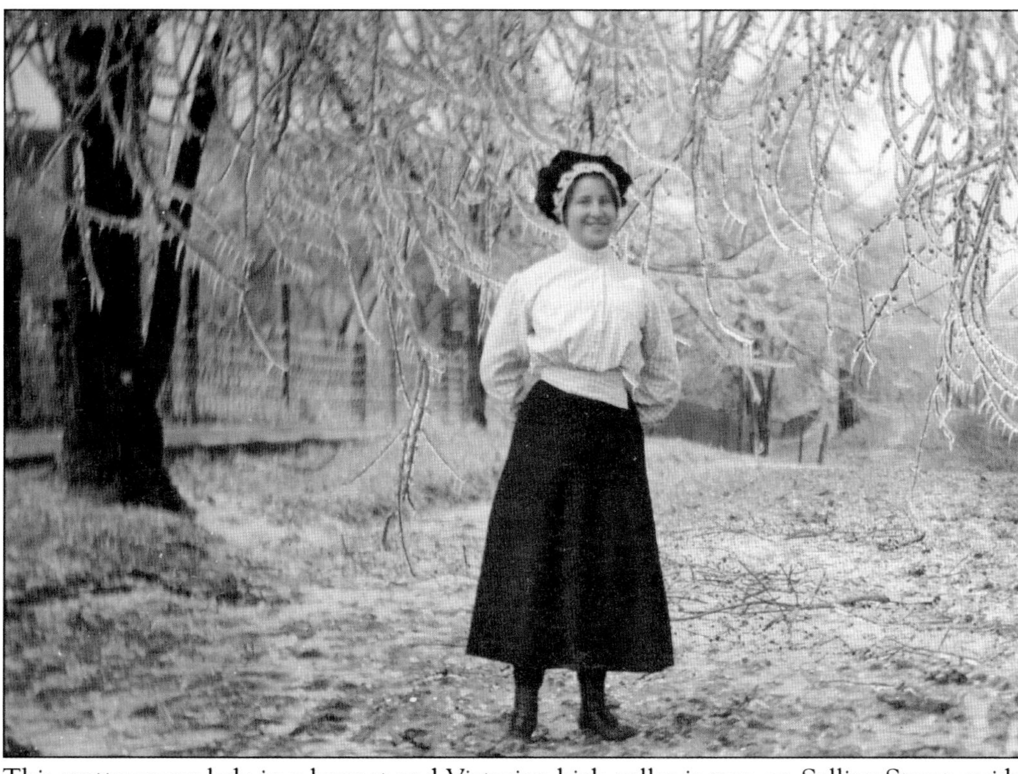

This pretty young lady in a bonnet and Victorian high collar is seen on Salling Street amidst the crystal palace following an ice storm that struck Perry on January 15, 1911. The ice lingered several days, snapping off fruit trees and utility poles and cutting electricity and telephone service. (Author.)

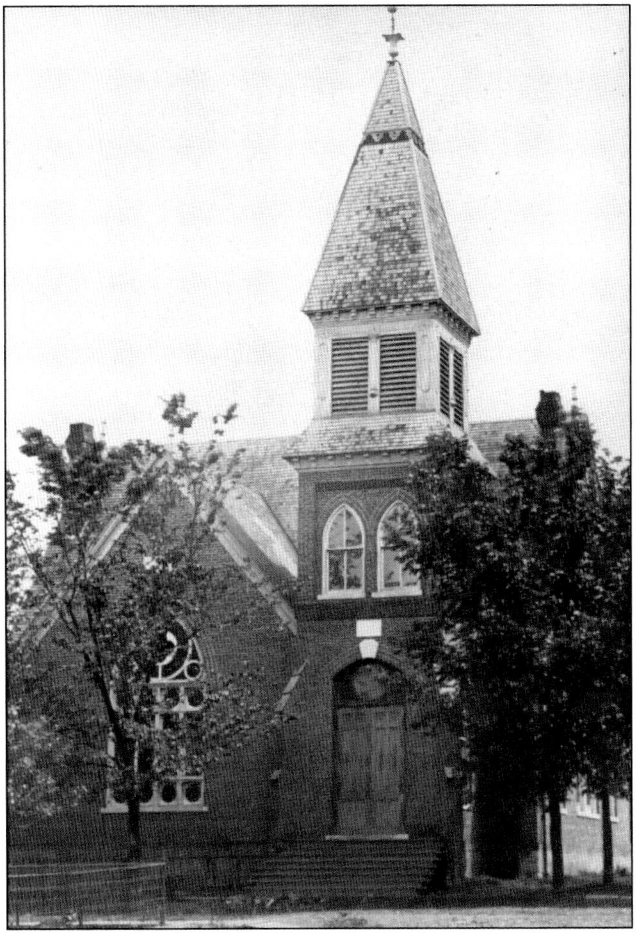

Here is the New London First Christian Church at Fourth and Church Streets, the church's second structure since organizing in 1838. The early congregation met in homes and early courthouses until erecting three different buildings, beginning in 1852, at this location. The first was destroyed by a storm on May 1, 1887; with W.H. Pinkerton as pastor, this one was lost to fire the afternoon of May 19, 1911. (New London First Christian.)

On December 30, 1914, young folks returning late from a party reported a fire at the Charles McCoy Poultry House on Palmyra Street (below). In minutes, fire engulfed the entire structure, endangering buildings abutting it. McCoy's fixtures were saved but 450 chickens and geese, 100 pigeons, 2,000 rabbits, and $250 worth of feathers were "cremated" according to the *Perry Enterprise*. (RCHS.)

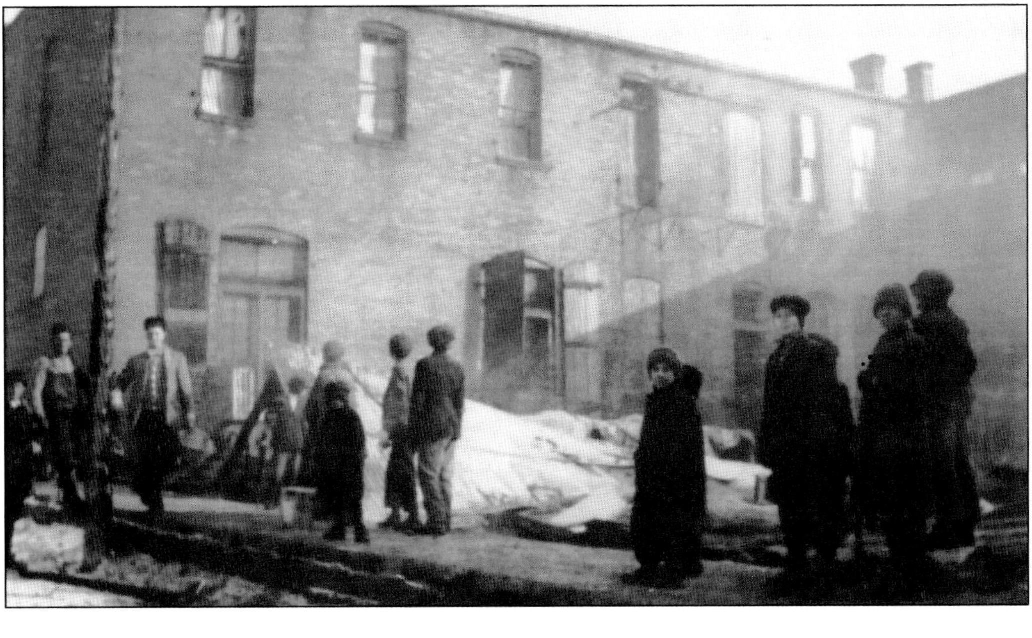

Minnie Stehle took this precious portrait of Hugh Edward Barr, son of Martin and Annie (Menke) Barr of rural Perry. Tragically, little Hugh died five days short of his second birthday on August 5, 1915, when he accidentally ingested arsenic from a dairy flytrap. His family was devastated. (Author.)

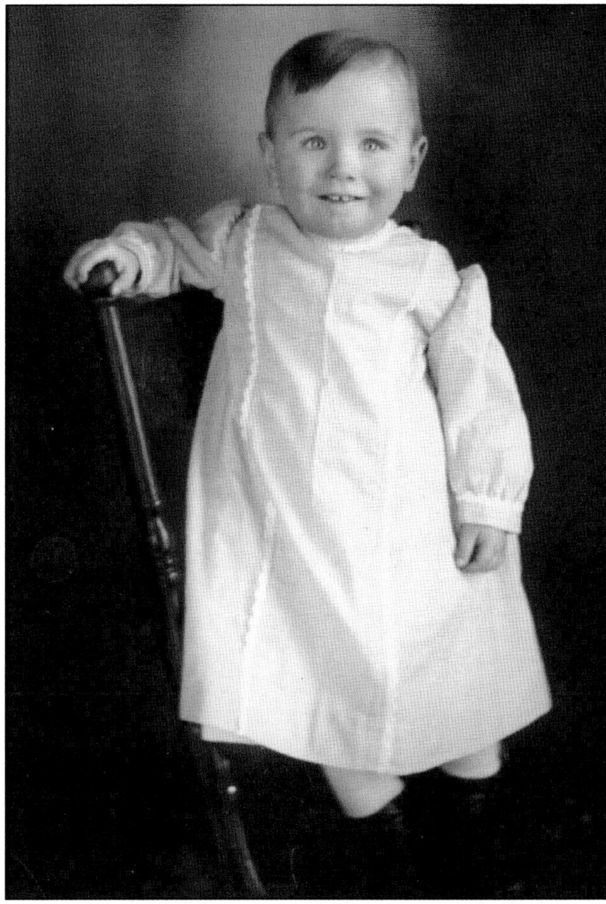

Around midnight on June 8, 1916, a fire began at C.F. Rowland's grocery store, sweeping New London's Fourth Street district. It destroyed the *Ralls County Times*, Park Hotel, A.G. Kennedy's grocery, E.A. Eddings's Barbershop, and Woods and Weaver's Gem Moving Picture show, and damaged local telephone cables. Sheriff Pritchett's daughter Mary discovered the fire. The loss was estimated at $40,000; the Park Hotel was uninsured. (Archie Hayden.)

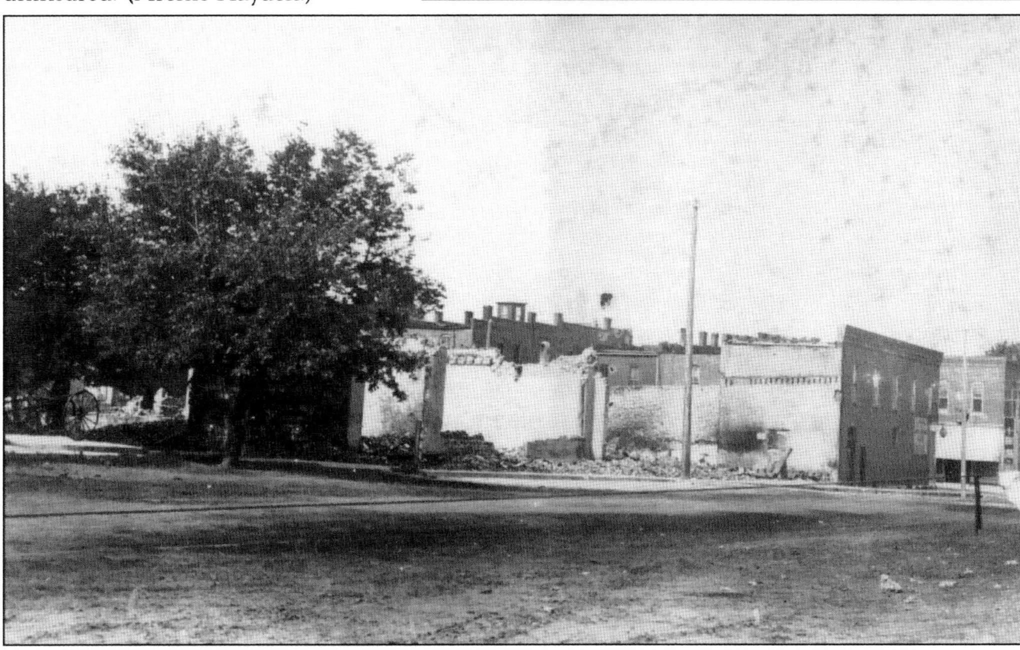

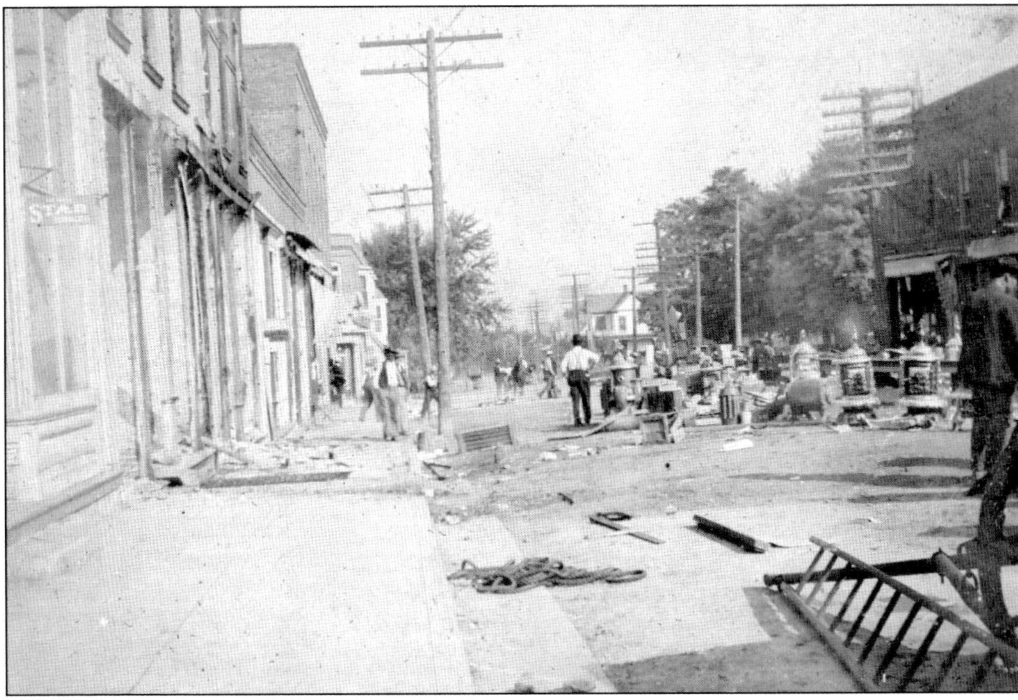

On February 8, 1923, at 7:15 p.m., a fire started in Owen Briscoe's Grocery in the Newlon building. It spread fast, destroying the second-floor home of O.D. Helms's family, his barbershop, and Dr. Ragan's office. G.E. Yager moved stoves and hardware into the street before Briscoe's wall fell on his store. Hannibal's Chief T.B. Parks brought an engine and crew to assist New London in only 30 minutes. (Archie Hayden.)

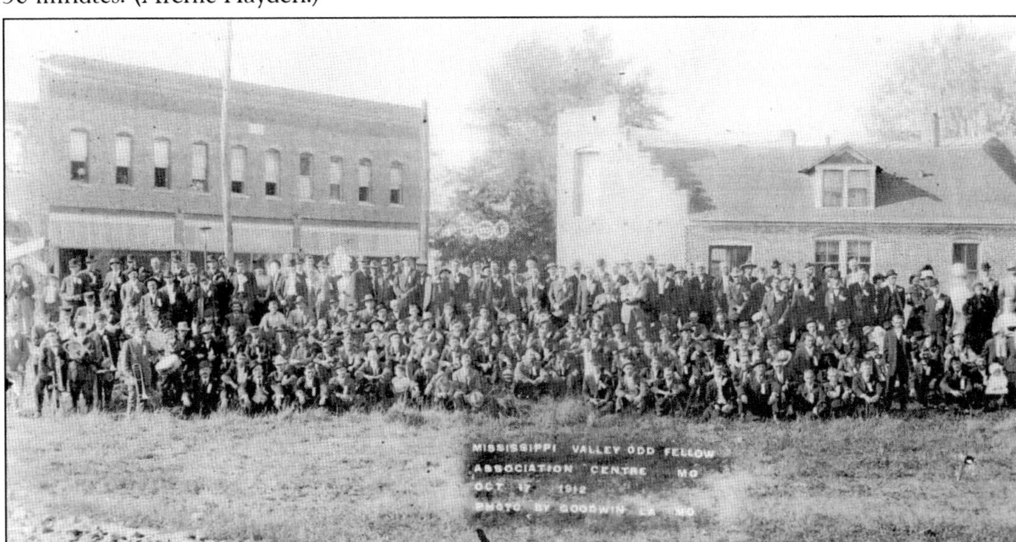

Behind this gathering of Odd Fellows in Center are buildings of the Ralls County Mercantile (RCM) Company in 1912. RCM was the Short Line's largest freight customer until fire erupted on December 26, 1923, destroying 3,500 live chickens, $1,000 of cream, $50,000 of dressed poultry, $1,000 of feed, and the company's $25,000 building at Lamb and Foster Streets. A total of 35 employees lost their jobs during their busiest season. (RCHS.)

On June 20, 1927, nearly five inches of rain fell on Center in one hour, causing this near Biblical deluge. The water at Public Street and Highway 19 by the St. Louis & Hannibal Railroad crossing was four feet deep. W.B. Myers had two inches of water inside his grocery. Center is flat former-prairie grasslands with inadequate drainage even today. (RCHS.)

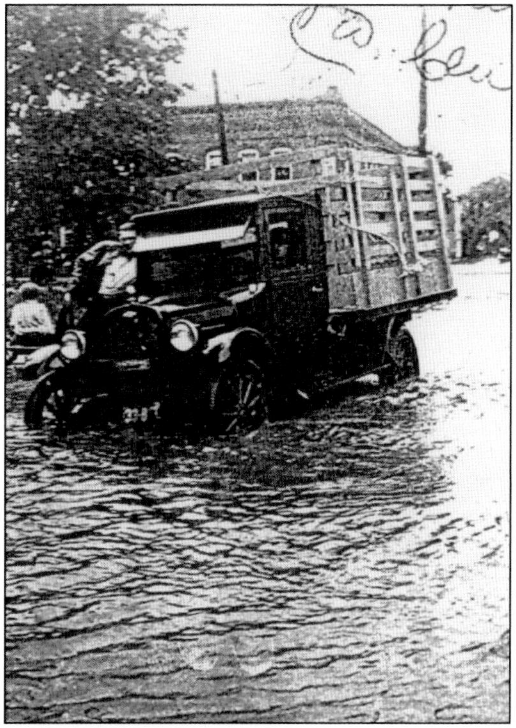

On February 6, 1937, this Swift Meats truck struck and killed Texas Empire Pipeline employee Archie Pierce near the Highway 19 double curves at Olivet Road, east of Center. Pierce died the following day in Hannibal, leaving behind a wife and three children. This photograph was taken in Center looking at the long-gone buildings on the west side of South Public Street. (Author.)

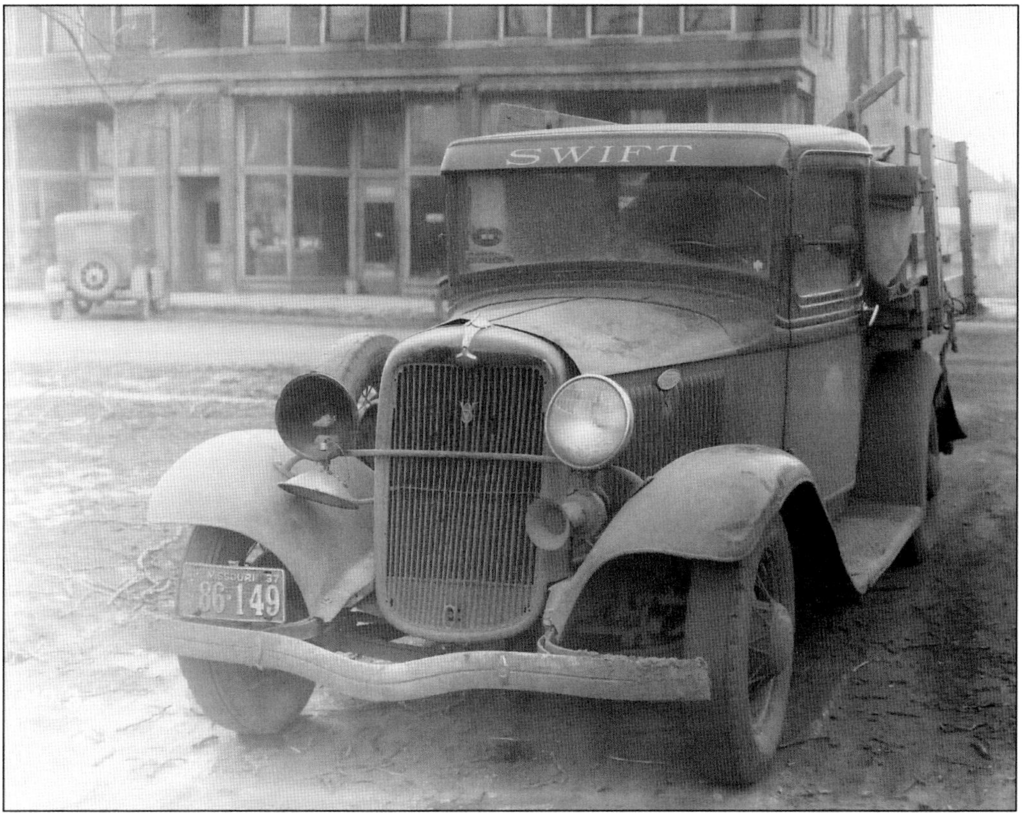

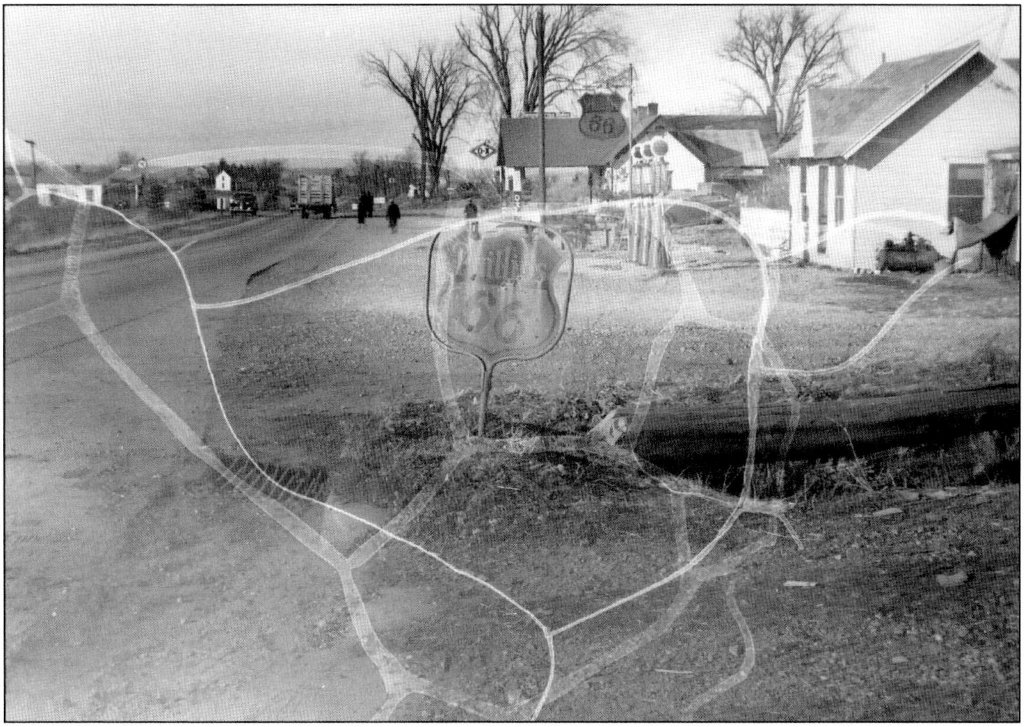

This is Main and First Streets, New London, Missouri, following a fatal accident. Frankford nurse Freda Blount, 26 years old, and New London resident Mary Mudd, 61 years old, were accidentally struck by an automobile 100 feet south of the intersection. The tragedy occurred November 16, 1937, at 9:00 p.m., the evening before this photograph was taken, in front of the Charles Fields D-X filling station. The men in black coats are highway patrol investigators. (Author.)

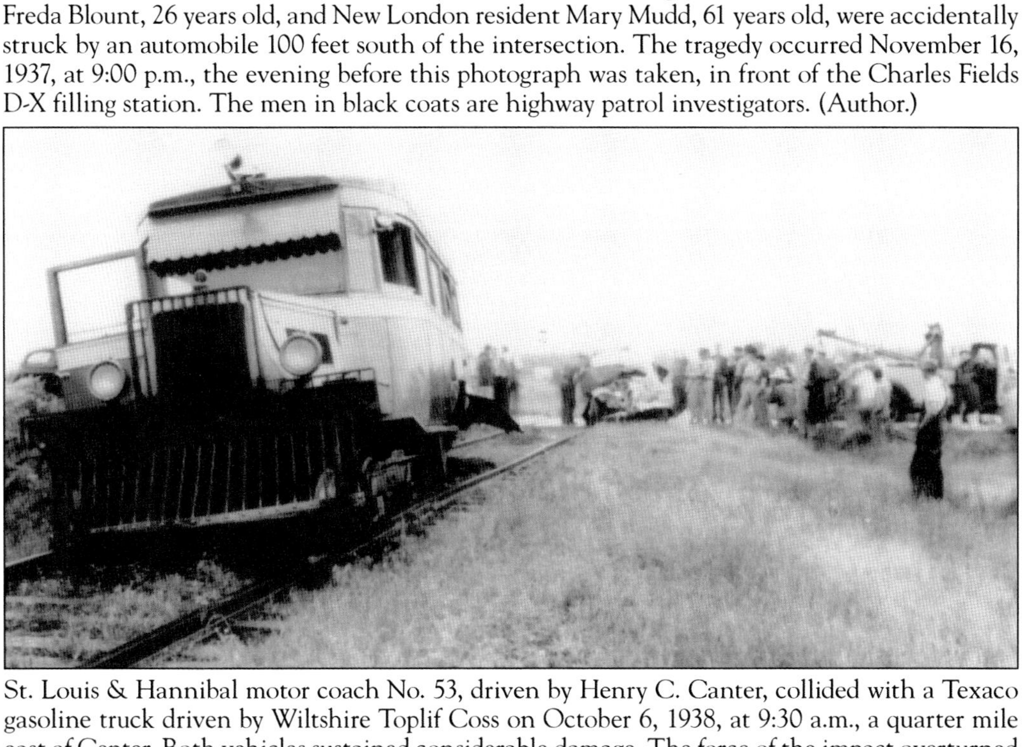

St. Louis & Hannibal motor coach No. 53, driven by Henry C. Canter, collided with a Texaco gasoline truck driven by Wiltshire Toplif Coss on October 6, 1938, at 9:30 a.m., a quarter mile east of Center. Both vehicles sustained considerable damage. The force of the impact overturned the oil truck. Neither man was injured, and there were no passengers on the coach. (RCHS.)

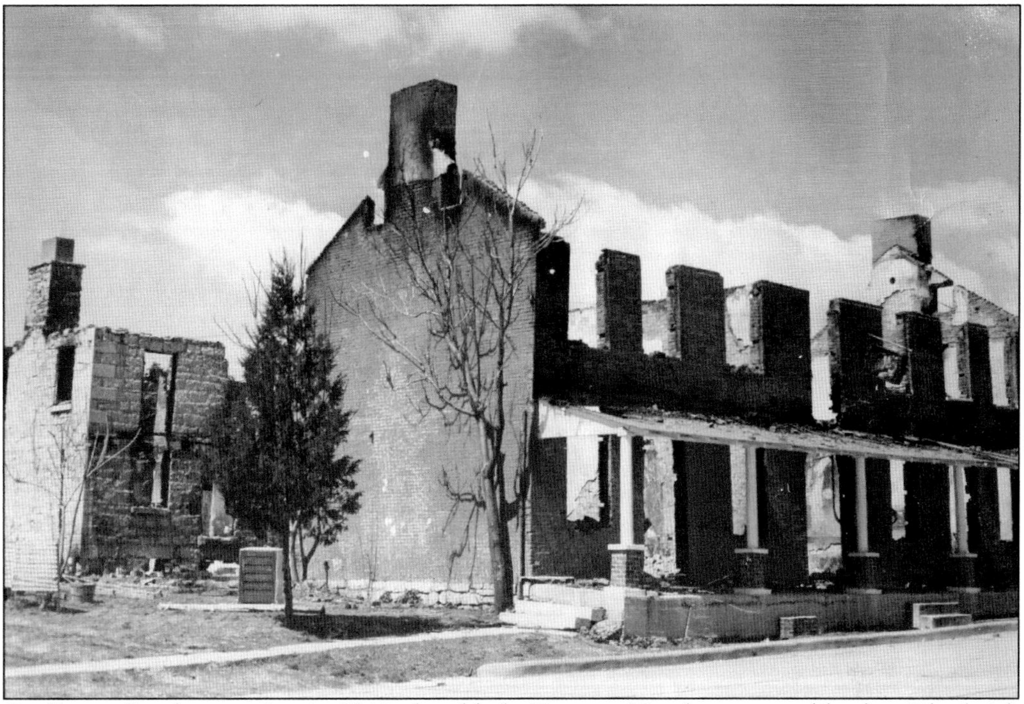

On Easter Sunday evening in 1944, the elderly Century Hotel was gutted by fire. The brick building dated to 1829 and was originally a way stop with a bad reputation on the stagecoach route to Palmyra. The hotel ended life as a tavern and apartment house. (RCHS.)

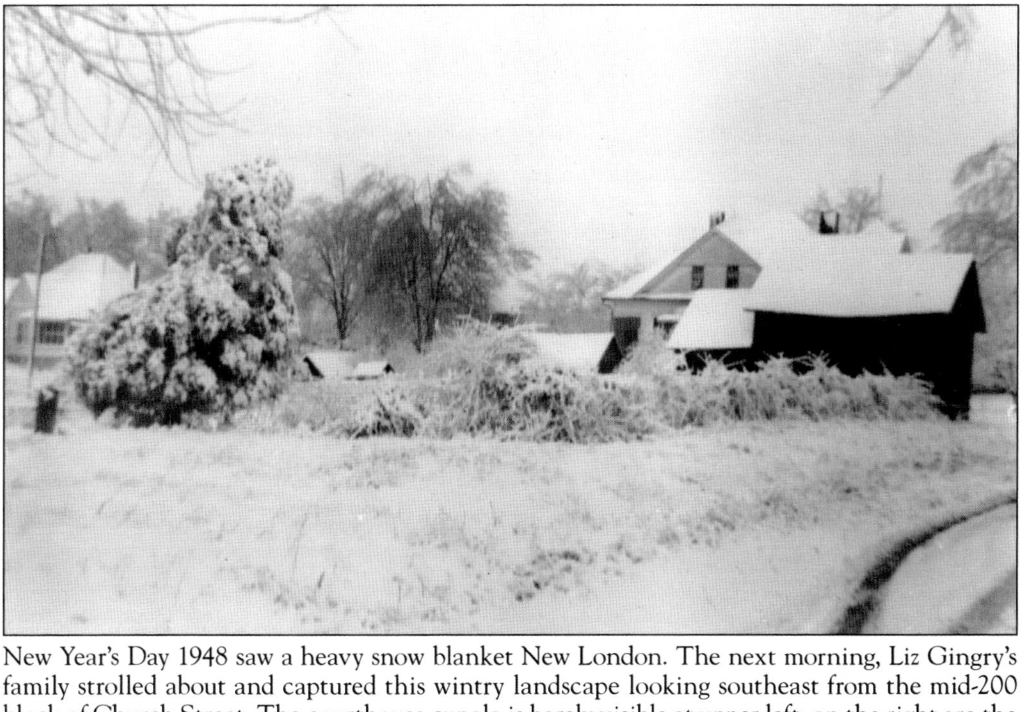

New Year's Day 1948 saw a heavy snow blanket New London. The next morning, Liz Gingry's family strolled about and captured this wintry landscape looking southeast from the mid-200 block of Church Street. The courthouse cupola is barely visible at upper left; on the right are the outbuildings and the Queen Anne Victorian of Dr. Waters. (Liz Gingry.)

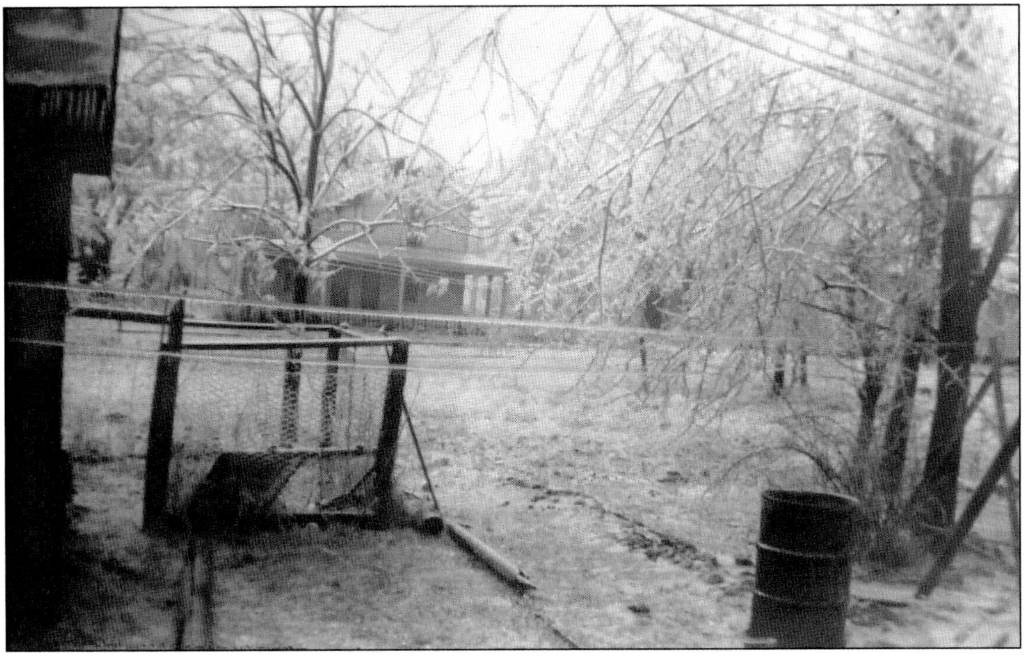

January 12, 1949, brought this storm to New London, leaving a glassy coat of ice and sleet in its wake. Even the clothesline is coated. Liz Gingry took this snapshot from her porch looking at a home on the northeast corner of Fifth and Ralls Streets. The icy trees on the right obscure Robey-Robinson lumber. (Liz Gingry.)

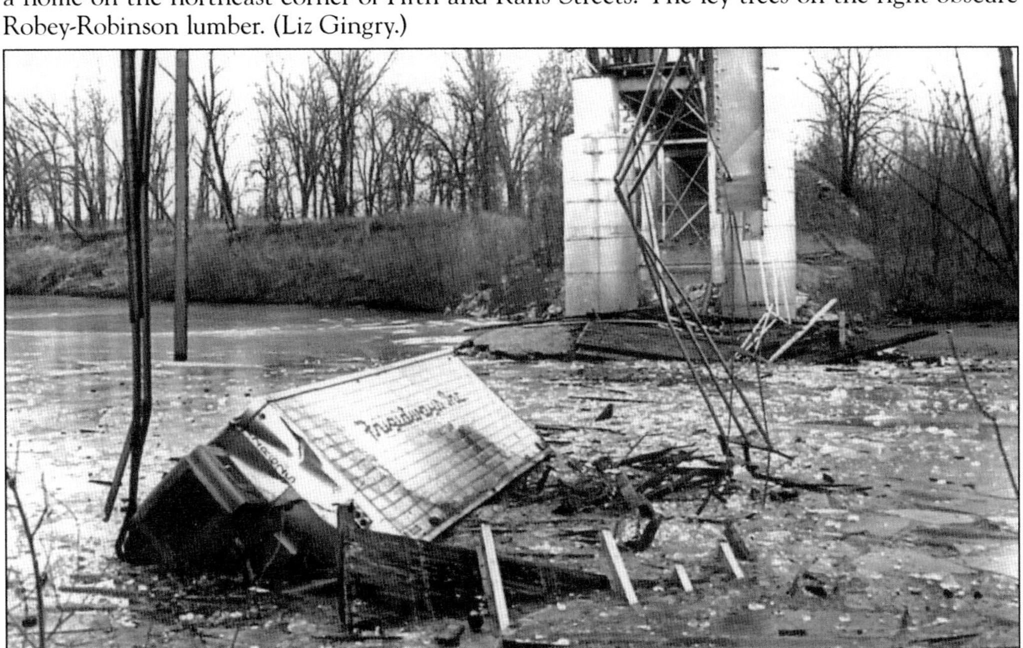

On Friday, January 13, 1956, at 11:00 p.m., the Organ Ferry Bridge was murdered. The weapon was a 1955 Mack semi truck loaded with 55,000 pounds of lard. With a posted six-ton weight limit, the two Tennessee drivers attempted to cross anyway. It is unclear why they were off the main road, but it was rumored that a local young lady knew. Both drivers survived with cuts by crawling atop the cab until being rescued. (RCHS.)

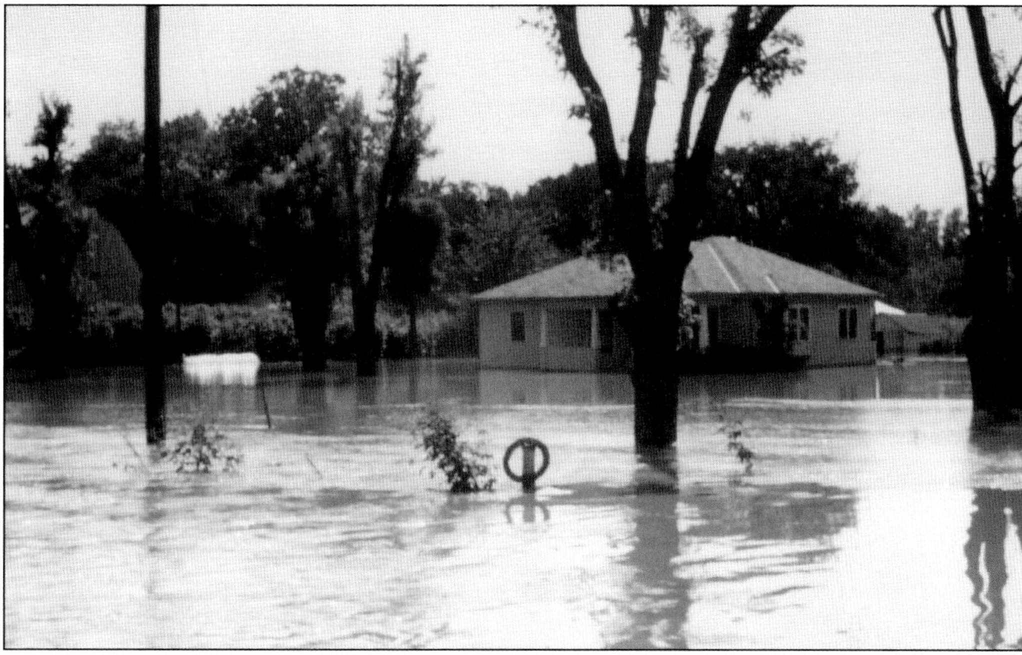

The Salt River is both a blessing and curse to Ralls County. On July 30, 1958, and again on August 2, it reached 29.95 feet, flooding homes and farms and endangering bridges. Shown above is a home on Choctaw, along the southbound 1931 US Highway 61 span (shown below). Flooding threats continued until 1984, when the Cannon Dam was completed and water accumulated forming Mark Twain Lake. Unfortunately, in 2008, these scenes repeated during the record Mississippi River flood coupled with a 13-inch rain near Kirksville, Missouri, severely testing the Mark Twain Lake and the dam's ability to release water fast enough. (Both, Liz Gingry.)

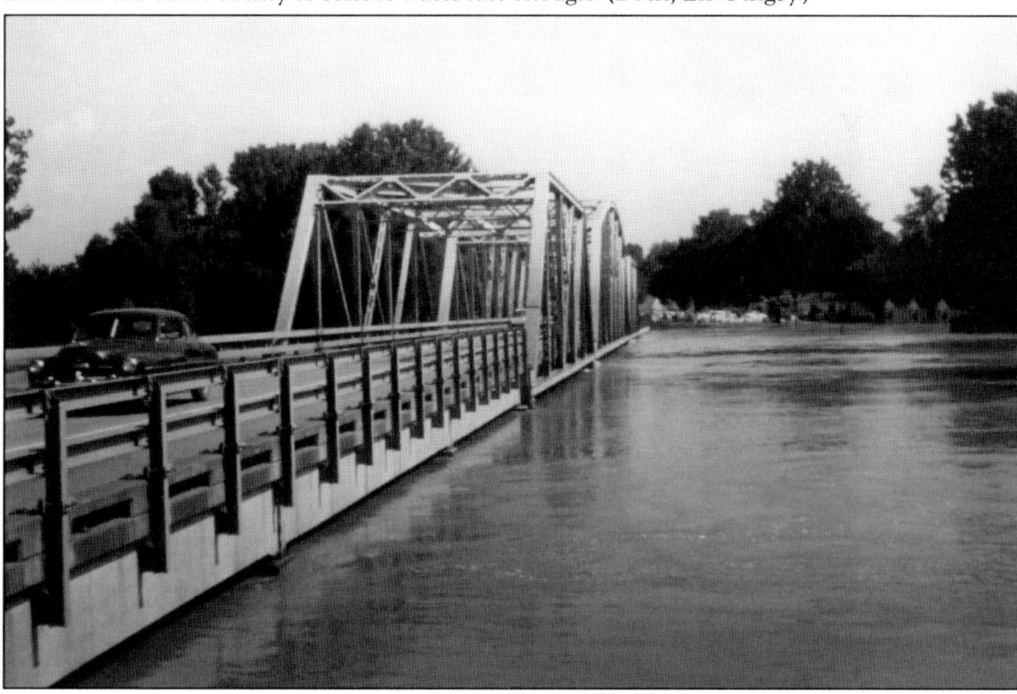

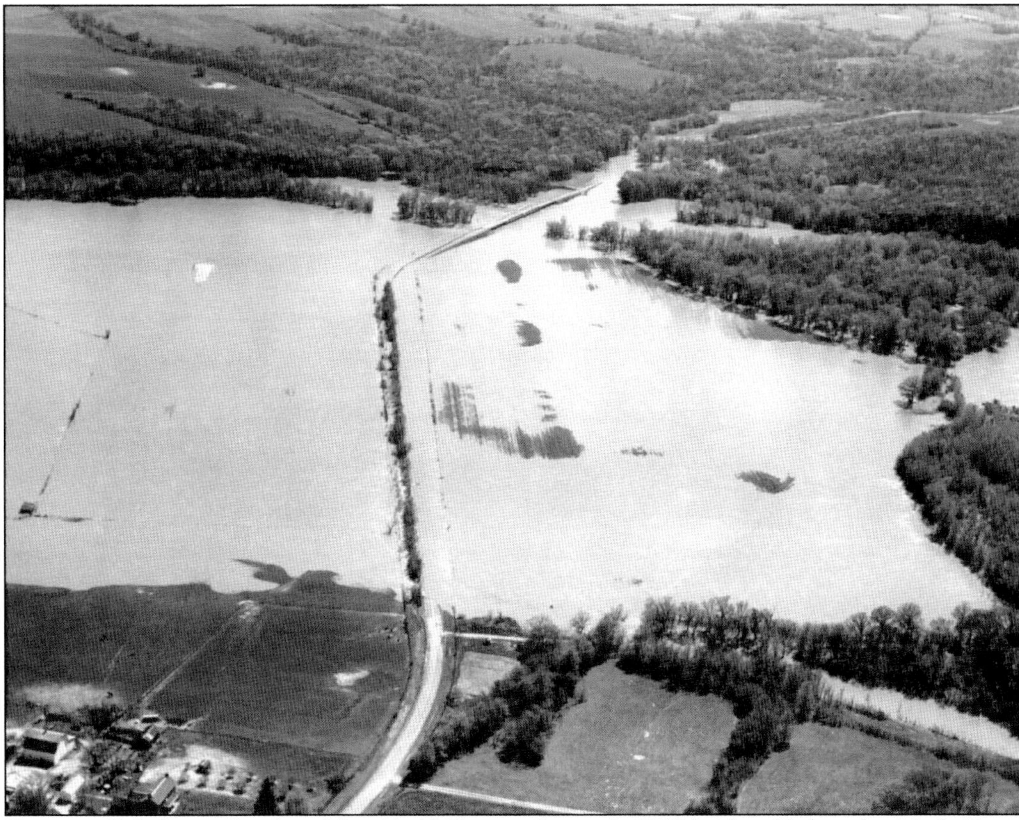

Here is a Salt River flood on May 11, 1961, near Joanna's 1957 bridge. Today, the Mark Twain Lake covers this area. (Hannibal Chamber of Commerce.)

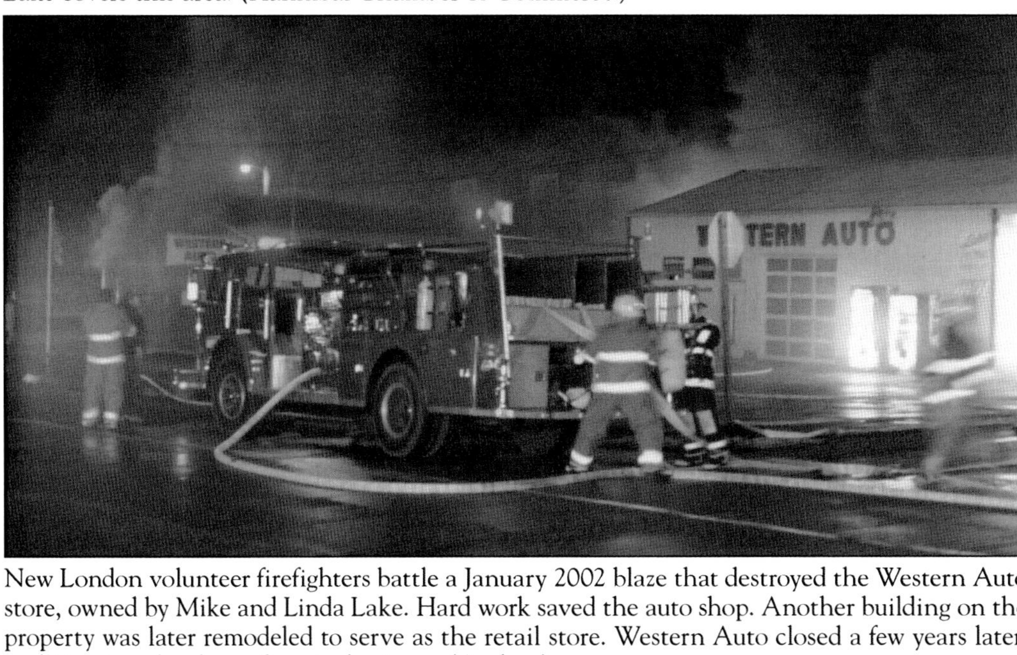

New London volunteer firefighters battle a January 2002 blaze that destroyed the Western Auto store, owned by Mike and Linda Lake. Hard work saved the auto shop. Another building on the property was later remodeled to serve as the retail store. Western Auto closed a few years later, and New London lost a favorite business. (Author.)

Eight

Celebrations and Remembrance

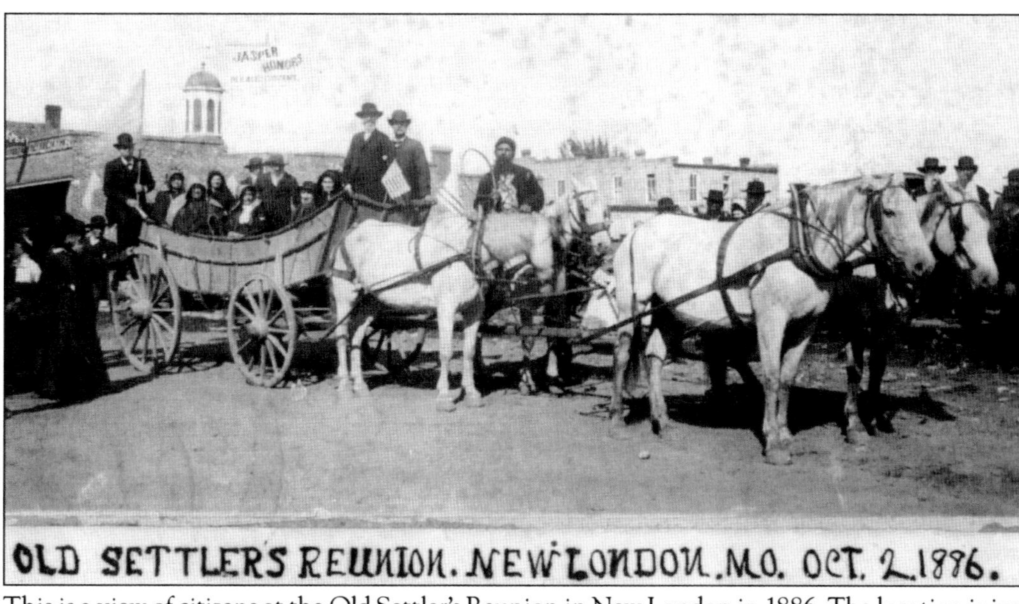

This is a view of citizens at the Old Settler's Reunion in New London in 1886. The location is just south of Fifth and Main Streets in front of present-day Little Steps Daycare. There is a four-horse team hitched to a Prairie Schooner wagon; at extreme left is Elzea's Grocery, and the courthouse cupola is visible at upper left. (RCHS.)

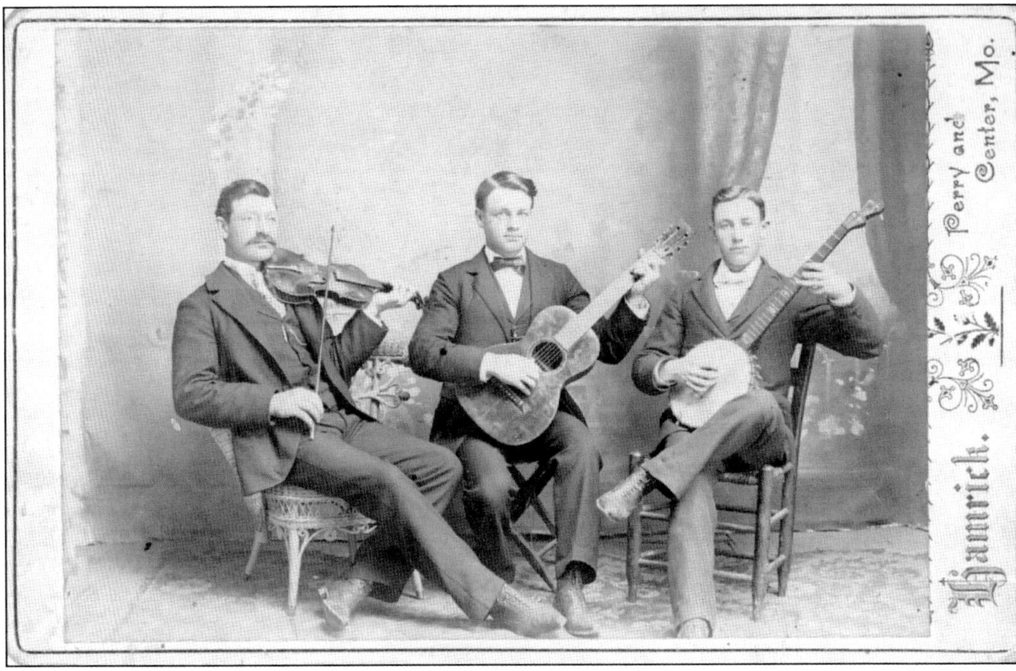

This is a cabinet-card photograph of Perry-West Hartford musicians. From left to right are Carr Bailey, violin; Ellegood Johnson, guitar; and Oscar Johnson, banjo. (Ben Akers.)

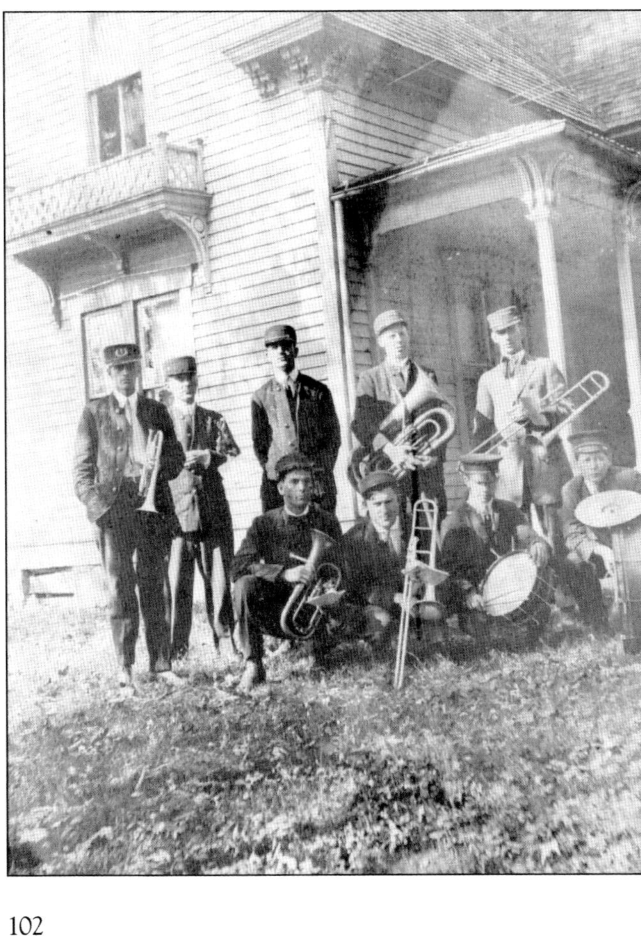

Like most Midwestern towns and villages, Ralls County had several good brass bands and instrumental groups. Newspapers of the day note that Center had a particularly fine group of musicians. This is New London's Town Band at a home somewhere on Main Street. The man playing the tuba is John Porter Fisher; the others are unidentified. (Archie Hayden.)

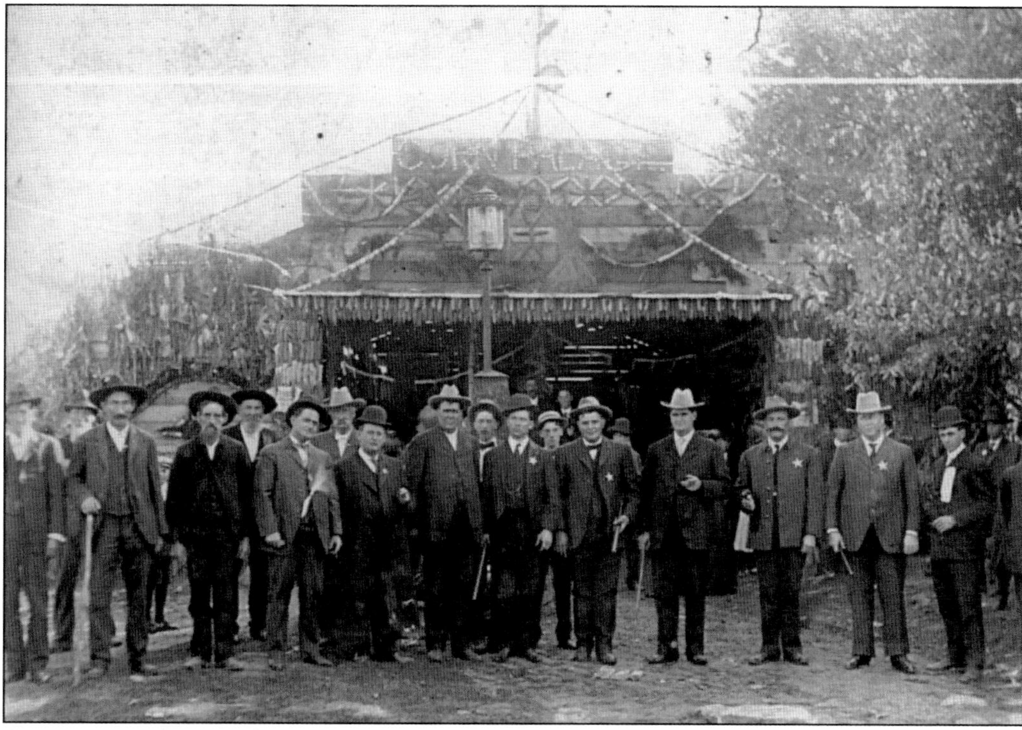

Corn Carnivals and Chautauquas were popular Ralls events. Even though Perry's were better documented, Center and New London hosted them as well. This image shows a Center Corn Palace facade in 1907. (RCHS.)

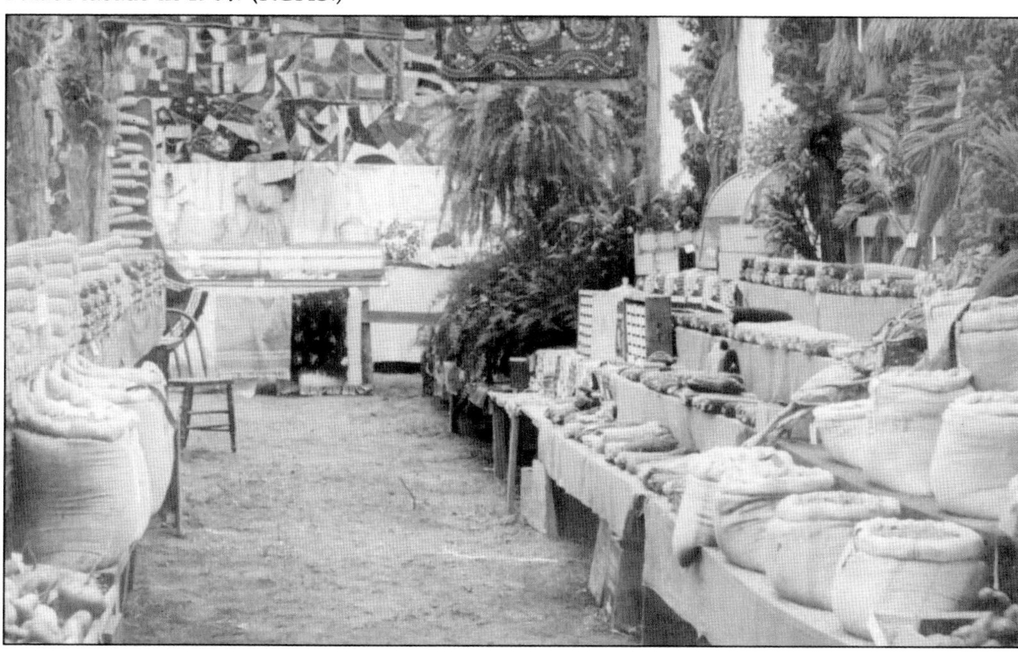

Here is an interior view of a 1908 Perry Corn Carnival exhibit; everything from old relics, fruits, vegetables, flour, meal, canned goods, quilts, tatting, embroidery, pies, livestock, and of course, corn in stacks of 21 were on display. Premiums were awarded for the best entries. (David Polc.)

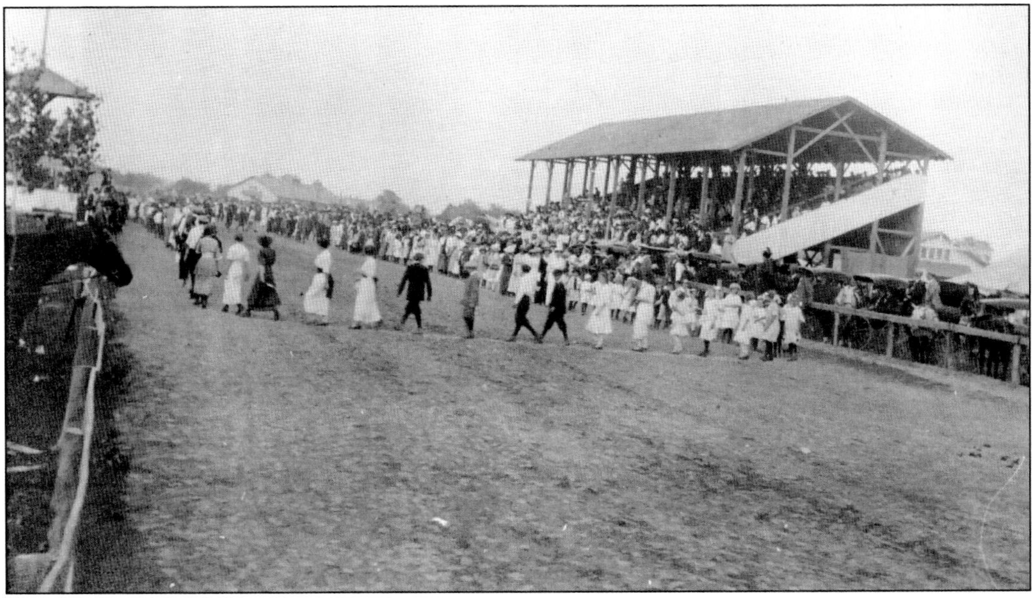

The success of earlier Corn Carnivals and Chautauquas brought construction of first-class fairgrounds near Ralls Junction in 1909, costing $12,000. Each year, no expense was spared for new or improved buildings, grandstands, livestock shows, cooking and hobby judging categories, prize premiums, or entertainment. The St. Louis & Hannibal Railroad offered more frequent trains and reduced fares to accommodate fairgoers. Pictured is the 1912 fair. (Archie Hayden.)

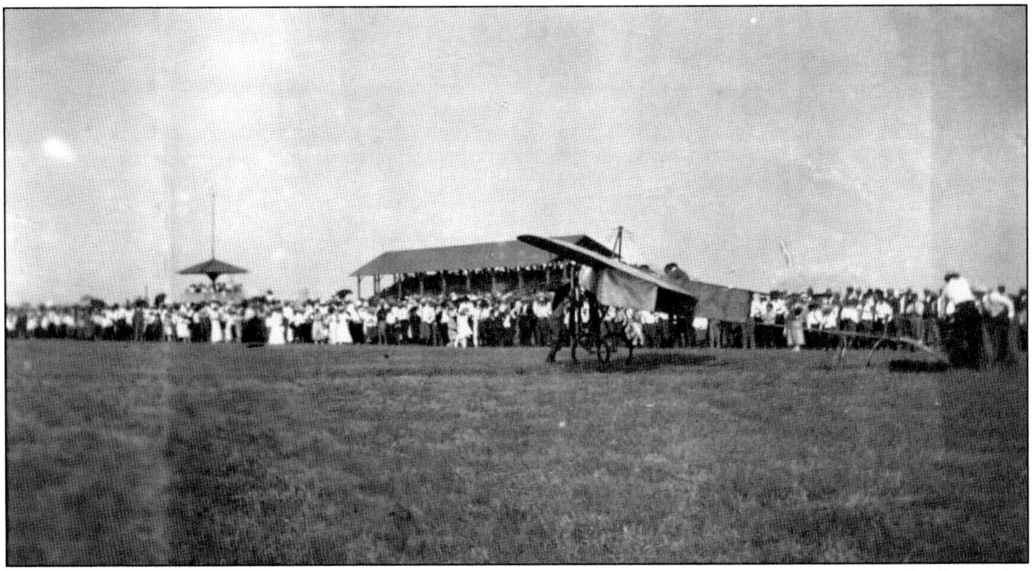

Harold Kantner prepares his 70-horsepower Moisant-built Blériot XI monoplane for flight at the 1912 Ralls County Fair. Kantner earned his license in France in 1911; his boss John Moisant was killed in 1909 in a Blériot Type X. Kantner and Matilde Moisant carried on, setting many early aviation records. Flying his Type XI, Louis Blériot was the first to fly across the English Channel in 1909. Kantner is considered an aviation pioneer today. (Archie Hayden.)

Sporting events were numerous and competitive in Ralls County, including women's events. Here are members of the 1919–1920 New London girls' basketball team. They are, from left to right, (first row) Mart Sayres and Martha McCune; (second row) Vera Bradley, Edna Jackson, and Olivia Waters; (third row) Ruth Roy, an unidentified professor, and Mary Elliott. (RCHS.)

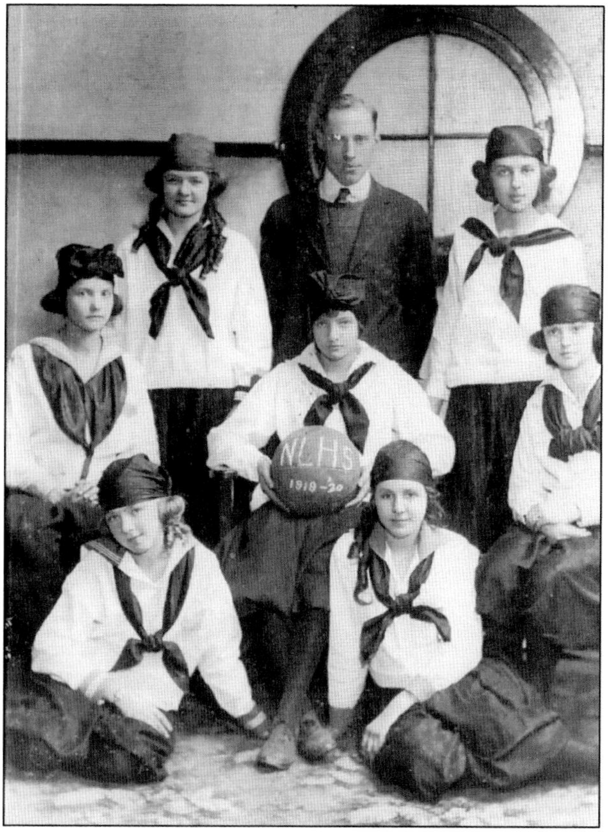

This gathering at the 1912 Perry Corn Carnival is in front of the temporary corn palace at Main and Gill Streets. Edgar Dye stands in front of a fine horse ridden by his sister. The corn palace was the later site of Brashears Motor Co. and present-day city hall. Behind is the Thomas Gill seven-gabled raised cottage, which was Perry's first brick home. Today, Casey's convenience store occupies this lot. (Author.)

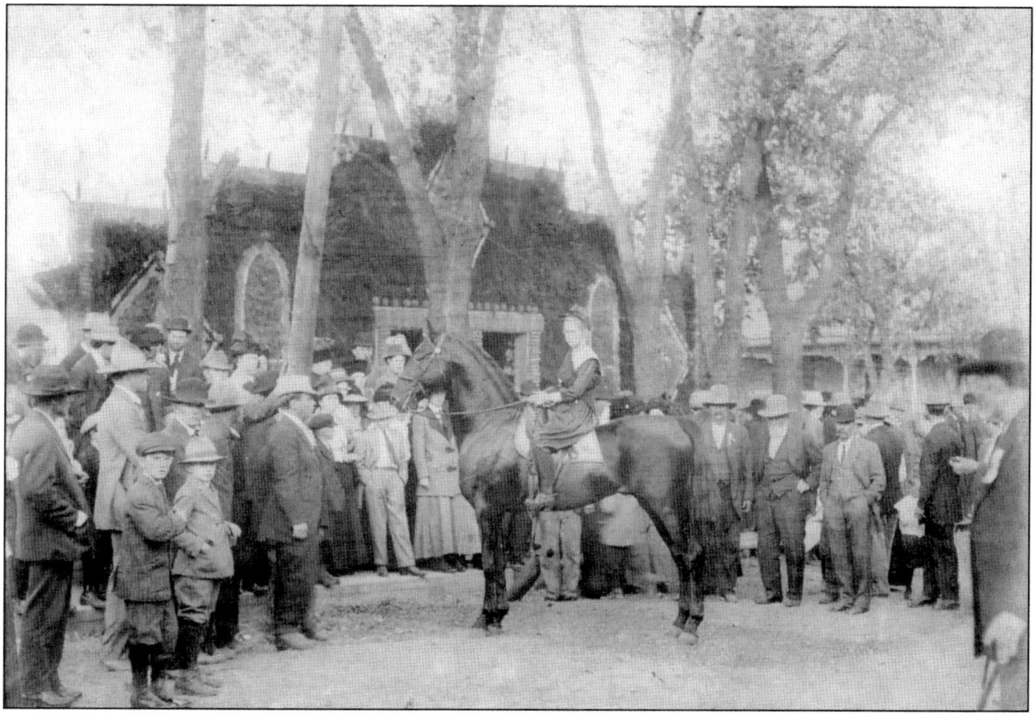

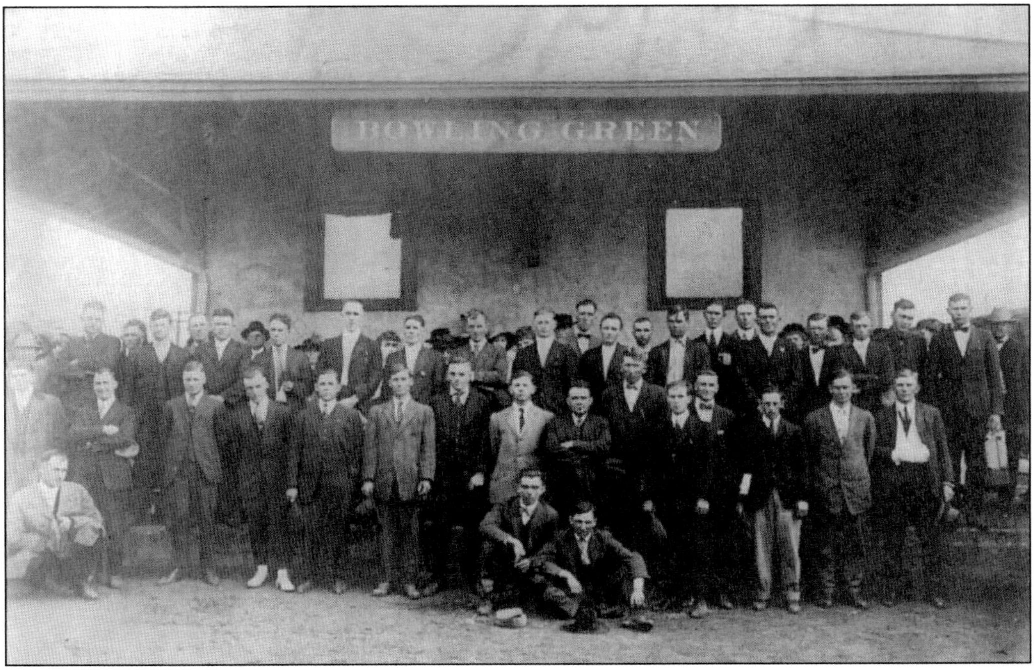

These men are waiting at the St. Louis & Hannibal Railroad depot on their way to military training camp. Departing from Bowling Green on November 10, 1919, they are the final Ralls County men called to duty in World War I. Upon arrival in Kansas the following day, they learned that the armistice had been signed. The War to End All Wars was over. (RCHS.)

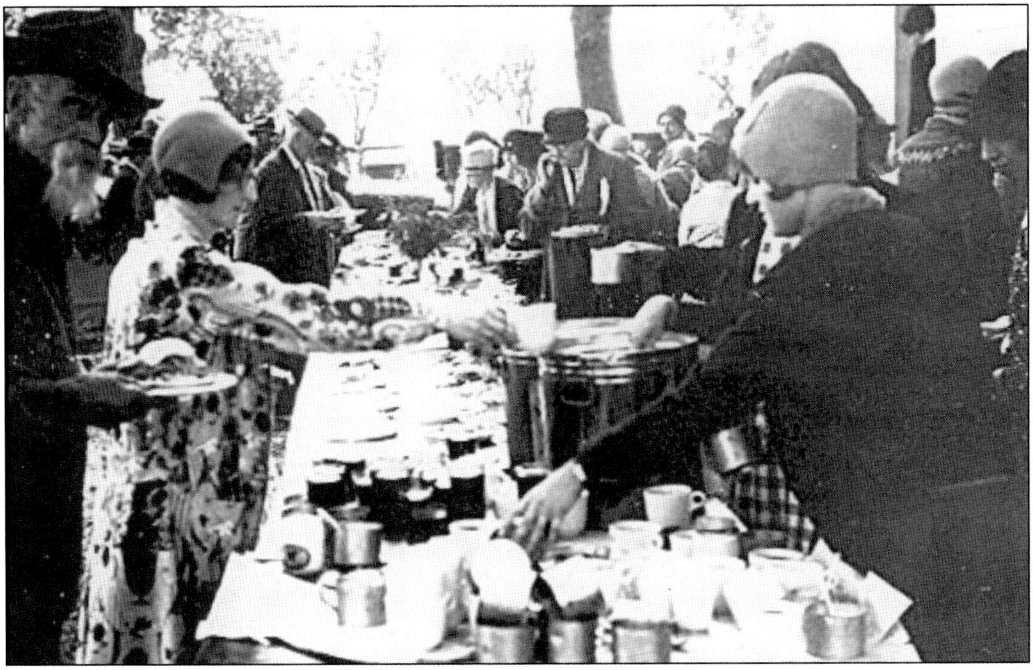

Liberty community is located at the intersection of Missouri 154 and Route P in southern Ralls County. Residents presented programs and hosted picnics and ice-cream socials, like this one, in the 1920s. Liberty has a Wide Awake 4-H Club today. (RCHS.)

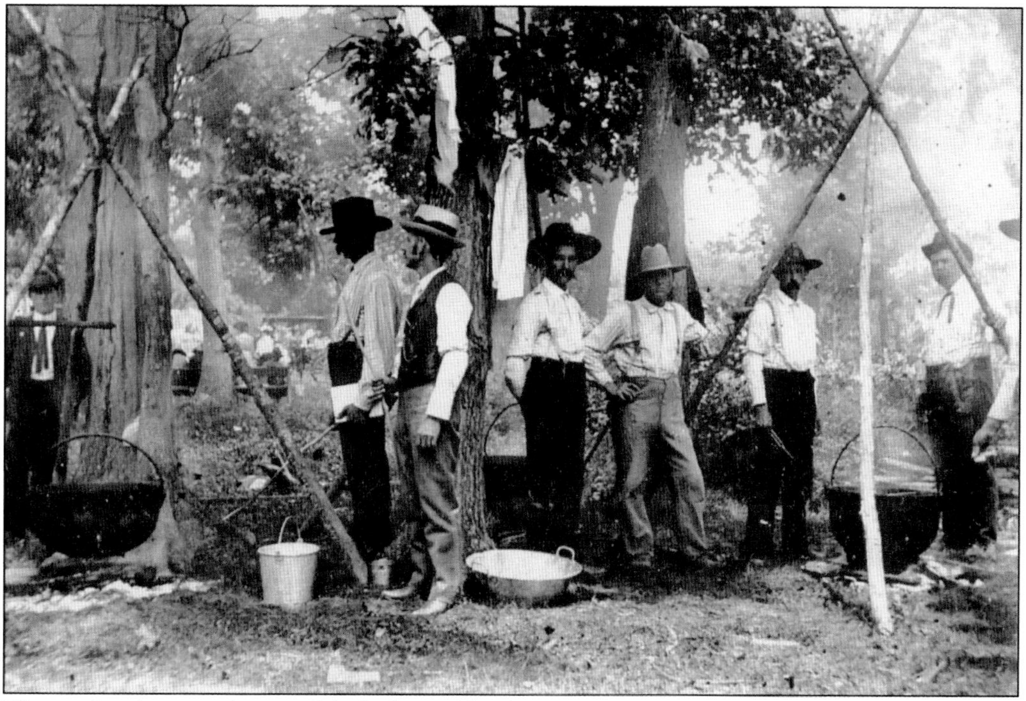

This undated image shows a fish fry hosted by the men of Madisonville, held annually for many years. Madisonville is south of Center and sits atop a ridge above Spencer Creek on the old Vandalia Road. Laid out by Jeptha Crosthwait in 1836, it was named by him for his half-brother Madison. When the railroad passed through Center, Madisonville's population began declining. (RCHS.)

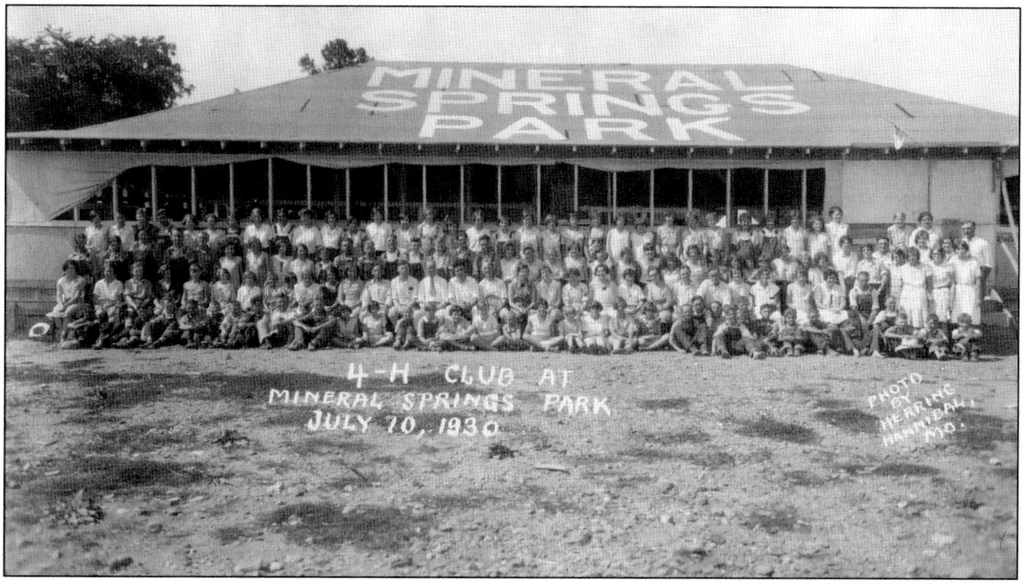

A popular place to unwind was Mineral Springs Park on the Ralls-Pike border near present-day Wedemeier Farms. There was a large sulphur pool to swim in and this tent shelter for gatherings, as seen here on July 10, 1930. Leona Lake of New London said that she and her brother swam here; her brother would immerse himself up to his chin and jokingly sing "I Ain't Got No Body." (Author.)

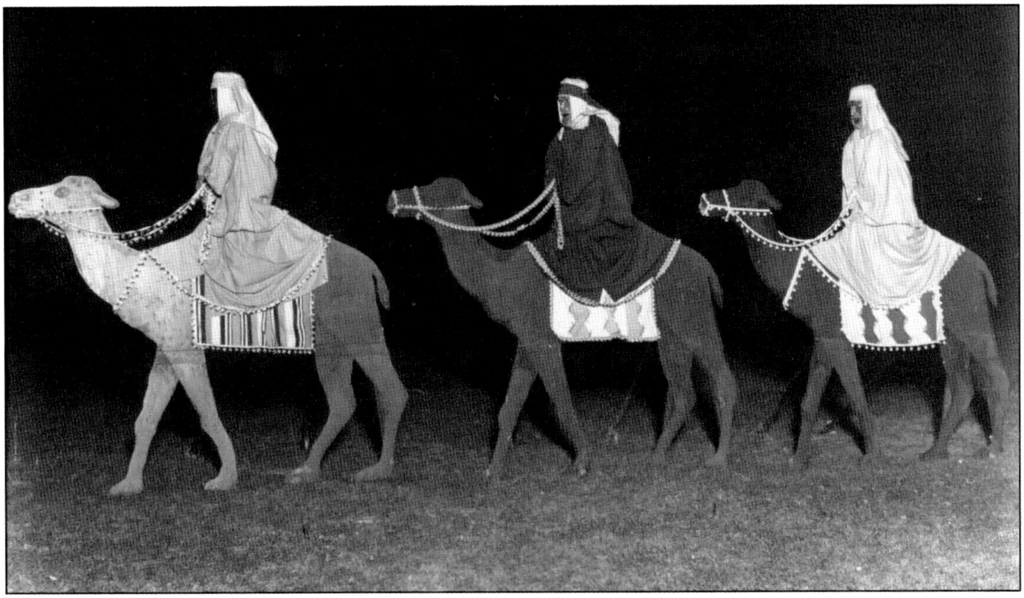

Led by the Star of the East, the Three Magi apparently passed through Ralls County on their way to present gifts to baby Jesus and his parents. Or perhaps, they returned home this way to avoid King Herrod. Actually, this photograph is part of a multi-vignette Nativity scene at Grandview Burial Park on December 26, 1947. (Author.)

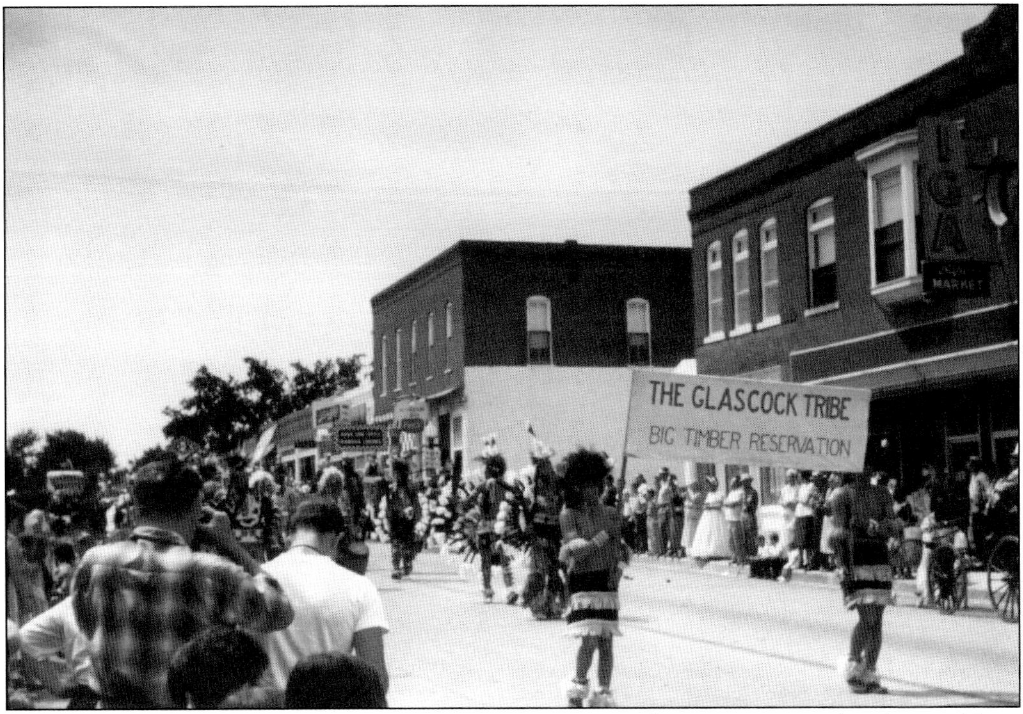

In July 1958, Ralls County commemorated its landmark courthouse's centennial with a weeklong celebration. The event featured a church service, priceless historic displays, contests, vendors, a parade, rededication ceremony, guest speakers, and seven queens of the courthouse, one from each township. At the time, it was the largest event ever held in Ralls. (RCHS.)

Nine

Farmers, Merchants, and Occupations

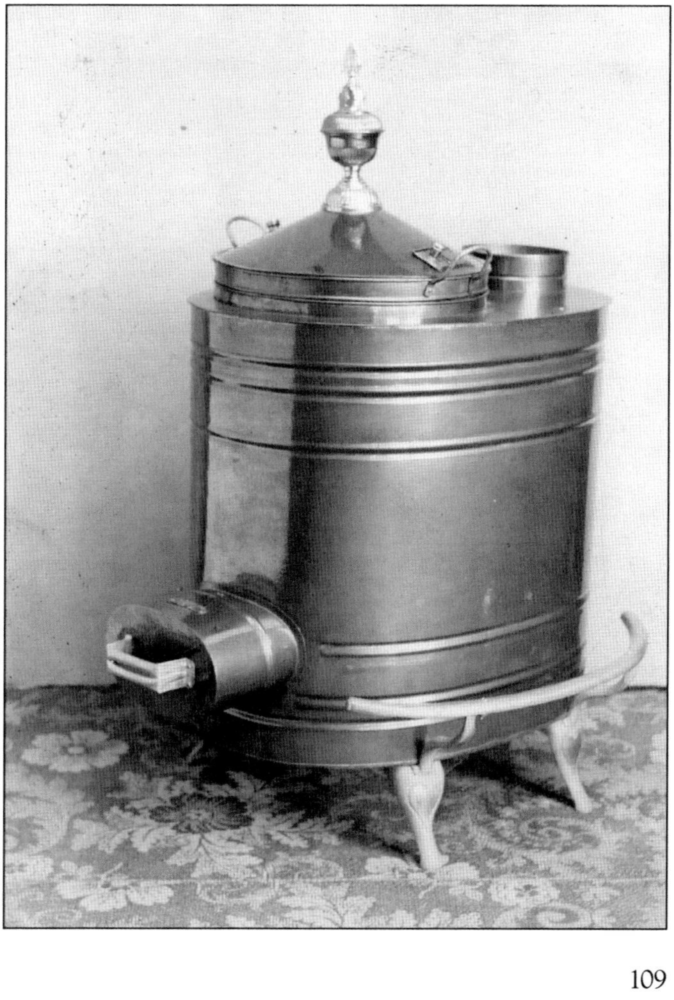

This is a cabinet-card photograph of a Stehle and Sons Co. stove, manufactured in Perry. Martin Stehle was from a French tinsmith family from Kirkwood, Missouri. He moved to Perry around 1875 and made stoves until his death in 1916. From 1894 to 1897, US Patents Nos. 527380, 575179, and 582703 were issued to Martin and his son Will for a combined heating cook stove and stovepipe joint. Original sample models survive in Perry. (Ben Akers.)

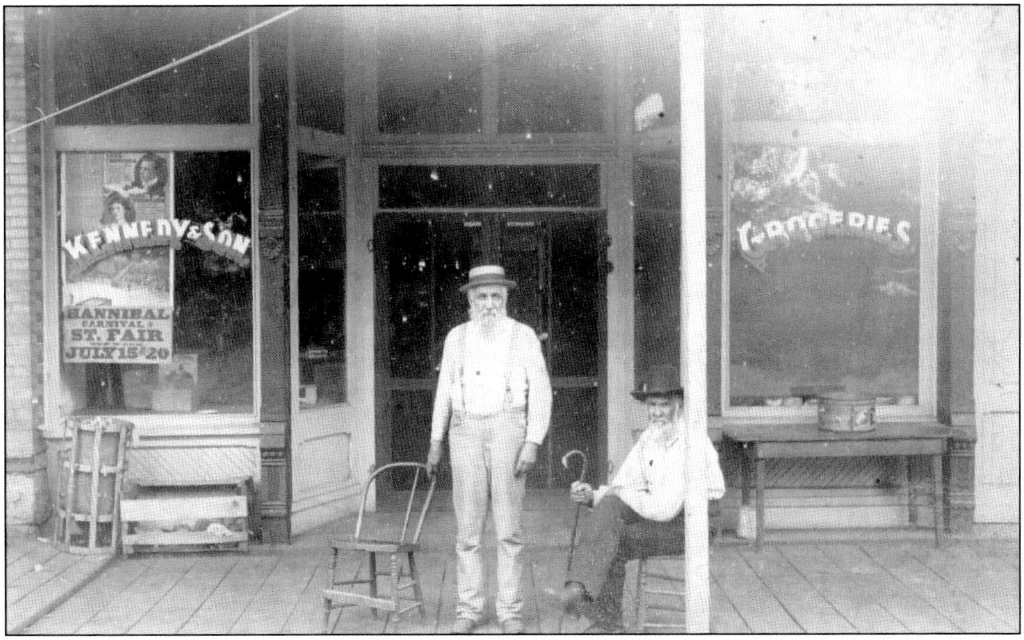

"Hayge" Jones (right) and George Washington Kennedy (1833–1908) are in front of Kennedy's Fourth Street grocery store in New London around 1890. The store was on the west side of Main Street. Kennedy was another citizen who started on the bottom rung of life as a gristmill worker but eventually became a prominent businessman in the late 1800s. (Frances Hays.)

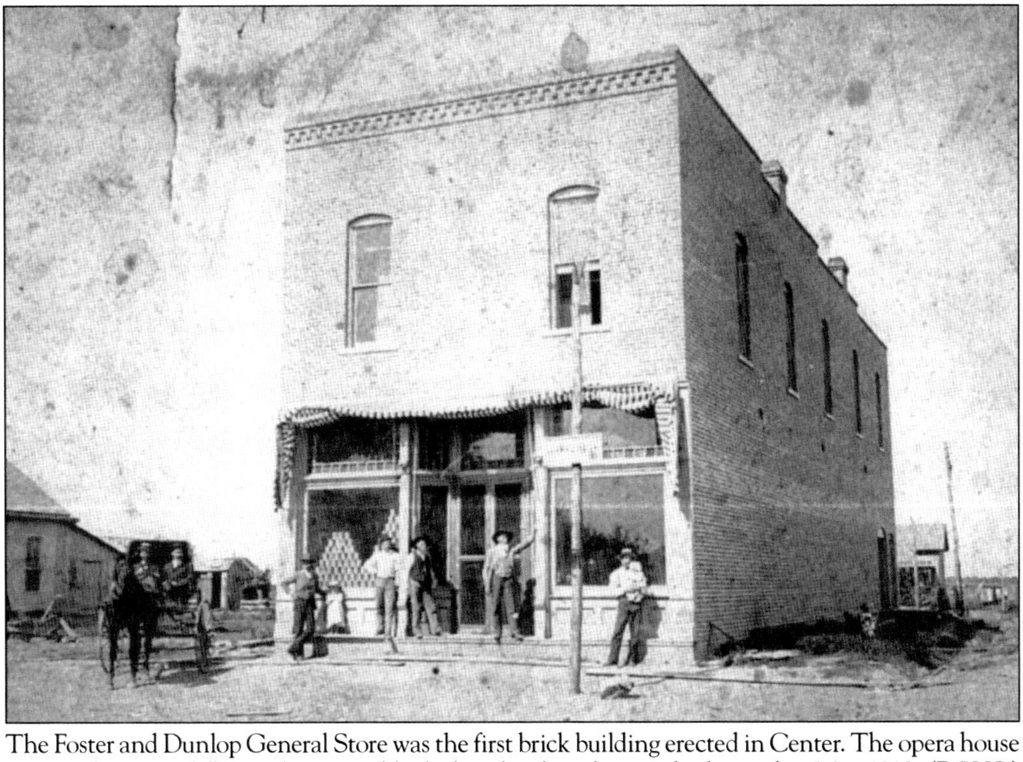

The Foster and Dunlop General Store was the first brick building erected in Center. The opera house was on the second floor. The entire block that developed around it burned in May 1912. (RCHS.)

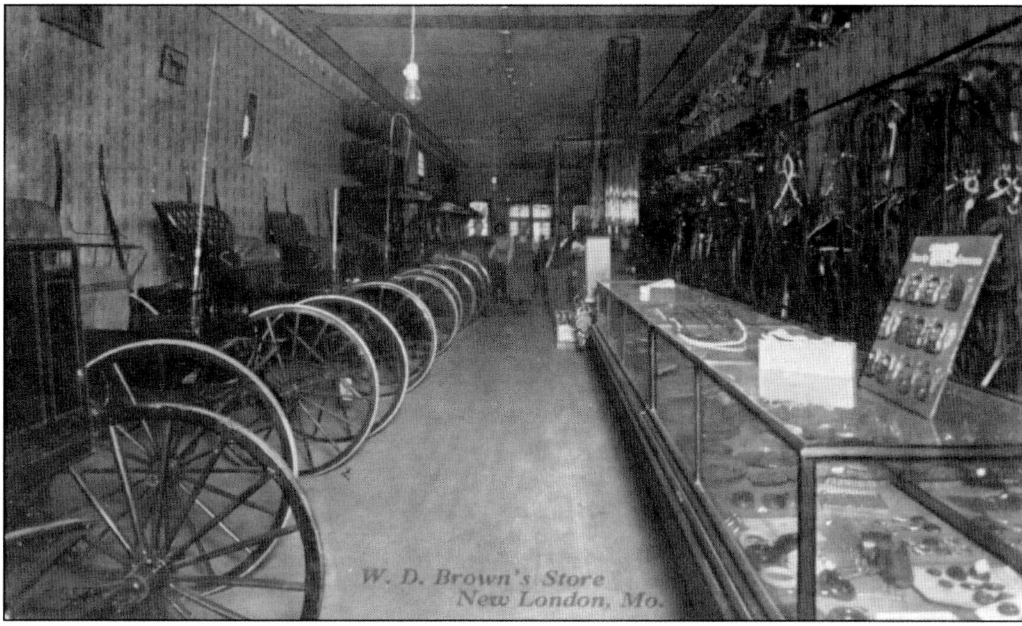

This postcard shows W.D. Brown's Buggy and Harness Store on Main Street in New London. Brick buildings were the standard for these kinds of businesses until the new century, when the Kennedy-Indorf block was completed with a multi-occupant building, as seen below. Early business buildings in New London were log or wooden construction. (Steve Chou.)

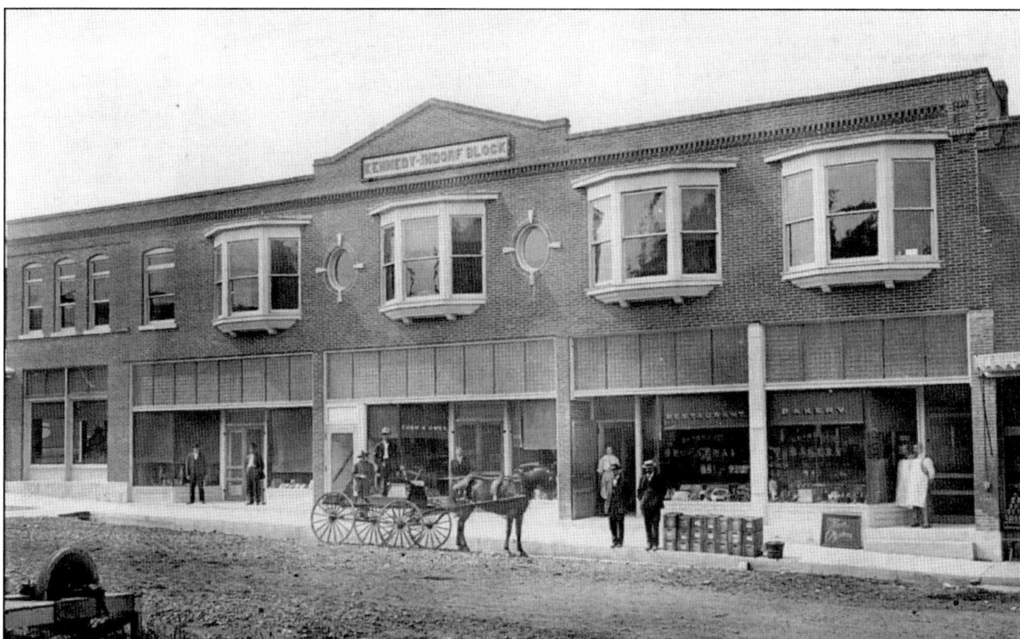

The Kennedy-Indorf Building was constructed by New London grocers James Kennedy and his son A.G. Kennedy. Grandfather G.W. Kennedy first began selling mercantile dry goods on the west side of Fourth Street and then the east side. From left to right are Ed Conn, unidentified, Ed Miller, Allison Evans (in buggy), the daughter of Mr. Brigham in doorway, two unidentified, and Mr. Brigham. (RCHS.)

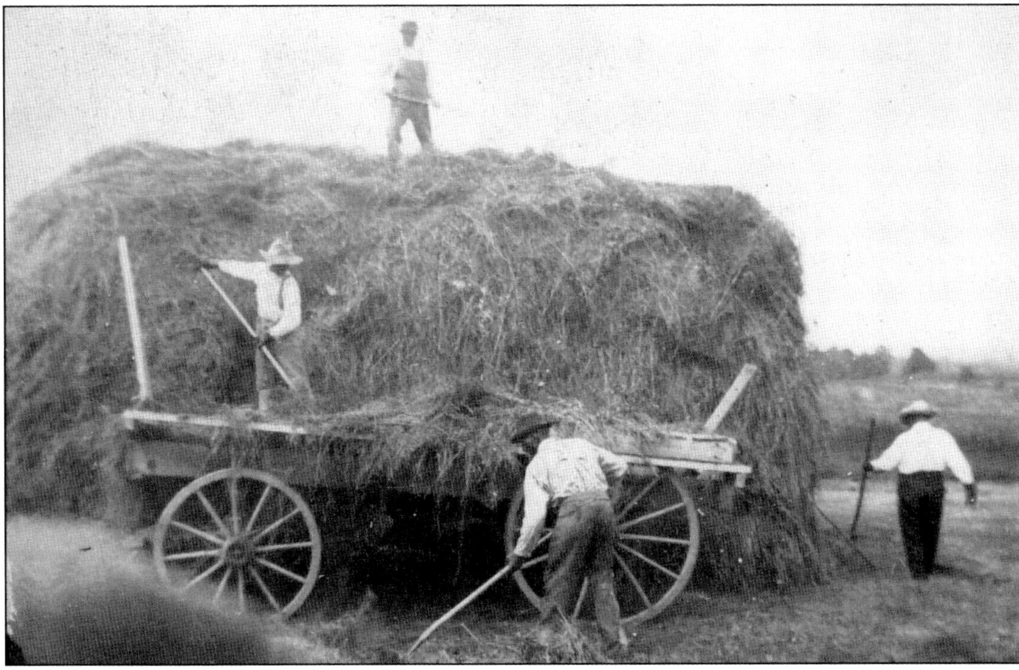

Hay "mounding" is underway at the Elijah Jameson Farm, southwest of New London, in the 1900s. Alfalfa cutting was done manually or by a horse-drawn sickle bar mower. Then the hay was brought in loose by wagon. The first small baler was not invented until 1910, although stationary balers came into use shortly after. The first commercially available small baler was Allis Chalmers's pull-behind Roto baler in 1947. (Archie Hayden.)

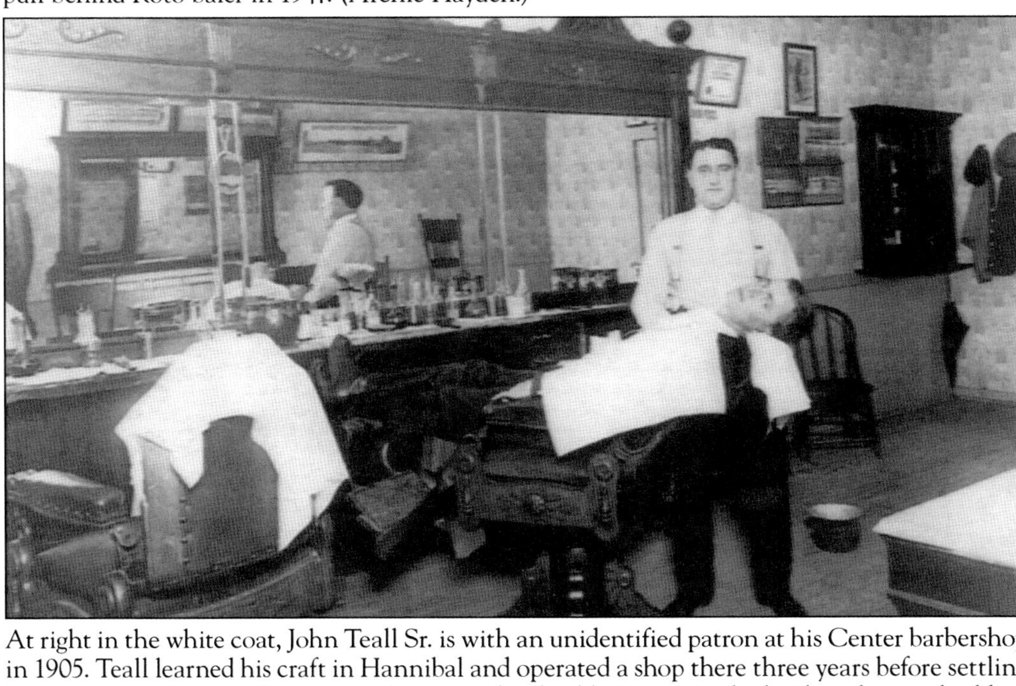

At right in the white coat, John Teall Sr. is with an unidentified patron at his Center barbershop in 1905. Teall learned his craft in Hannibal and operated a shop there three years before settling in Center. His shop was located on the west side of Public Street in the brick real estate building owned by E.N. Paulding. (RCHS.)

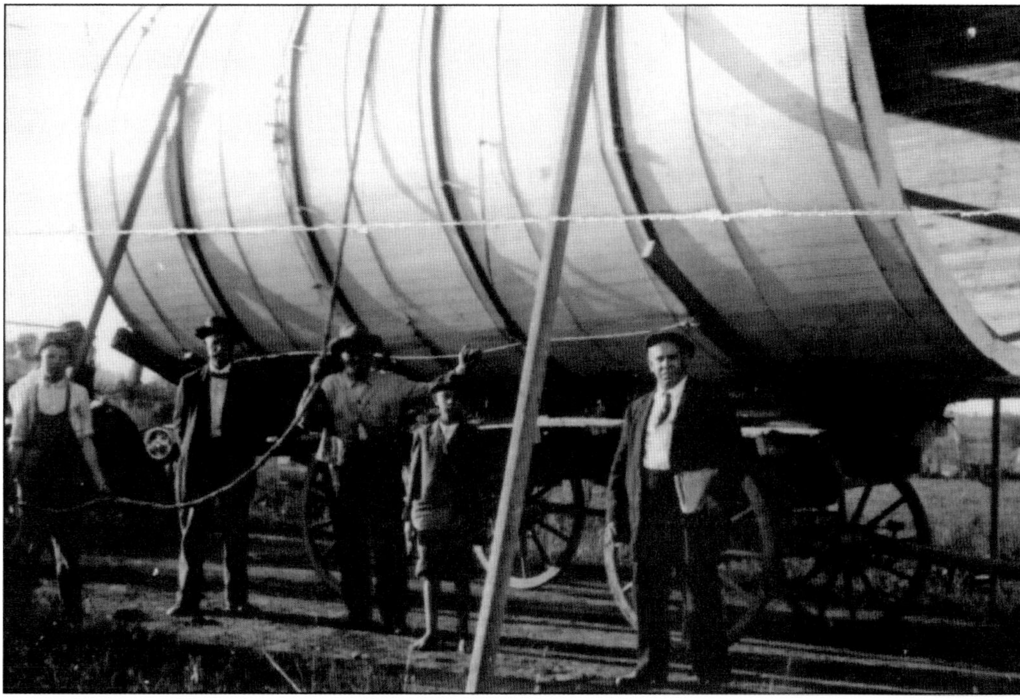

Several men and boys have paused during the difficult task of moving a wooden silo to the John T. LaFrance farm in Perry. One has to marvel at the workmanship to render such a structure as this from wood and then transport it safely by a heavy horse-drawn wagon to its site. (RCHS.)

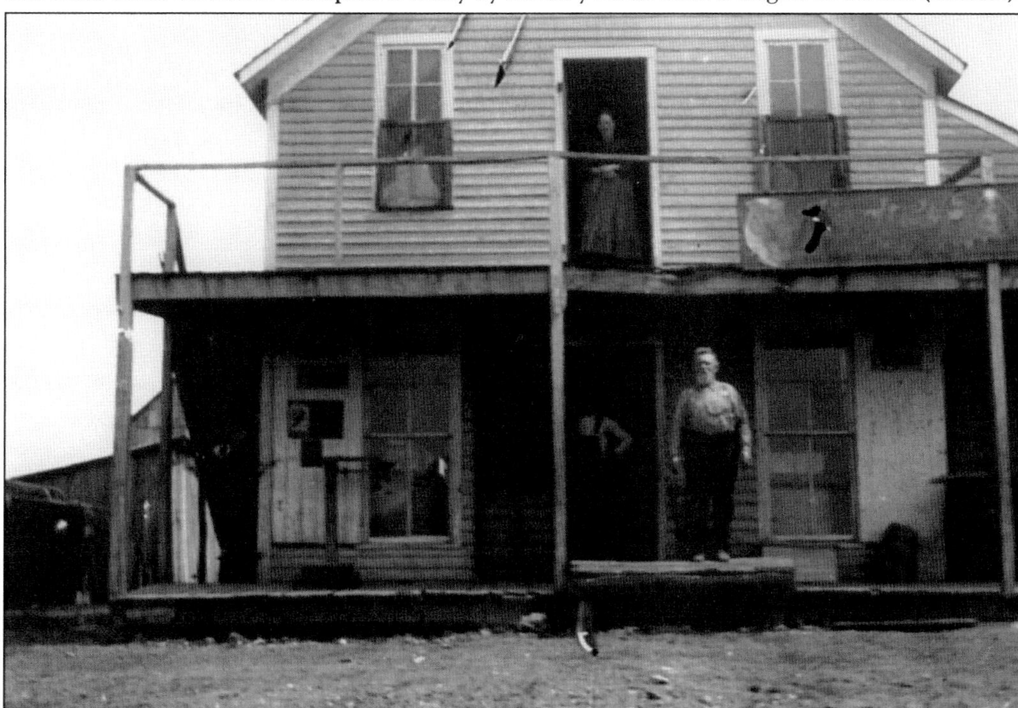

This is an early-1900s view of the Greenlawn store, north of Perry, Missouri. (RCHS.)

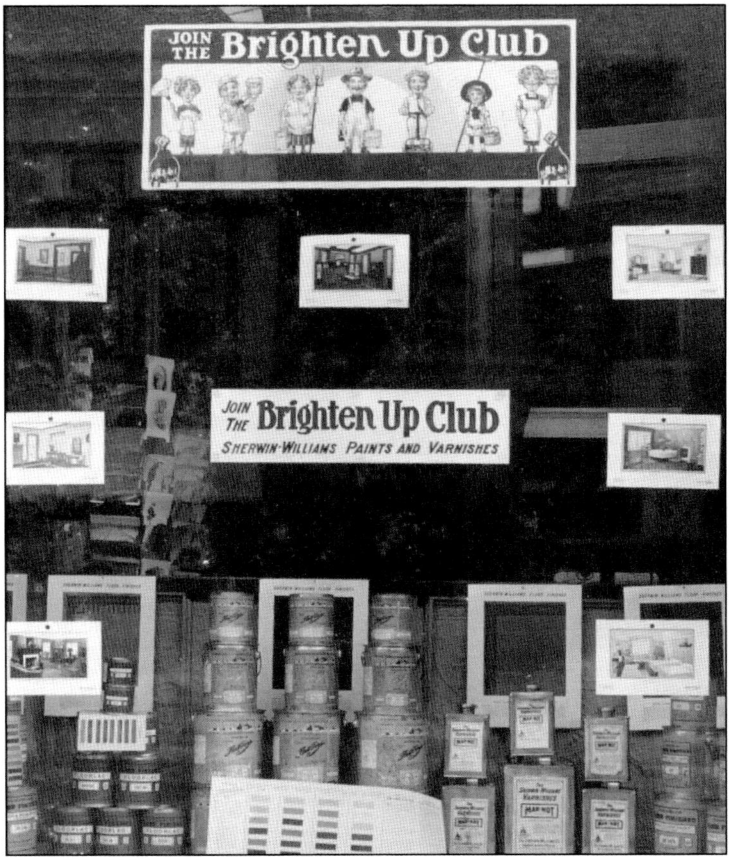

At left is a 1913 window display at Young's Drugstore in Perry. Young's carried a full line of Sherwin-Williams paint products. The signs encourage folks to join the "Brighten Up Club" for S-W's Brighten Up line of finishes. The "BUC" club began in 1911 as a ladies' philanthropical effort by the company to fund relief and charitable groups nationally. (Author.)

People are gathered on the front steps of the Kendrick Store in Hassard around 1920. Judge Jerome Kendrick was an early Ralls County settler in Saline Township near the Monroe City area. (RCHS.)

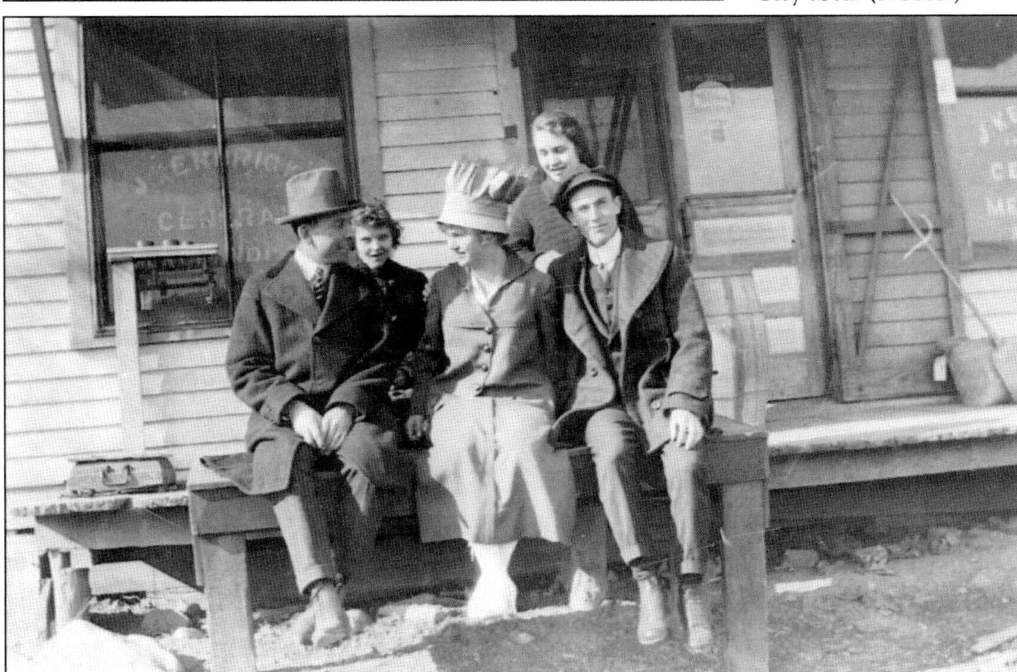

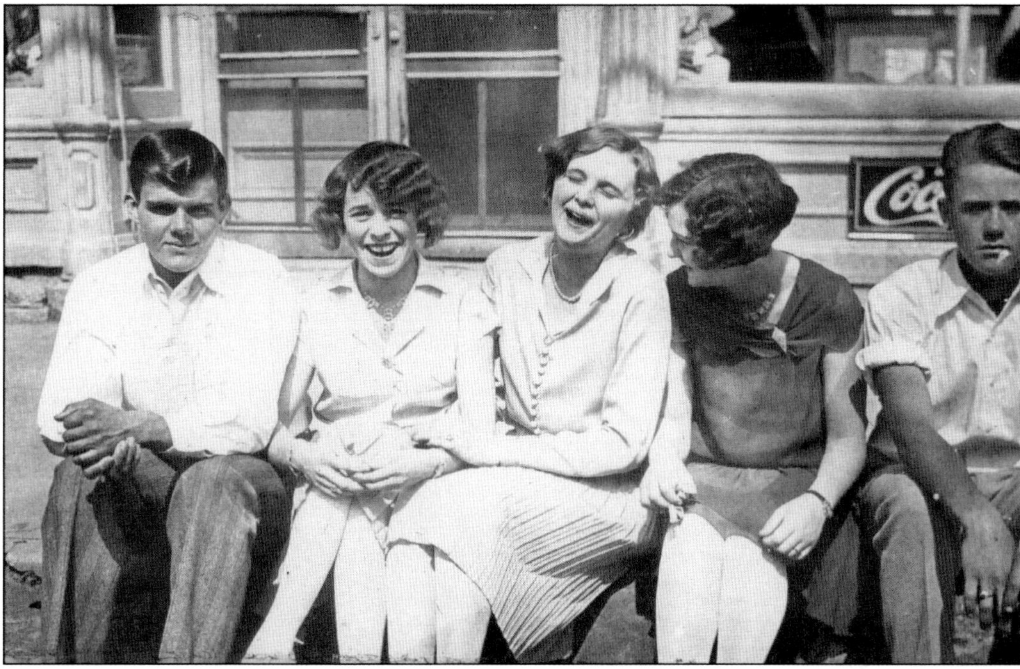

The Tearoom was located at 422 Main Street in New London and was managed by Myrl Conn. Outside on the sidewalk are, from left to right, Harold Haden, Mary Brashears, Virginia Gatewood, Juanita Johnson, and Charles Northcutt. The Tearoom's ad in the June 24, 1927, *Ralls County Record* offered Cherry Nut Cream and Orange Ice as its Friday and Saturday special. (Liz Gingry.)

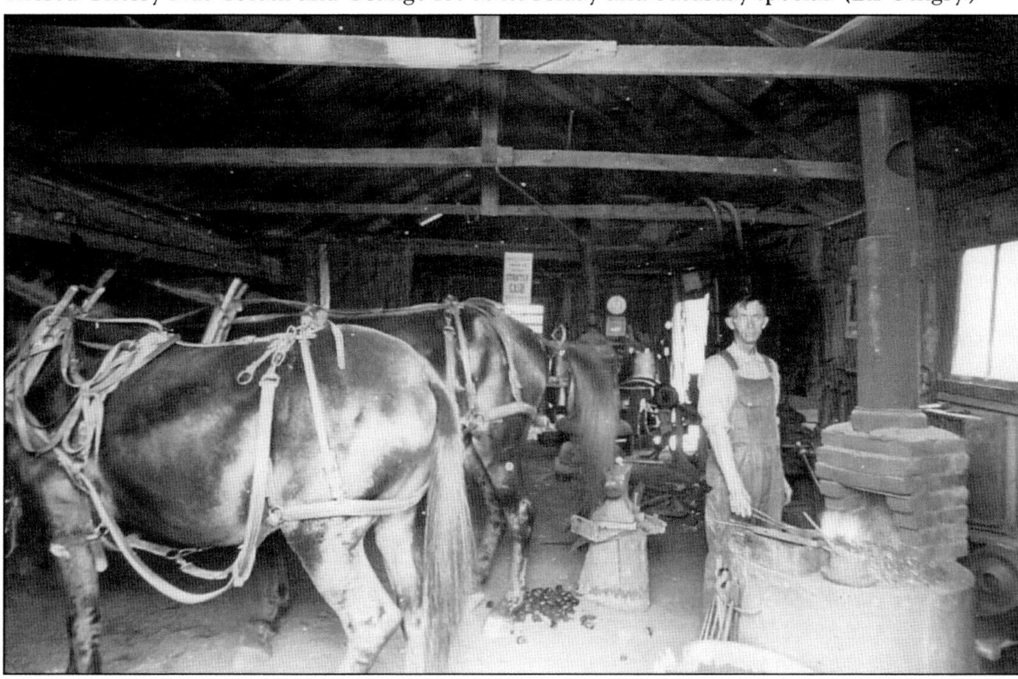

Theodore G. Campbell's blacksmith shop was in Center in 1931, between North Public and Foster Streets on Hawkins Street behind the present-day Ralls County Library. Campbell died on May 1, 1932, at age 55, from a ruptured duodenal ulcer. (RCHS.)

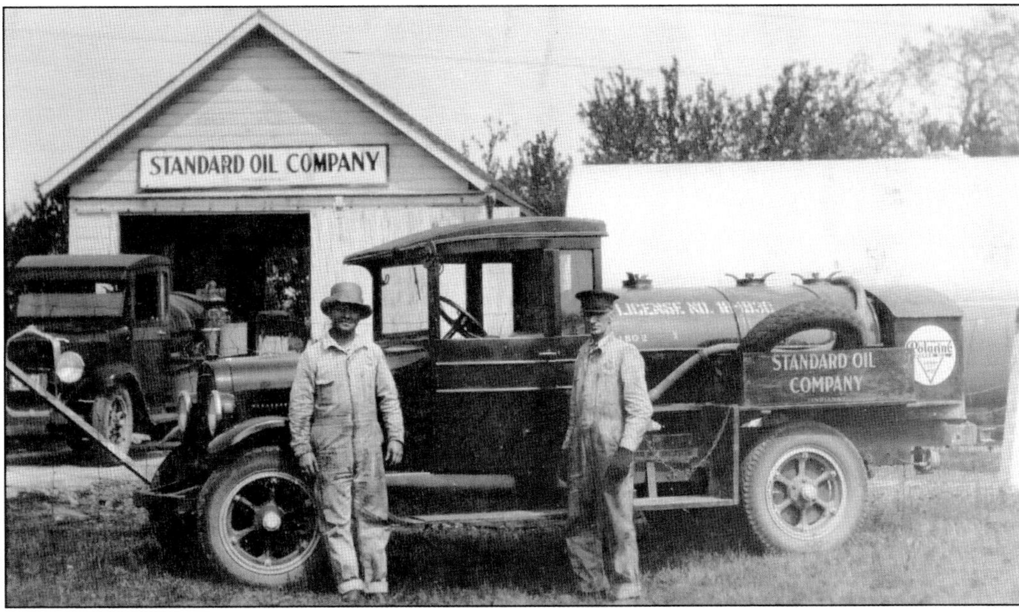

Standard Oil Co. in Center, Missouri, in 1938 was a little north of the St. Louis & Hannibal siding near the west edge of Center. The rail siding here served several other businesses including Illinois Oil Co. Pictured are Harry Hays (left) and Bill Small in front of their tanker truck. (Frances Hays.)

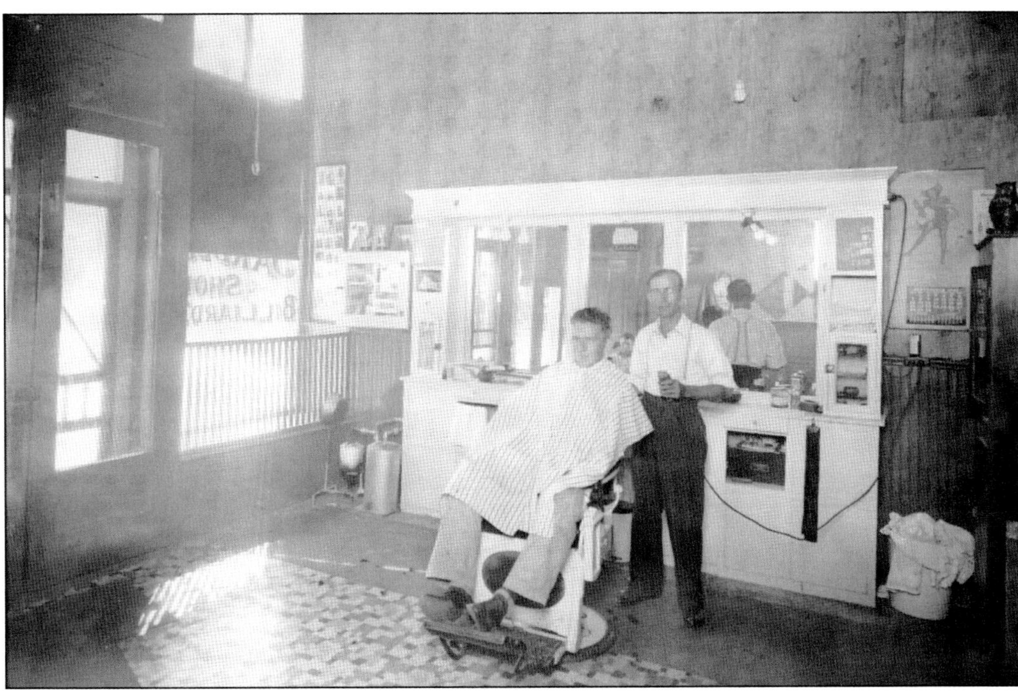

Perry Barbershop and Billiards was operated by R.C. "Buster" Riley. His patron is unidentified, but the ubiquitous girlie calendar says it is September 1941, three months before Pearl Harbor. (RCHS.)

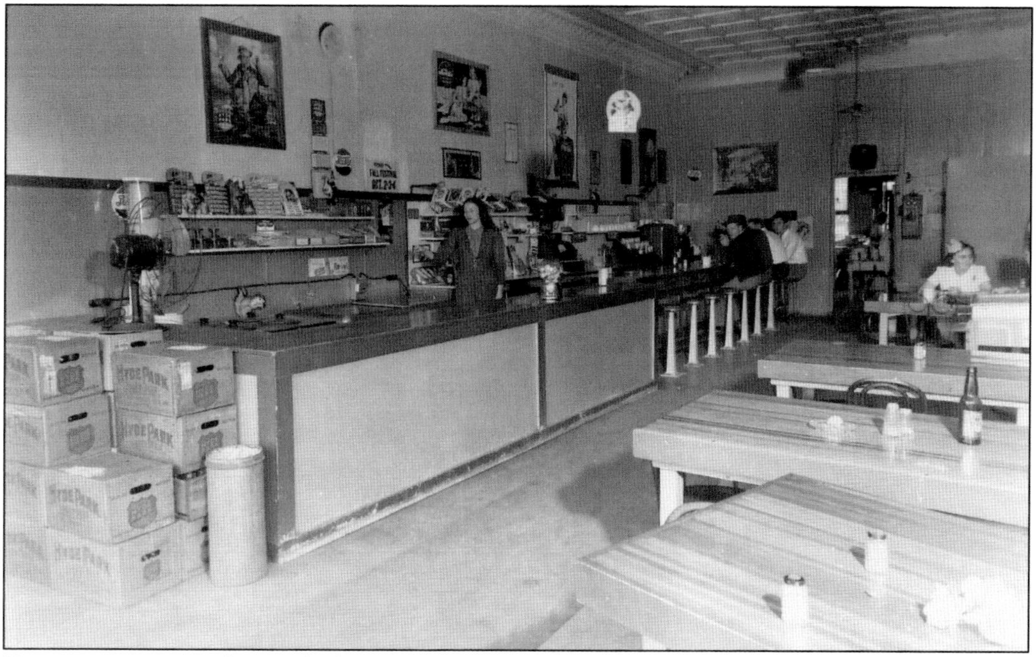

Hermann Herring of Hannibal, Missouri, took this photograph of the interior of Perry Café on October 3, 1947. Café operator Fanny Alston is seated at the table behind the pinball machine. Hyde Park beer appears to be a local favorite. Behind the counter is a full array of products from pain relievers to gum and smokes. Today, this building contains Ralls County Historical Society's genealogical resources. (Author.)

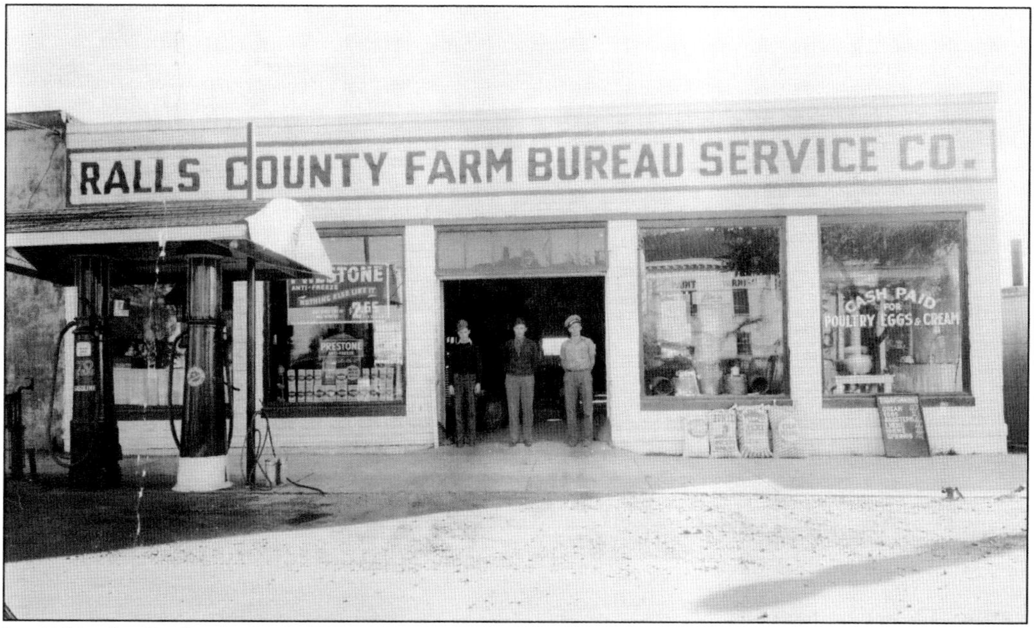

In 1950, the Ralls County Farm Bureau was on Fourth Street across from the Ralls County Courthouse, seen reflected in the windows. From left to right, Charles Fuqua, Roy Dowell, and Leonard Burroughs stand in the garage doorway. It is hard to see, but gas is 17¢. New London COOP occupies this building today. (Jim and Dorothy Quinlin.)

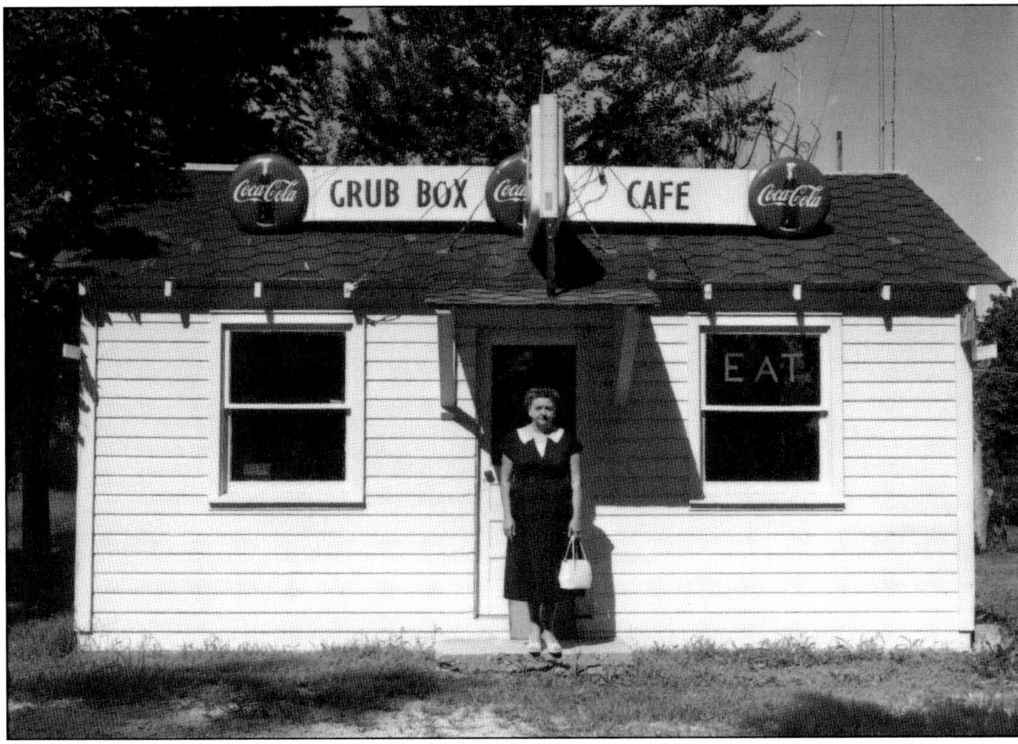

The Grub Box, on the 800 block of South Main street in New London, is pictured in June 1954. This café was a Highway 61 roadside eatery when this photograph was taken with proprietor Mary C. Janes out front. Prior to this, Sherwood "Ozzie" Gann and his wife, Bob Ruth, operated the café and a gas station next door beginning in 1946. Only the tiny filling station still stands. (Author.)

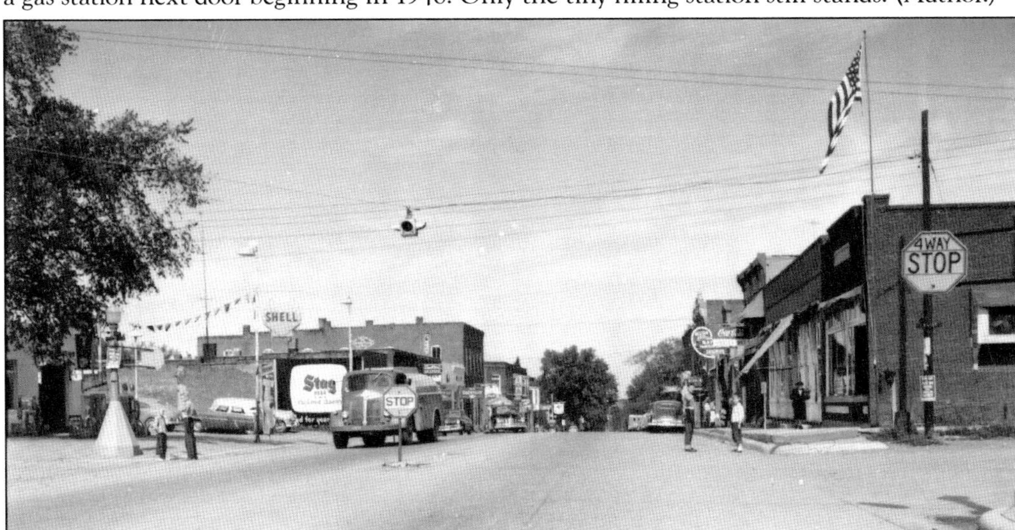

This June 1954 photograph is of New London's Fifth and Main Streets. The crossing guard indicates school is in session. This is a great view uptown showing Eber's Shell station, which is where RCS Bank would be built in 1994. On the west side are cafés and taverns, Ralls County Bank, IGA, a liquor store, and Mobil Gas; on the east are Charles Market, Naylor's Fountain Service, Tiny Potts's Western Auto, and an armored car that is barely visible. (Author.)

Ten

Here and Now

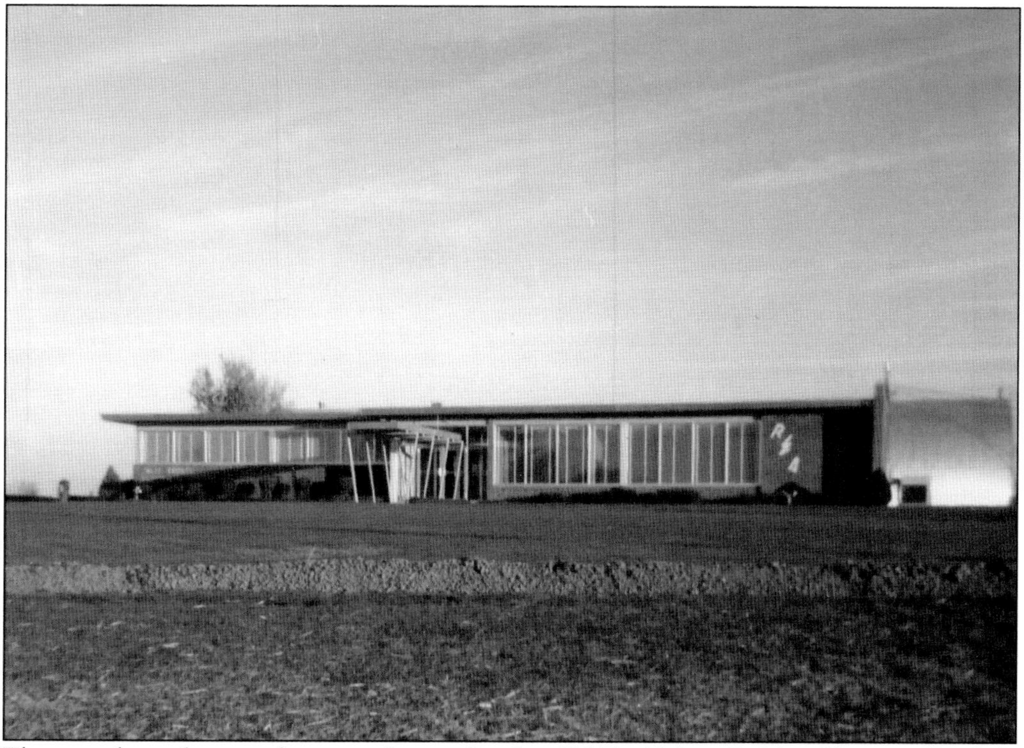

The next three photographs were taken in October 1964 by Nelson Stehle of Perry and include the Ralls County Rural Electric Association (REA) Building at the intersection of Highway 61 and Missouri 19. Today, the REA is Ralls County Electric Company (RCEC), and the building has been much remodeled. A new 911 emergency call center is next door. The RCEC occupies land where the 1909 Ralls County Fairgrounds were built near the St. Louis & Hannibal Railroad's Ralls Junction. (Author.)

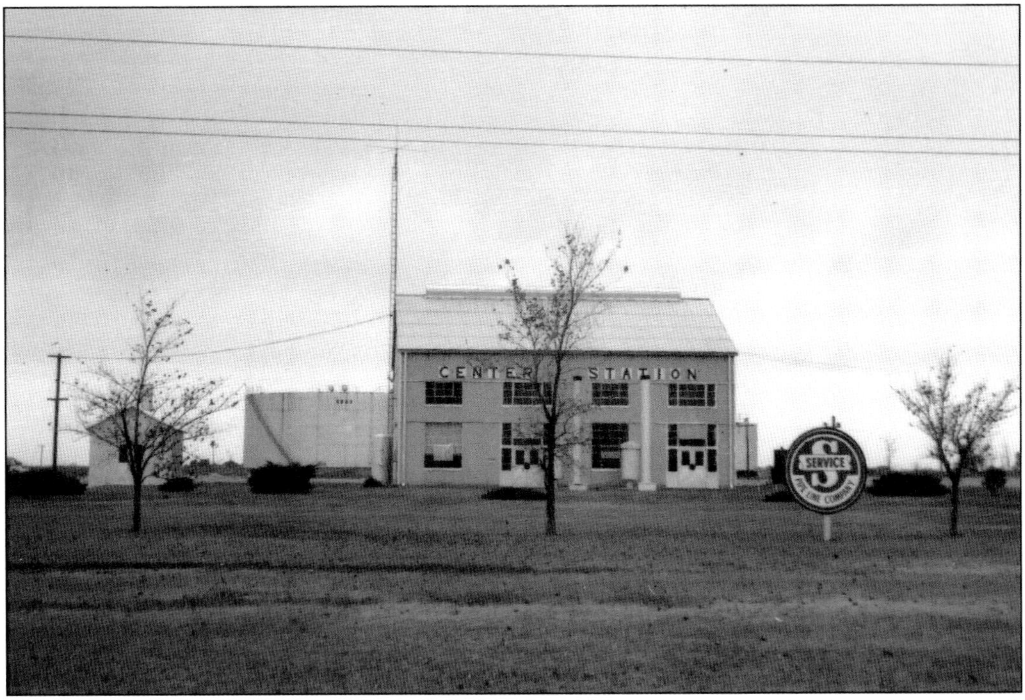

This is a view of Center Pipeline Station No. 2 west of Center, Missouri, on Highway 19. (Author.)

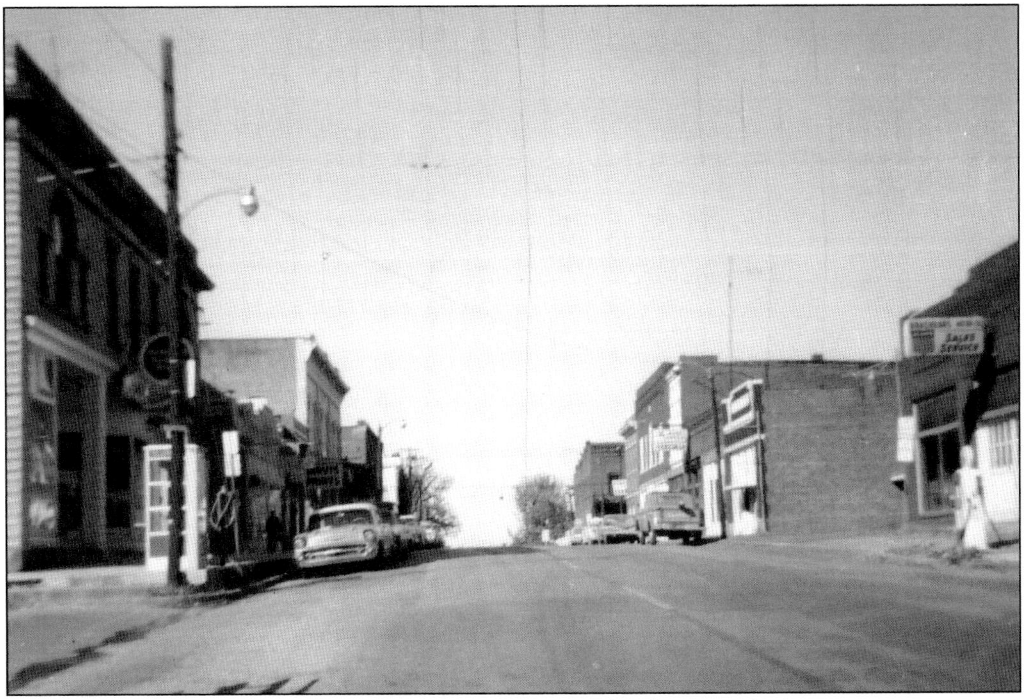

Downtown Perry has been photographed from Main and Gill Streets looking west many times. This is how it appeared in 1964. Today, the Brashears Motor Co., at right, has been remodeled into city hall. Three buildings on the left, found on either side of the Pepsi sign, currently house the Ralls County Historical Society. (Author.)

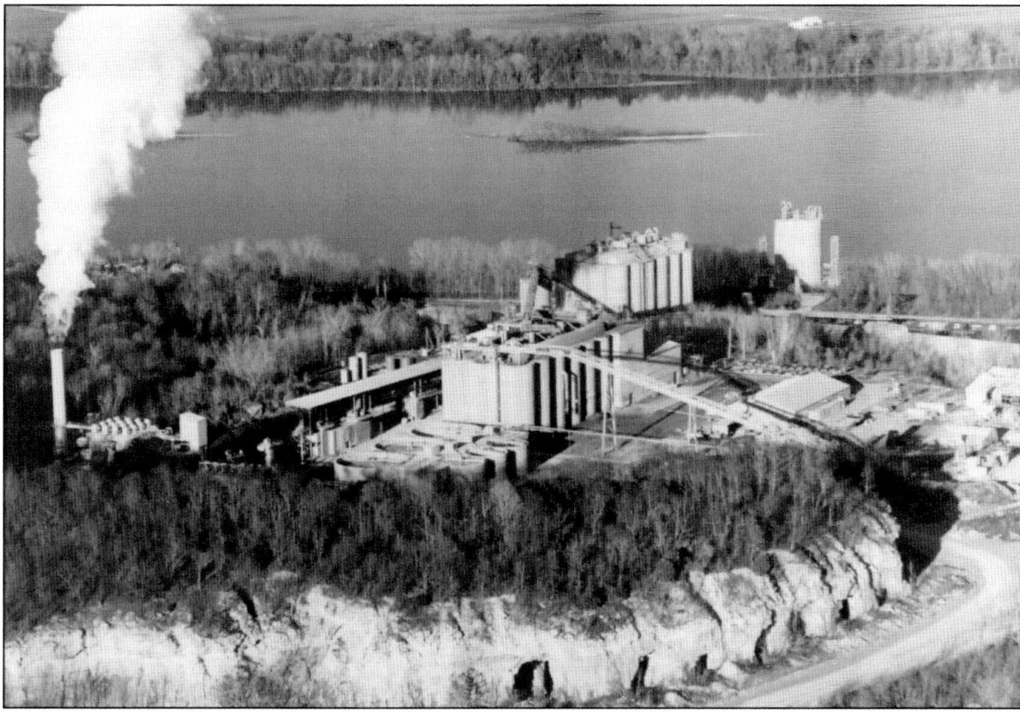

This is a 1980s aerial view of Continental Cement Complex. Limestone tunnels are in view as well as the Mississippi River and Illinois bottoms. The 662-foot-long Allis Chalmers kiln heats raw solid materials to near transparency at 2,600 degrees Fahrenheit. The process produces "clinkers," which are pulverized into Portland Cement. Since 1986, the plant has cleanly burned 7,500 tons of liquid and solid hazardous wastes monthly as green fuel and was upgraded in 2009. (Author.)

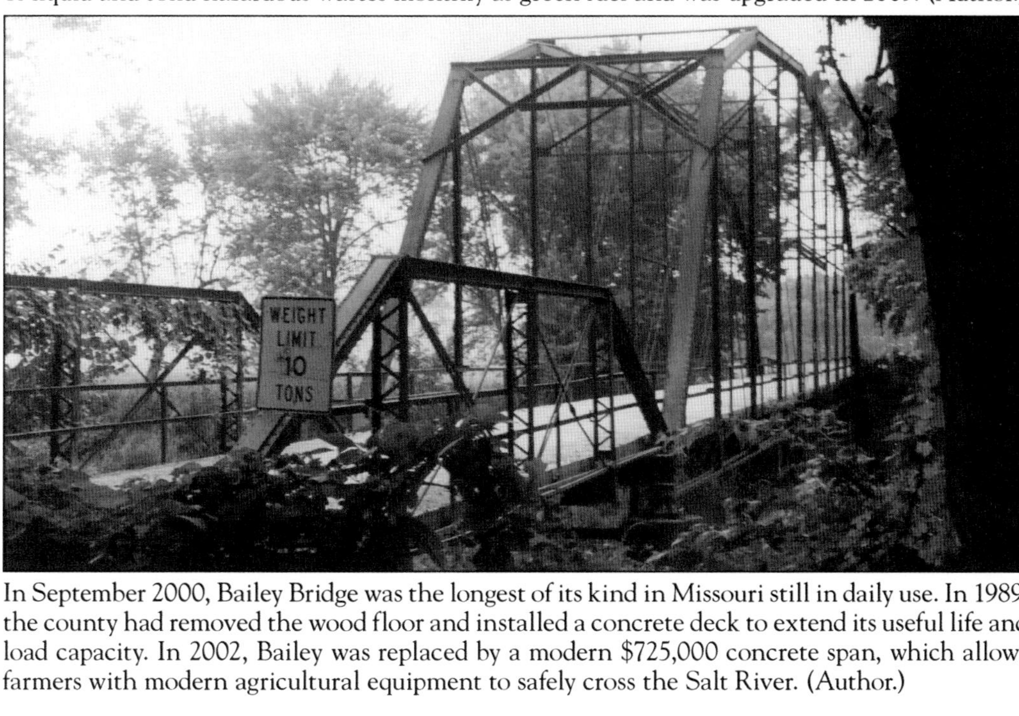

In September 2000, Bailey Bridge was the longest of its kind in Missouri still in daily use. In 1989, the county had removed the wood floor and installed a concrete deck to extend its useful life and load capacity. In 2002, Bailey was replaced by a modern $725,000 concrete span, which allows farmers with modern agricultural equipment to safely cross the Salt River. (Author.)

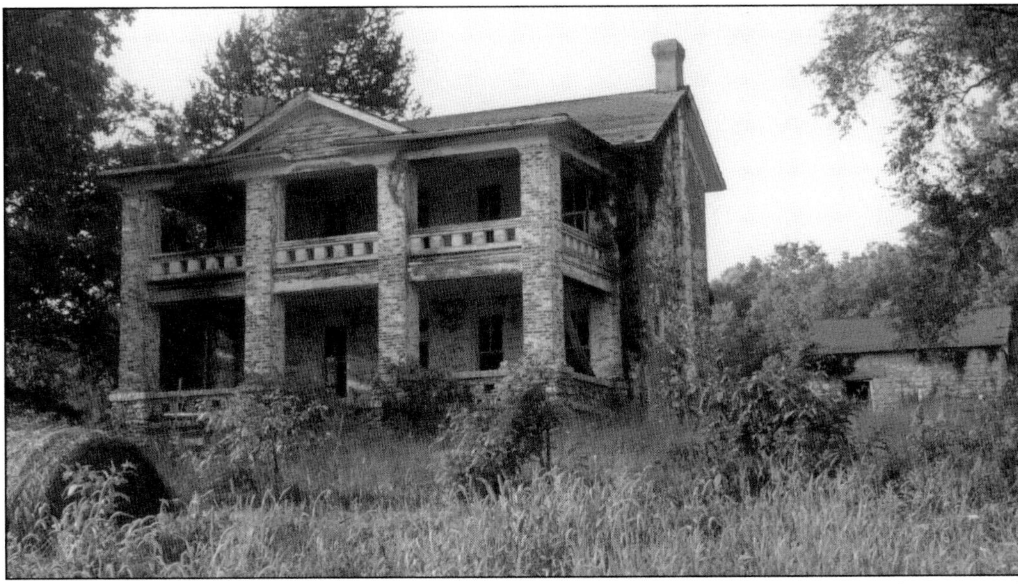

Cleve Yeager constructed this long-abandoned but once beautiful mansion at the foot of Yeager's Hill above the old Red Ball Highway. The house was later sold to the family of Paul C. Stark (brother to Gov. Lloyd Stark), then the Sparks family in 1943, and later Dean Hamilton. There was an L-shaped barn nearby, but it succumbed to arson after this September 2000 photograph. (Author.)

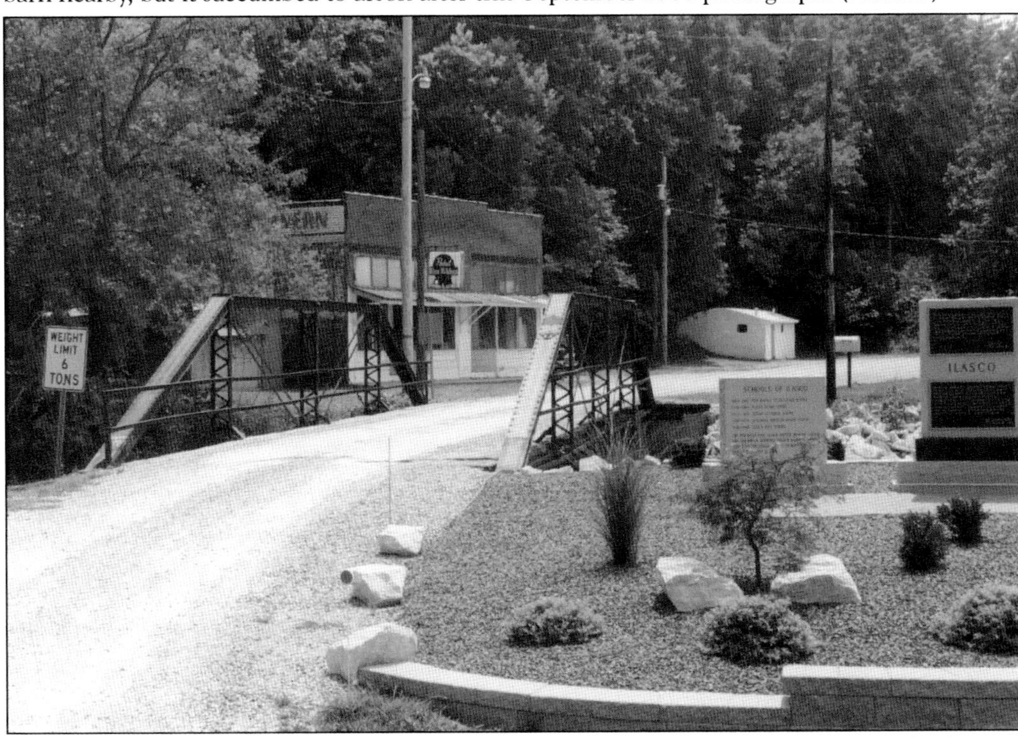

Today, one can visit Ilasco and view memorial markers at the foot of the old pony bridge over Marble Creek. Ilasco has a very dedicated historical society that keeps the town's memory alive and well. In this August 2001 photograph, the tavern, store, and old jail are visible; out of view is the Methodist church, and beyond is the former site of the Ilasco High School. (Author.)

Built in 1911 by Stupp Bros. of St. Louis, this is Ralls County's last large Pratt truss pin-through span still in use, pictured in September 2000. Over time, it has been called Anderson or Rismiller Bridge, with the original name being lost. The Spencer Creek span is near the site of early French settler Marcellin St. Vrain's stone gristmill. In 2012, the county road department installed a new wooden deck. (Author.)

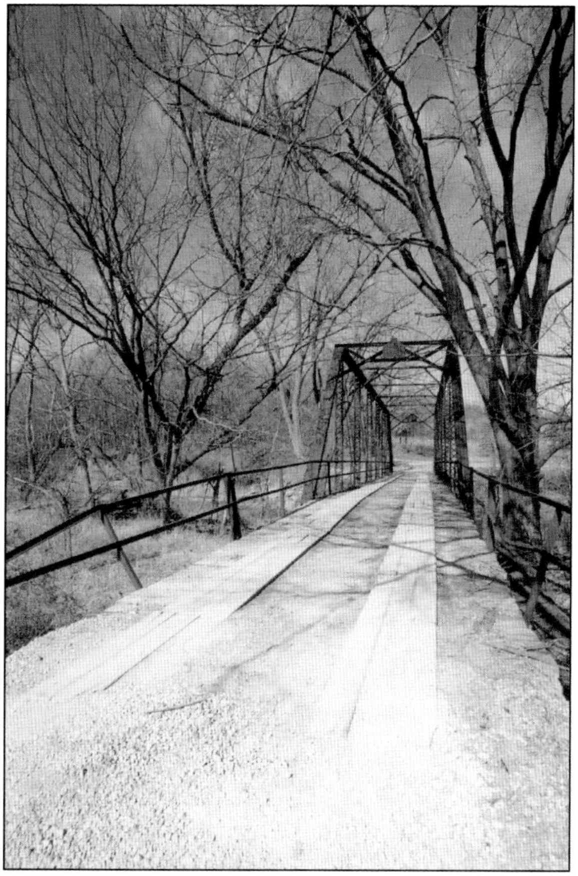

Pictured in September 2002, the 1872 Centenary Methodist Church near Fools Creek was built of hand-hewn logs. In 2003, local residents installed a new roof and made the old church weather-tight, intending to restore it for use as a community house. Tragically, around midnight on March 29, 2004, an arsonist burned it to the ground. The perpetrator has never been caught. (Author.)

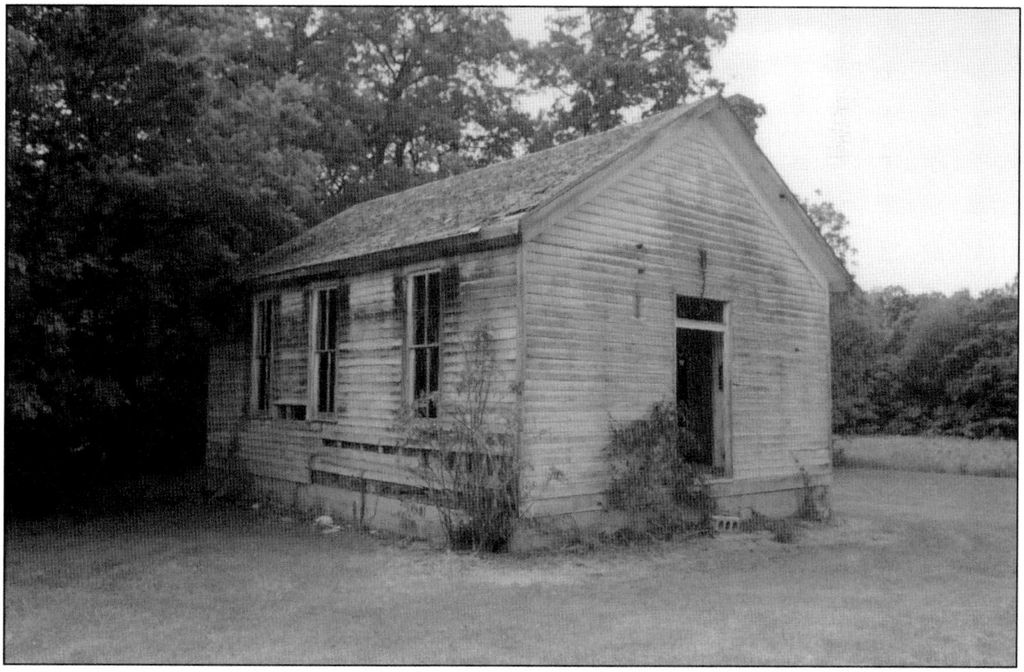

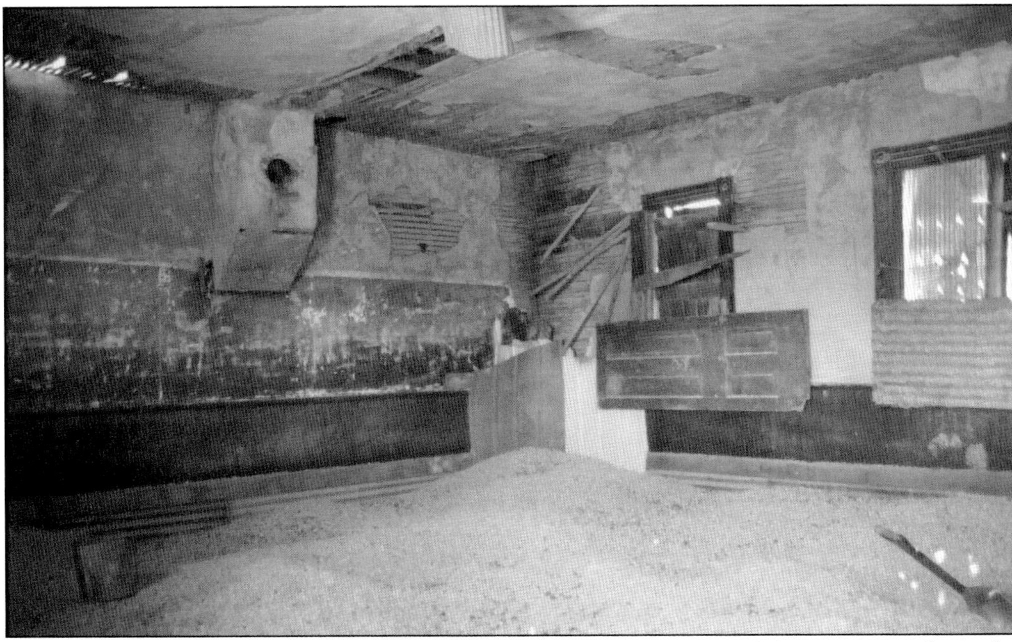

So what becomes of an old country school? In this case, landowner Ralph Rooney on the Ralls-Pike border near Spencer Creek used the old Seely School for feed corn storage. The original slate blackboard and wainscoting remained. Seely was finally torn down in the late 2000s. (Author.)

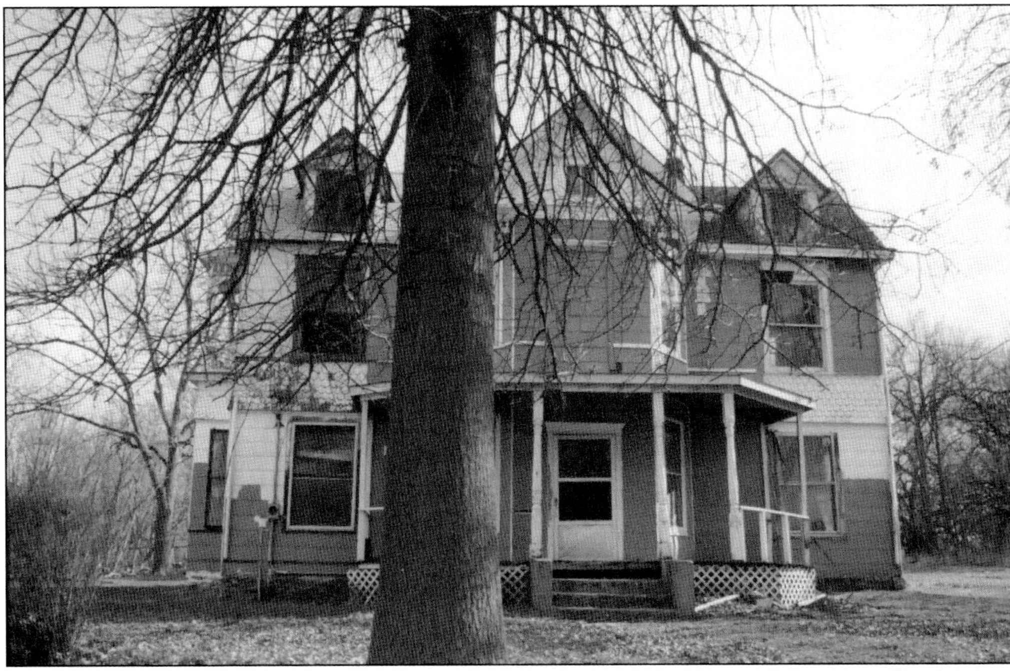

Here is the G.W. Jameson home in April 2003, days before demolition. The summer kitchen was moved to Bob Schoenemann's 1893 Queen Anne at Fourth and Ralls Streets. Most of the ornate trim is gone, while the rear of the house is open to the elements and critters. Some remaining gingerbread exterior, trim, wainscoting, pocket doors, and old-growth lumber were salvaged and reused in other local historic homes. (Author.)

In 2004, Ralls citizens passed a $2 million bond to renovate the 1858 courthouse, including electrical work, computer wiring, a new elevator, and energy upgrades. Klinger and Associates Engineering oversaw completion; New London's Jamie Page was project manager. Work was completed and followed by a 2008 Sesquicentennial Courthouse Celebration. The events were similar to 1958 and featured a concert by Nashville artists Leroy Van Dyke and Helen Cornelius, a Ralls native. (Robert Ventverloh photograph/author.)

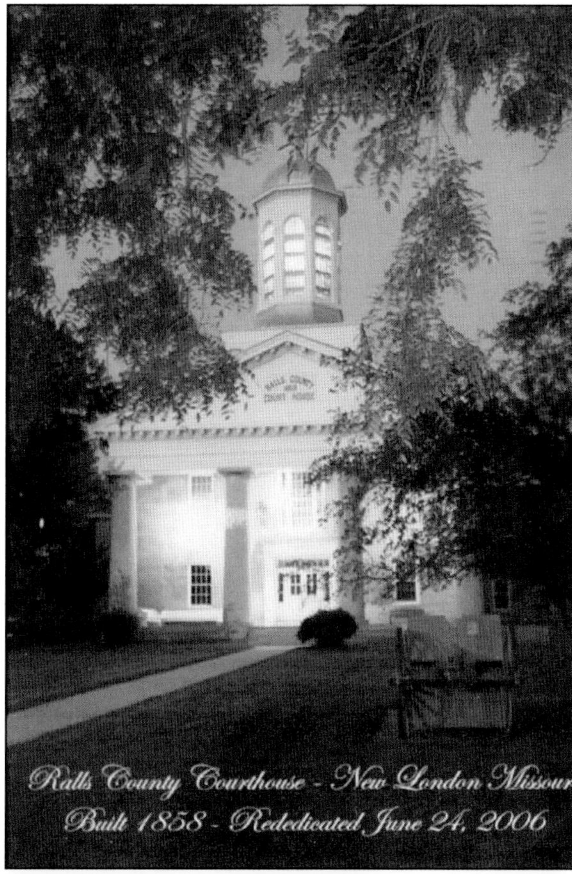

Just off Missouri Route F, two miles down Kingbird Lane, lies the remains of this St. Louis & Hannibal boxcar. It was probably acquired by Ringling from the New York Central and sold as excess inventory to a 1930s landowner. Although the trucks are gone, the rungs and handbrake remain. Despite its forlorn rustic look, it still served as useful storage at the time of this June 2008 photograph. (Author.)

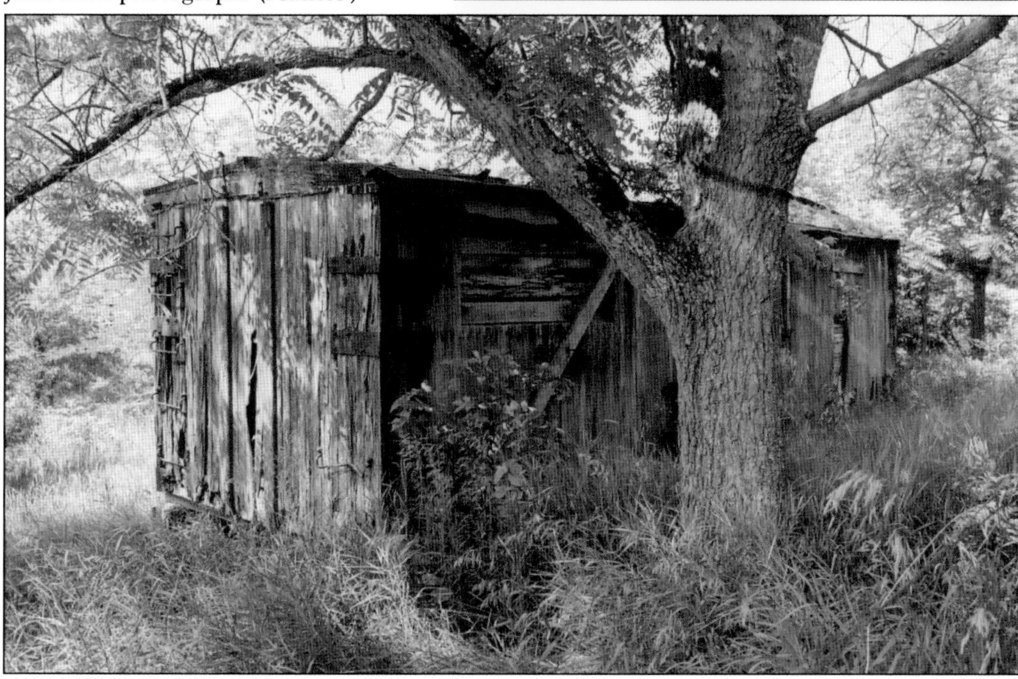

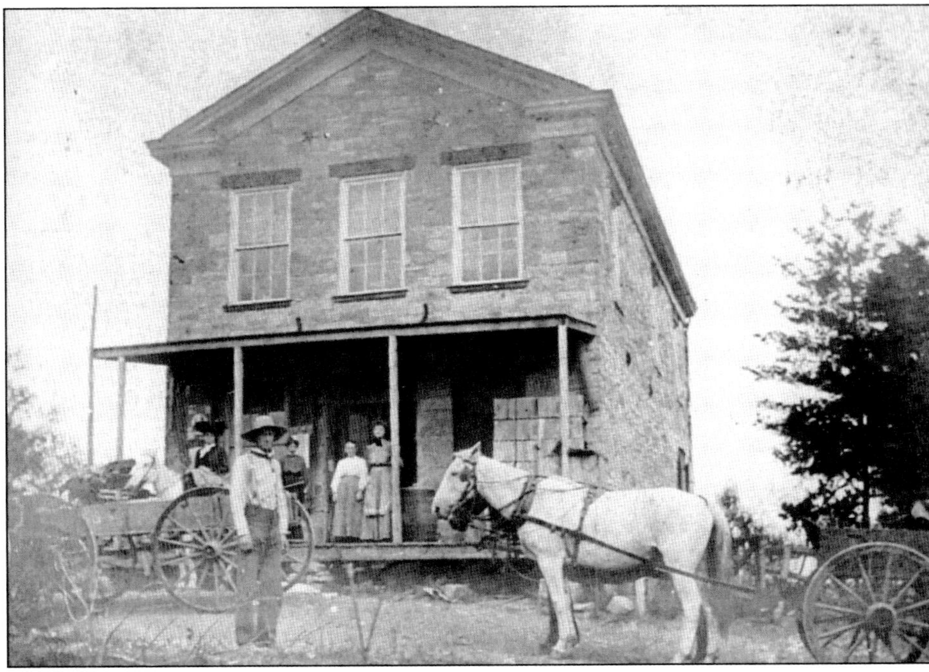

Sidney was established in 1855 south of Huntington on the Hannibal-Paris Plank Road. Hard to believe, but morphine and other drugs were sold over the counter as well as whiskey, dry goods, chain, and carpet warp. The post office closed in 1876 and reopened in 1898, but the name changed to Shiel. The photograph above dates to the 1880s. Time moves on, becoming history. In 1850, this once important trading post sat along the plank road, now Huntington Lane. Settlers and residents passed alongside, stopping for mail or obtaining vital supplies; some headed farther inland, westward, crossing rich lands waiting to be possessed, improved, harvested, and passed down to their children. Today, this gravel road is lightly used, and the store has fallen in. However, 165 years ago, both were essential to life in this part of Missouri and Ralls County. (Above, RCHS; below, author.)

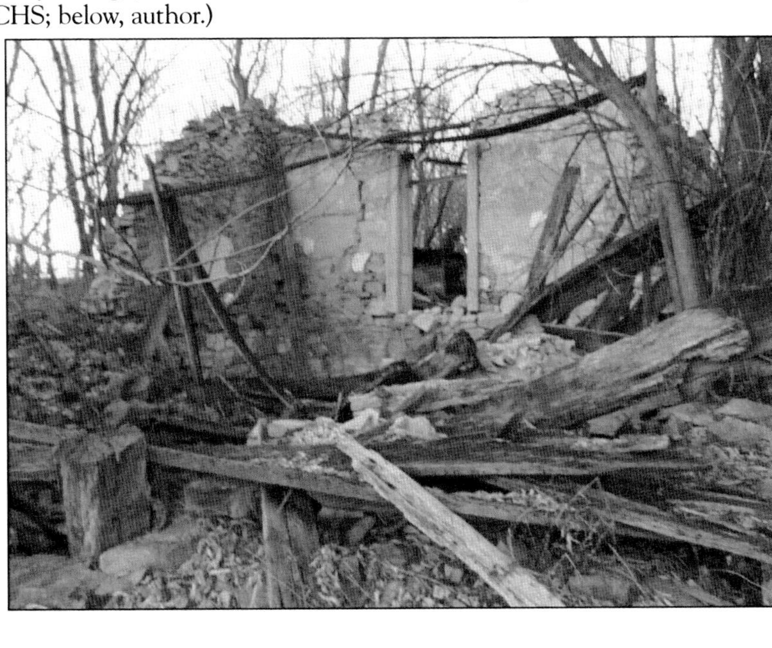

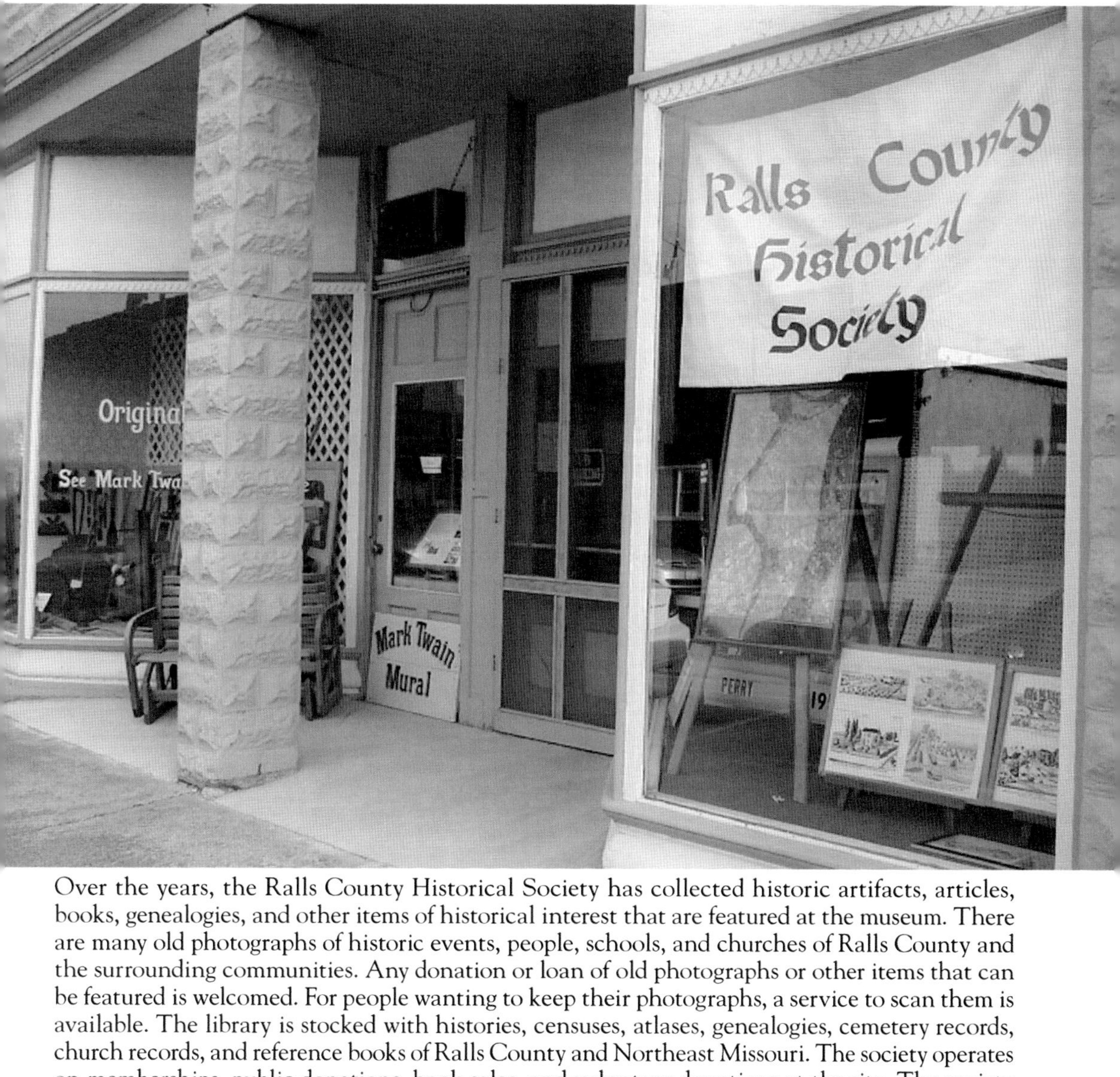

Over the years, the Ralls County Historical Society has collected historic artifacts, articles, books, genealogies, and other items of historical interest that are featured at the museum. There are many old photographs of historic events, people, schools, and churches of Ralls County and the surrounding communities. Any donation or loan of old photographs or other items that can be featured is welcomed. For people wanting to keep their photographs, a service to scan them is available. The library is stocked with histories, censuses, atlases, genealogies, cemetery records, church records, and reference books of Ralls County and Northeast Missouri. The society operates on memberships, public donations, book sales, and voluntary donations at the site. The society is a qualified 501c3 tax exempt organization.

Ralls County Historical Society
PO Box 463
Perry, Missouri 63462

Ralls County Historical Museum and Library
120 East Main Street
Perry, Missouri 63462
Open Tuesday to Saturday 10:00 a.m. to 5:00 p.m. and Sunday and Monday by appointment.
Phone: (573) 248-6147 or (573) 565-2025 for an appointment.
www.rootsweb.ancestry.com/~morchs/
You can also find us on Facebook.

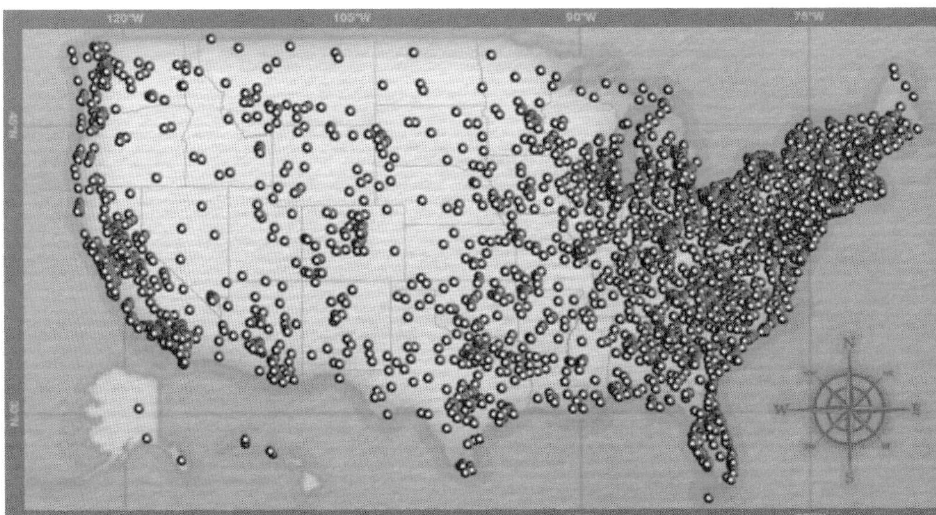